P9-AOH-465

BRUMBACK LIBRARY

3 3045 00140 2151

$29.95

941.08   Hindley, Geoffrey
HIN   The House of Windsor
          : a history
1/99

THE BRUMBACK LIBRARY
OF VAN WERT COUNTY
VAN WERT, OHIO

The
House
of
Windsor

A HISTORY

The House of Windsor

of

A HISTORY

JG PRESS

941.08
HIN

BT

Published in the USA 1998 by JG Press
Distributed by World Publications, Inc.

The JG Press imprint is a trademark of
JG Press, Inc.
455 Somerset Avenue
North Dighton, MA 02764

Produced by
Brompton Books Corp.
15 Sherwood Place
Greenwich, CT 06830

Copyright © 1998 Brompton Books Corp.

All rights reserved. No part of this publication may be
reproduced, stored in a retrieval system, or transmitted
in any form by any means, electronic, mechanical, photo-
copying, or otherwise, without first obtaining the written
permission of the copyright owner.

ISBN 1-57215-266-4

Printed in China

Picture Credits
Thanks to BBC Hulton Picture Library which supplied all of the illustra-
tions in this book except for the following:

Archive Photos/Express Newspapers: 2, 173top, 176, 177, 178bottom, 182,
    184-85, 187, 188top, 189.
Archive Photos/Press Association: 1, 179.
Brompton Picture Library: 83bottom, 131.
Guildhall Art Gallery, City of London/Bridgeman Art Library: 4-5.
Her Majesty The Queen: 6-7, 9, 11, 19top, 34.
Her Majesty Queen Elizabeth, The Queen Mother: 98.
Anwar Hussein: 94-5, 110bottom, 113, 114-15, 140-41, 145both, 147,
    149bottom, 152, 156, 157all, 159, 160right, 161left, 164both, 165,
    166top, 168, 169, 170.
The Illustrated London News Picture Library: 65, 66bottom, 68bottom,
    69bottom, 71bottom, 72both, 74bottom, 77, 83top, 99top, 123, 144.
Imapress/Romuald Meigneux/Archive Photos: 178top.
Imperial War Museum: 53.
Leeds City Art Galleries: 70bottom.
Mansell Collection: 13, 17top, 32, 36, 39bottom, 43top, 44both, 45, 47,
    49bottom, 51top, 52top, left and right, 56, 97bottom, 100top.
National Portrait Gallery: 64right, 75, 87, 102, 160left.
New Zealand High Commission, London: 167both.
PA News Ltd/Archive Photos: 173bottom.
The Photo Source/Central Press: 109.
The Photo Source/Fox: 119bottom.
Reuters/Archive Photos: Bob East III: 171; Paul Hackett: 183; Ho 180;
    Andy Mettler: 188bottom; JM Ribiero 172; Mike Segar: 181; John
    Stillwell: 186.
S&G Press Agency: 91bottom, 92bottom, 93, 106, 111, 121, 122top, 124,
    126bottom, 134, 135, 136both, 137top, 139, 142, 143, 146, 150top,
    151both, 153, 154-55, 163bottom, 166bottom.
The Scotsman Picture Collection, Edinburgh: 91top.
John Scott: 110top, 122bottom left and right, 133, 137bottom, 148,
    149top, 162.
Sotheby's, London/Cecil Beaton: 76.

29.95

Contents

Victoria

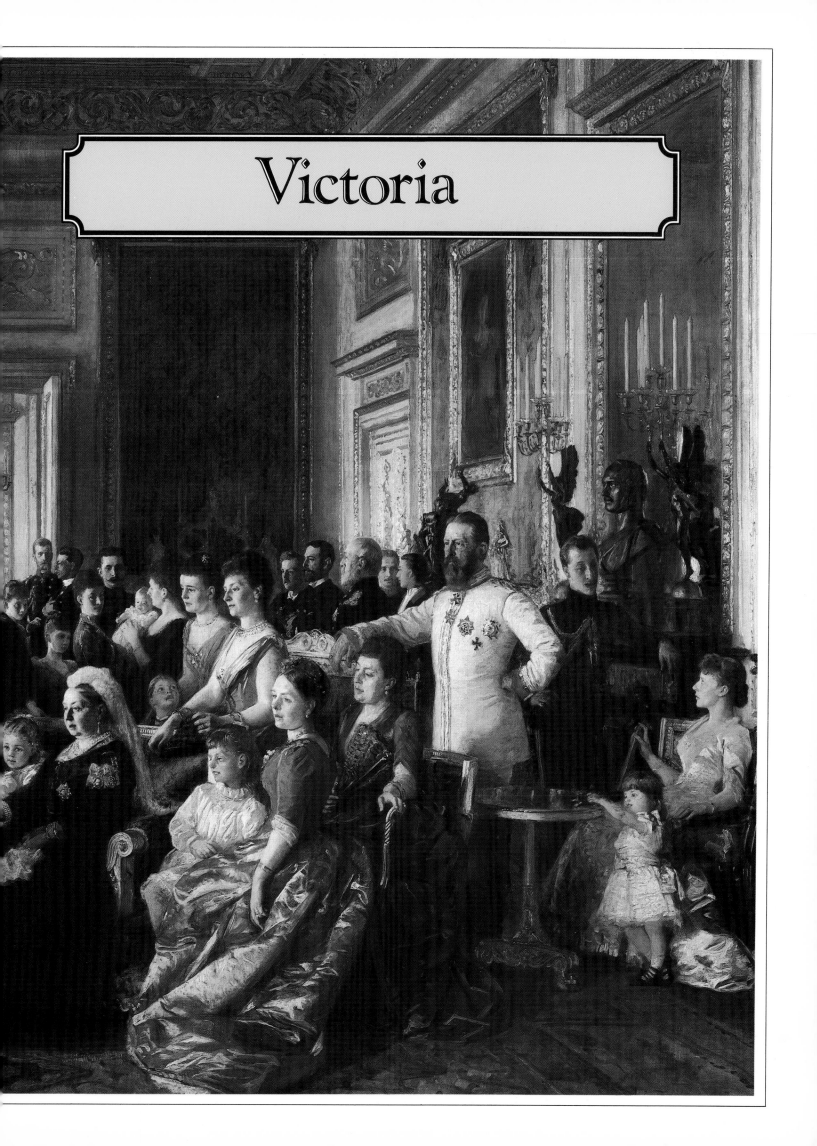

Pages 6-7: Queen Victoria, surrounded by members of her extensive family on the occasion of her Golden Jubilee in 1887. The picture includes the Queen's many German relations, including the future Kaiser, members of the Battenberg family, ancestors of Prince Philip as well as Russian Grand Dukes and Duchesses.

When Queen Victoria acceded to the throne in 1837, many people in Great Britain breathed a sigh of relief. The performance of the Queen's immediate predecessors had been less than stellar, and it was felt that Victoria might be able to restore some sense of stability and dignity to the monarchy.

There was every reason to believe that the image of the monarchy could be restored. After all, the institution had survived for more than a millennium, despite numerous scandals, long periods of social upheaval and repeated attacks from foreign powers. Indeed, if we take into account the entire history of the monarchy, the problems inherited by Victoria – not to mention the problems that have plagued the monarchy in recent years – seem rather insignificant.

The precise origins of the English monarchy are difficult to pinpoint. The first man to call himself 'king of the English' was Offa, an eighth-century ruler who seized control of most of the country south of the river Humber. Today, most history books list Egbert of Essex as the first sovereign because, between A.D. 825 and 830, he managed to unify all the vari-

Below: The Queen aged four. Those who saw the young Victoria at this age considered her an alert and lively child; she later lamented a sad childhood.

ous regions of present-day England. Forty years later, Alfred the Great, Egbert's grandson, became the country's first national hero, after achieving a decisive victory over the Danes in England.

One important fact that emerges from the study of this period is that the monarchy, from the very beginning, was inextricably linked with Christianity. Alfred, and the other early kings, saw themselves as defenders of the Christian faith. Subsequent eras would be characterised, to varying degrees, by friction between kings and clerics. And eventually, of course, the country would break away from Rome and form the Church of England. Nevertheless, all British monarchs, from the seventh century onward, have regarded themselves as agents of God and Christ.

The performance of individual monarchs, however, has not always been inspired. A century after the reign of Alfred, for example, Ethelred II tried to control the Danes with bribes. To say that the policy was ill-conceived would be an understatement. He managed to buy only short-term peace, and by A.D. 1016 he was forced to seek refuge with the Duke of Normandy.

Other kings were brought down by their own indulgences. Edward II, for example, was said to be unusually fond of baths. What's more, as Sir Winston Churchill so delicately put it, 'he carried his friendship for his advisors beyond dignity and decency.' These friendships so disgusted his wife, Isabella, that she eventually turned on him. In 1324, she traveled to France, ostensibly on a diplomatic mission. While she was there, she became the lover and confidante of one of the king's arch enemies. The two soon staged a coup and had the king executed.

Fortunately for Britain, Edward's son acceded to the throne and ruled, successfully, for 50 years. But many dark days lay ahead: Richard II, grandson of Edward III, was deposed in 1399; Edward V, his great-great grandson, was murdered in the Tower of London, and Richard III – whose reputation was shaped by Shakespeare – died in battle after reigning for only two years.

Then there was Henry VIII – a great king, in many respects, but a man who, nevertheless, is remembered more for his ruthless treatment of his wives than for his role in establishing the Church of England.

The point of all this is not to chronicle the history of the British monarchy, but to put the subject of this book – the history of the House of Windsor – into perspective. When we understand this history, we can see the profound irony in Shakespeare's phrase 'divinity doth hedge a king.' Indeed, the history of the monarchy is made up of a series of tragedies of Shakespearean proportions. It is the story of men and women who rose to a position of supreme power but, in many cases, were brought down by their own shortcomings – by tragic flaws, if you will.

And yet, in the wake of each tragedy, a new sovereign has stepped in to reinvent the institution. There was, of course, the brief period in the mid-seventeenth century when England became a Commonwealth under Oliver Cromwell. But by 1660, the monarchy had been restored under Charles II, and it has remained in place ever since, despite repeated upheavals. As Jessica Hodge has pointed out in her book *The Royal Family Today,* the post-Restoration monarchy has survived the Glorious Revolution, when Charles II's brother James II was deposed; it has survived the reign of George III, who lost control of the American colonies and who eventually went mad because of a rare disease. And it has endured despite all sorts of problems within the domestic spheres of the royal families. George IV, for example, had been in love with a commoner but was forced to abandon her and marry Princess Caroline of Brunswick after falling deep into debt. He never even pretended to be happy about the arrangement, however, and when he was crowned in 1820 he refused to invite Caroline to the ceremony. After George's death, his brother William IV proved to be a more successful king, although he too exposed himself to scandal. Over time, he fathered 10 illegitimate children.

William's failure to provide a legitimate heir to the throne led to the accession of Victoria, a granddaughter of George III. Princess Alexandrina Victoria was born at 4.15am on 24 May 1819 at Kensington Palace on the outskirts of London. Her mother had arrived there only weeks before, having been conveyed across Europe from her home in the miniature German principality of Sachsen-Coburg during the eighth month of her pregnancy so that her child, confidently scheduled by her husband Edward Duke of Kent as the future monarch of Great Britain, should be born on British soil.

The Duke was the fourth son of King George III and, until two years before, had been living in affectionate fidelity with a French lady known as Mme de St Laurent. It was an arrangement more or less common-place among the middle-aged Princes of the House of Hanover. William (later King as William IV) lived with a sturdy family of bastards by his actress companion Mrs Jordan and neither he nor any of his brothers (most of them unmarried) had a legitimate heir. Hopes

for the succession rested with Princess Charlotte, the daughter of the Prince Regent and wife of Prince Leopold of Saxe-Coburg. When she died in childbirth in 1817 the whole nation mourned – not for the dynasty but for the Princess herself who alone among her dreadful family had captured the hearts of the people.

And the dynasty did face a crisis. Mistresses were retired and the royal dukes, preparing to do their duty, looked for wives. The Duke of Kent's choice fell on the widowed Princess Victoire of Leiningen, daughter of the Duke of Saxe-Coburg and sister of Prince Leopold. The lady was comfortably off and took some persuading to leave her secure life at the little German court for an uncertain future with a total stranger up to his eyes in debt. In fact Kent was living abroad to avoid his creditors. Reluctantly, Parliament voted him funds so that the family was back in England for the birth of the child. The 'little Mayflower' was a fine healthy baby to the delight of her parents who, despite the circumstances of their courtship, were rapidly falling in love.

But clouds were on the horizon. The Prince Regent disliked his brother intensely and, himself without an heir, was mortified that

Above: Louise Lehzen, the faithful and beloved companion of the young Victoria. The drawing, dated 'Nov: 30th 1833' is by the Princess herself. If not inspired, the 14-year-old royal artist was already a competent draughtswoman. Later in life she took lessons from Edward Lear, the distinguished topographical painter. On his first visit to Windsor Lear blurted out: 'Where did you get all these wonderful paintings?' Amused, Victoria replied: 'They belonged to my family, Mr Lear.' Today, this picture is part of the royal collection – one of the great family art collections in the world.

Above: Victoria (left) and her mother, the Duchess of Kent, 'at the Chapel Royal Windsor'; a coloured lithograph (1837) commissioned as an advertising promotion by a contemporary magazine. The image of two virtuous women at church, it heralds the onset of 'Victorian morality.'

ue living in London and they rented a cottage at Sidmouth in Devon. Here on 23 January 1820 the Duke, having taken a chill, died of pneumonia. The widow, penniless and grief-stricken, was in a desperate plight. Her brother, Leopold, living at Claremont House in Surrey, made her an allowance from his £50,000 British government pension and intervened with the new King George IV, to ensure that his sister and her child should remain in England. They returned to apartments in the rambling old palace at Kensington. George's one wish was to see them out of the country, but not even he could evict his niece and her mother. He tolerated the arrangement with the worst possible grace.

Oblivious to the murky family politics that surrounded her home, the little princess flourished under her mother's watchful eye and the loving care of her governess Louise Lehzen. In later life Victoria was to complain of her 'sad and dull' childhood. True, she missed the company of children of her own age and the regime at Kensington was 'sensible' rather than stimulating. Yet she impressed all who saw her as a well adjusted and very bright little girl. At the age of four she was presented at court. The King had come to terms with an arrangement he could not change and on her fourth birthday gave her a diamond-set miniature portrait of himself. No doubt her own lively and affectionate nature softened the old King who 'expressed himself greatly delighted with his little niece.'

With his rouged cheeks and immense bulk, 'Uncle King' was a monstrous sight, but when he wished he could still be a charmer, and there were some idyllic days of carriage rides in the parkland around Virginia Water and fishing on the lake to the sound of band music from the island pavilion. This growing friendship between the King and his little successor did not suit everybody. Sir John Conroy, Comptroller of the Household to the Duchess and an adventurer with ambitions, looked forward to the day when he should be principal adviser to the Queen of England and did his utmost to isolate mother and daughter from the court. The Duchess, still harbouring grievances at her early treatment by the King, willingly fell under Conroy's spell. It is not necessary to accept the gossip that he was a lover to account for the increasing domination he exercised over her. Victoria came to hate him and cling ever closer to her beloved governess, Lehzen.

By the standards of the day, Princess Victoria enjoyed a decent education. Lessons were systematic and besides arithmetic, drawing, and music, included French, German and Italian. Like other young ladies of her time,

Edward of all people should father the eventual successor to the throne. On his orders the christening was a small affair over which he gloweringly presided. As the child's sponsor it was for him to select the name from those proposed by the parents. Ignoring the tearful Duchess he first of all gave just one name 'Alexandrina' and then grudgingly conceded that the child might have her mother's name also. It had been cruelly made plain that though she might one day sit on the British throne, Alexandrina Victoria was to be denied any of the traditional names of her royal predecessors.

The callous ill will of King George was to colour the Duchess's attitudes and behaviour for years to come.

Towards the end of the year it became clear that the Kents, lodging for the time being in Kensington Palace, could not afford to contin-

Victoria kept up her art and developed a modest talent – later in life she took lessons from Edward Lear, noted as a topographical painter. The 'Kensington system' as it was called introduced her to a fair selection of literature both English and French and from her music lessons she developed a passion for Italian opera that remained throughout her life.

With the death of George IV in June 1830 the life of the 11-year-old Victoria entered a more public and increasingly hectic phase. Parliament named her mother as sole regent in the event of a minority and increased the Duchess's income by £10,000 a year. In the opinion of one courtier, William IV seemed 'a kind-hearted, well-meaning, not stupid, burlesque, bustling old fellow' ñ he was 65 ñ who 'if he doesn't go mad may make a very decent king.' The new King and his wife Queen Adelaide, though they had not abandoned all hope of a child of their own, willingly recognised Victoria as heir presumptive and were prepared to see her take her place at court. But the Duchess and Conroy saw this as a threat to their grip on the Princess and their future ascendancy when she should become Queen. The intelligent girl who now found herself a pawn in court and family politics came to conceal her natural openness of nature behind a stony look which both hurt and angered the King.

The arrangements for the coronation opened the rift. Furious to learn that her daughter was to be preceded in the procession by the King's brothers, the royal dukes, the Duchess of Kent announced that the Princess Victoria would not attend the ceremony because 'the fatigue would put too great a strain on her health.' Victoria wept bitterly and her resentment against Conroy, who she was convinced was to blame, increased.

But there were more serious troubles in the air. Revolutions in Europe had driven King Charles X of France from his throne and forced the partition of the Kingdom of the Netherlands. At home, agitation for the reform of Parliament was producing conditions of public unrest which alarmed Society to the possibility of revolution in England. Queen Adelaide prepared to be a courageous Marie Antoinette while humbly admitting she would not be as beautiful. The Tory government of the Duke of Wellington fell; Lord Grey, his Whig successor won a resounding election victory for Reform. King William resigned himself to creating enough new peers to secure the passage of the Great Reform Bill if the House of Lords threw it out for a second time. But the diehards abstained and the Bill became law in June 1832.

Two months later Princess Victoria and her entourage headed north for a royal progress which was received with surprising enthusiasm. It took her through the grim heartlands of industrial England, 'a country very desolate everywhere,' as she recorded in her journal. 'The grass is quite blasted and black . . . engines flaming . . . everywhere smoking and burning coal heaps, intermingled with wretched huts and carts and little ragged children.' The Reform Bill had meant only a modest extension of the franchise, but its passage had defused the situation ñ the monarchy seemed once again secure and the pretty little princess was welcomed.

Behind the scenes the running battle between Kensington and the Palace continued. While Conroy egged the Duchess on to ever more outrageous demands her more sensible advisers urged restraint. When Victoria was 15 a new figure made his appearance in the Kent councils. This was Baron Stockmar, the confidant of Uncle Leopold who in 1830 had left England to become King of the new kingdom of Belgium formed by the partition of the Netherlands. Stockmar was to play a great role in the early years of Victoria's reign but in 1834 Victoria was more personally affected when her mother appointed Lady Flora Hastings as her lady-in-waiting, without consultation. Hastings rapidly allied herself to Conroy and so, in Victoria's mind, joined the 'enemy.' Lehzen seemed to be

Left: Victoria (aged 13) by George Hayter. Painter of miniatures to Princess Charlotte, he also did a painting of *The Trial of Queen Caroline,* George IV's estranged wife, whose trial for adultery (1822) incensed the public. Victoria appointed Hayter court 'portrait and history painter' and knighted him (aged 50) in 1842.

Left: Prince Albert (left) and his brother Prince Ernst of Sachsen-Coburg und Gotha, cousins of Victoria. The Queen found them both 'kind and good', and Albert 'extremely handsome.' Ernst is shown wearing antique armour of the kind that appealed to 19th-century romanticism. In 1839, for example, the Earl of Eglinton mounted a week long 'medieval' tournament on his estate. The picture, based on one by the miniaturist Robert Thorburn, is a print by Thomas Herbert Maguire, who became court lithographer to Queen Victoria.
Right: Queen Victoria in the first year of her reign, portrayed wearing the insignia of the Order of the Garter. The image of this lovely and vital young woman, adorned with the emblems of ancient chivalry perfectly matched the nostalgic dreams of the world's first industrialized society.

her only friend and resentment against her mother now began to be added to her hatred of Conroy.

As she grew into womanhood, the atmosphere of intrigue surrounding her deepened. Alarmed by the schemings of Conroy and the Duchess, King William publicly announced his hope 'that his successor would be of age when she came to the throne'. Victoria devoutly agreed – even a short regency by her mother and Conroy might establish them too firmly to be dislodged. The situation eased slightly when to her great delight, Uncle Leopold 'who has always been to me like a father' made a brief visit to England in September 1835. But shortly after his departure Victoria fell desperately ill. Conroy saw an opening and tried to force the weakened princess to sign a document guaranteeing his appointment as Private Secretary when she should become Queen. He was the first to come up against the iron determination which all who had dealings with Victoria encountered sooner or later.

Approaching the age of 18, Victoria was Europe's greatest heiress but among all the family politicking very little thought had been given to choosing a husband for her. Uncle Leopold, of course, had a plan and in May his brother, the Duke of Saxe-Coburg-Gotha arrived at Kensington Palace with his two sons Ernest and Albert. The Princess found both her cousins 'so kind and good' and thought Albert 'extremely handsome', but it was not love at first sight. She recognized her marriage was a political event. However, she thought Albert would 'do' very well and he had, besides, 'the most pleasing and delightful exterior and appearance.'

King William was now in his seventies and Conroy's hopes of manipulating a regency

through the Duchess seemed to be receding. He went to extraordinary lengths to secure his position – even forcing her to refuse an offer by the King to give her an independent household when she came of age. But still she refused to appoint him to any household office. With her 18th birthday on 24 May 1837 she reached the age of royal majority. The King's life was now ebbing and the court was rife with speculation because of 'the absolute ignorance of everybody of the character and capacity of the Princess . . . kept in such jealous seclusion by her mother.'

At 6am on the morning of 20 June Victoria was awakened by her mother at Kensington Palace to be told that the Archbishop of Canterbury and Lord Conyngham were there to see her. 'I got out of bed and went into my sitting room (only in my dressing gown) and *alone*, and saw them.' She learnt that she had been queen since shortly after two o'clock. At nine o'clock the Lord Melbourne the prime minister arrived 'whom I saw in my room, and of COURSE *quite* ALONE as I shall *always* do all my Ministers.' The words spelt the end to the schemes of her mother and Conroy. He was denied all access to the Queen and even the Duchess could see her only daughter by appointment. Now Lehzen came into her own.

Meanwhile, a curious crowd of courtiers thronged the Red Saloon at Kensington to see their new monarch emerge and receive the first oaths of fealty of her reign. They were amazed by her 'modesty, propriety, her deep sense of her situation and her firmness.' The reality of the composed and confident young woman shattered the image of the immature 18-year-old pedalled by the Kensington propaganda circuit.

She made a still greater impact at her coronation on 28 June 1838. Her air of command combined with her 'baby face, tiny figure and her pretty smile' to extraordinary effect. 'Everyone literally gasped for breath . . . and the rails of the gallery trembled in one's hands from the trembling of the spectators.' Victoria herself was entranced by the whole event.

'Seated upon St Edward's chair, the Dalmatic robe was clasped about me by the Lord Great Chamberlain. Then followed all the various things; and last the Crown being placed on my head – which was, I must own, a most beautiful, impressive moment; *all* the Peers and Peeresses put on their coronets at the same instant . . . The shouts, which were very great, the drums, the trumpets, the firing of the guns, all at the same instant, rendered the spectacle most imposing . . . I came home at a little after six, really *not* feeling tired . . . My kind Lord Melbourne . . . asked kindly if I was tired and said the Sword he carried was excessively heavy. I said that the Crown had hurt me a good deal.'

The youthful monarch and her elderly prime minister compared notes in a mood of mutual admiration and affection which had been growing since the first day of the reign. Court wits spoke of the new 'Mrs Melbourne.' Certainly, the ageing statesman was enchanted by his young Queen while she depended on his advice

and company as much as she did that of her beloved Uncle Leopold. But as that summer advanced she was subject to moody fits of lethargy and irritability – her youthful prettiness was fading and there were those, including even Melbourne, who said she ought to lose weight.

The Queen's honeymoon with court and country ended abruptly. Gossip reached her that Lady Flora Hastings, never her favourite, was pregnant. Victoria was ready to believe the worst and Lady Flora submitted to a humiliating medical examination. Even this did not silence the scandal and the Hastings family leapt to the defence of their young kinswoman, while the Duchess of Kent openly took their part. Determined to be rid of her mamma, Victoria returned to the project of her marriage to Albert though she 'dreaded the thought of marrying as I was so used to getting my own way.'

But now, a new crisis broke. Melbourne's government was defeated in the House of Commons and to the Queen's dismay he resigned. The Tory leader, Sir Robert Peel, insisted that before he form an administration the Queen dismiss some of her ladies-of-the-bedchamber who were connected with leading Whig families. At that time the court was by no means 'above

Below: *Lord Melbourne instructing the Young Queen*, an engraving of 1837 giving an artist's impression of Victoria in council with her first Prime Minister. The picture cannot have been very far from the reality of the early months of the reign. Queen and minister shared a mutual admiration and respect that was cosy – almost domestic. The artist was rather flattering to Melbourne, at this time approaching 60, but no doubt Victoria would have approved. Her affection for her Prime Minister was an open secret – some society gossips nick-named her 'the new Mrs Melbourne.'

Opposite: *Her Majesty in Her Robes of State* (1859), by Franz Winterhalter, the most fashionable society painter of the time.
Right: A loyal pun at the time of the royal wedding, prompted by the introduction of a new pear, the 'Nonpareil' – *A Pair for the Royal Table*.

Below: A lithograph at the time of the Queen's last official Opening of Parliament. Within a border depicting her ministers, it shows Victoria at her first council (top), reading the Speech from the Throne and riding in procession for the opening ceremony.

politics' as it is today and the staid Sir Robert had a point. But the Queen refused to budge and, astonishingly enough, Peel withdrew. The Bedchamber Crisis was one of the last public achievements of the royal prerogative – but Victoria had 'dear Lord Melbourne' once more as prime minister and had kept out the Tory friends of Lady Flora Hastings.

This poor woman had in fact been suffering from a tumour on the liver, diagnosed too late, and on 5 July she died. A contrite Victoria had visited her that morning but her enemies in the press charged that Lady Flora had died of a broken heart from the Queen's ill treatment. Conroy had left the country in disgrace the month before and the Duchess of Kent, estranged from her daughter and deprived of two friends by death and disgrace, had to be reluctantly re-admitted to the family circle. Uncle Leopold was at Windsor that August still talking of the arrangements for a second visit of

THE NONPAREIL.

A NEW AND MUCH ADMIRED PEAR TO BE INTRODUCED AT THE

ROYAL TABLE.

his nephew Albert. Even this could not raise the spirits of an increasingly fractious Victoria who was 'anxious it should be understood' that she had never given any promise to marry him.

But things went according to Uncle Leopold's plan. When Albert arrived at Windsor in October, the Queen quickly found herself enchanted. Only a little embarrassed – 'such things were usually done the other way' – she sent for him in her closet to let him know that it would make her '*too happy* if he would consent to what I wished (to marry me).' Duty and a warm affection for his cousin pointed the way and he nobly accepted, yet it was with mixed feelings that he renounced the quiet life of a little German princely court for the untidy turbulence of northern Europe's greatest royal family. With the stiffest of upper lips he reflected in his journal that 'with true resolution and zeal' he could not fail 'to continue noble, manly and princely in all things.' There were many times, in the years that lay ahead, when he would need all his resolution.

The announcement of the forthcoming marriage aroused hostility. The nation resented the prospect of a petty German princeling meddling in its affairs; the court objected to this new Coburg coup; Parliament docked £20,000 from the £50,000 proposed for the Prince's annual income, and refused to give him the high precedence of rank the Queen wanted. But she, too, stood on her dignity as his monarch. She insisted on choosing the gentlemen of his staff and even curtailed the two-week private honeymoon he proposed to a mere three days. They were married on 10 February 1840 in the Chapel Royal, St James's, and returned through rain-swept but cheering streets to Buckingham

Palace from where, at about 4pm, they set off for Windsor Castle. They were both in their 21st year.

From the first Victoria doted on her husband, but for the early years denied him access to state papers. Albert, whose prodigious talent for work, great tact and obvious devotion to his new country eventually earned him grudging respect on all sides, found the first scope for his restless energy at Windsor. He began the business of cataloguing and ordering the art collections and archives and set the farm running at a profit. Then, in 1844, he and the Queen acquired the estate of Osborne on the Isle of Wight to be a family retreat from the capital. Tough and businesslike, he bargained down the price and then embarked on the delightful job of replanning the estate and designing the considerable extensions to the modest Georgian mansion, walking the site and poring over plans with his builder, being his own architect. Additions in the grounds included the Swiss Cottage and the Dairy where the children of the growing royal family spent many happy childhood hours.

Their first child, the Princess Royal Victoria, always 'Vicky' in the family, arrived in November 1840 and over the next 17 years the Queen endured nine pregnancies. The royal pair had strong views on the sanctity of marriage. For both of them this may have been a reaction to their ancestry – the amorous adventures of Albert's father and brother could match even the Hanoverians. But comments in Victoria's journals, allusive but unmistakable in their meaning, show that her devotion to her husband was for something more than his public virtues. It was not because she doted on children that she had so many. When 'Vicky' was on the way she bemoaned the restricting prospect of motherhood on her life-style. As to the act of birth . . . she hated it. Late in life she quizzed

Opposite: *The Wedding Morning* a painting of Victoria and Albert in February 1840.
Above: A print of Osborne House in the late 1840s.

Below: *The Christening of the Princess Royal at Windsor* (1841), by Charles Robert Leslie. This was the first use of the christening robe still used today.

Above: Victoria and Albert and their five eldest children, engraved after a painting by Winterhalter. The original picture was exhibited to the public, by the Queen's special permission, at Buckingham Palace in 1848. Despite the formality of dress and the artistic conventions of pose and composition, Winterhalter's painting must have appeared to contemporaries to be as intimate and domestic a scene of royalty as could be expected; that it was to be viewed in the royal home gave the showing as much impact at the time as the TV presentation Royal Family in the 1960s. In the conditions of 1848 when crowns all over Europe were falling to revolution the idyllic family life of their own royals was a heartening symbol of stability to British hearts.

her granddaughter Marie of Roumania as to whether she had been given chloroform during her confinement. Marie, shamefacedly confessed she had – her own mother-in-law (something of a poetess) believed that to bring a child into the world was 'a moment of such poetical rapture that nothing must be allowed to allay the ecstasy of its pain.' Victoria had no time for such tosh. She had received chloroform at only one of her confinements and, she went on, 'I assure you my child, I deeply deplore the fact that I had to bring eight children into the world without its precious aid.'

She was prone to post-natal depression which, added to her unpredictable moodiness, made her a trying companion at times so that even Albert's good nature broke. At the outset he had helped ease her awkward relations with Sir Robert Peel so that she came to respect his qualities as a statesman. In the spring of 1840, a crazed young man discharged a pistol in the direction of her carriage as it rolled up Constitution Hill. Victoria saw that he was treated leniently – but heeded the warning of her own mortality and had Albert designated Regent in the event of her death.

For much of Europe the nineteenth century was punctuated by bloody revolutions and still

bloodier government repression. For a moment, during the 1840s, even England seemed to be teetering. Agitation for further liberalization of the political process, including universal manhood suffrage, had been mounting under the banner of the People's Charter and in 1842 thousands of Chartists marched in London to present a petition with more than a million signatures demanding reforms. Troops were mobilized and the drawing rooms nervously talked of revolution. But the moment passed, and the fashionable world giggled somewhat hysterically when it was learnt that some subversive wag had added the Queen's name to the Great Charter.

Across the Channel in 1848, the Year of Revolutions saw many thrones totter and the French royal family in flight. But to Victoria's disgust her foreign secretary, Lord Palmerston openly sympathized with the revolutionaries. Her displeasure contributed to his resignation in 1851. By now Albert's ascendancy over the Queen in state business was becoming established and also increasingly respected by her ministers. But it was only one aspect of his multifarious activities. An amateur composer of some ability, and an outstanding shot, he was revealing himself as England's most talented and versatile royal since the days of Elizabeth I.

With the Great Exhibition of 1851 he achieved his most notable public triumph. The world's first international exhibition of industry, trade and the arts, it was housed in the Crystal Palace, a monument of futuristic architecture prefabricated in iron and glass, so immense that full-grown elm trees were comfortably embraced by its arching girders. The displays ranged from music to machinery; the public flocked in their thousands; the new railway companies laid on cut price excursion trains; the show made a profit which served to finance the museum and college complex which still survives in South Kensington, London around the Victoria and Albert Museum. Behind it all lay the inspiration and organizational genius of Prince Albert.

Four years later saw the completion of another of his enterprises – the new castle at Balmoral, on the River Dee near Aberdeen in Scotland. The royal couple, who had first visited the area more than a decade before, were in love with the Scottish Highlands. They and their family roamed the glens, camped in remote cottages, drank the whisky and, in Albert's case at least, battled with the complexities of the Gaelic language. The Queen dressed in satin tartan, the boys in kilts; the Prince was equipped with sporting gun, she with sketch-book and journal; the politicians were dismayed by these royal

excursions 600 miles from the capital. In 1848 the royal pair took a lease on Balmoral House with its 17,000 acres – 'a pretty little castle in the Scotch style' – and four years later bought the place. The Prince could now get to work in earnest. Seconded by a local architect he designed a grand new castle which took just three years in the building. Thorough as always, he also designed a Balmoral tartan.

When Balmoral was completed, Britain was in the throes of the Crimean War. Victoria found Palmerston, now back in power and as prime minister, so 'zealous and able' in his conduct of affairs that she offered him the Garter.

Above: *The Opening of the Great Exhibition by H.M. the Queen, in the Crystal palace.* The immense iron and glass exhibition hall, the most advanced building of its time and the Exhibition itself owed their inspiration to her beloved Albert.

Below: The Royal Family in Scotland; Albert was a keen shot (and angler).

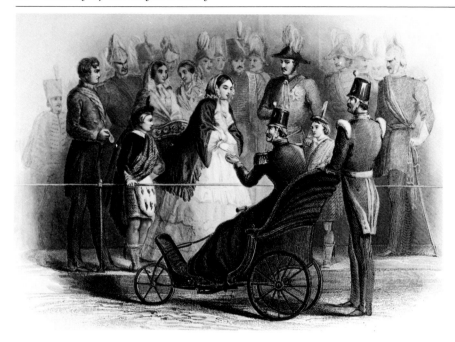

Above: Victoria distributing medals to veterans of the Crimean War in May 1855 – the Victoria Cross, first presented at this time, was her concept.

Below: Albert and Victoria with Napoleon III and Empress Eugénie at the Paris Opera during their state visit in 1855.

So moved was she by the heroism of her troops in that bloody and dire conflict that she instituted what is still Britain's highest award for gallantry – the Victoria Cross. Its inscription 'For Valour' was her idea and she presented the first sixty-two medals, cast from captured Russian guns, at a review in Hyde Park. The War witnessed the improbable alliance of France and England. The Queen, who was in the habit of writing to all her friends and relations among the sovereigns of Europe – often in good French

– was captivated by Napoleon III and his empress Eugénie who had been guests at Windsor in 1855.

On this occasion the castle was the setting for a brilliant reception; on less formal occasions there were parlour games and country dancing. At Christmas, the chandeliers in the Queen's private sitting room were taken down and Christmas trees, aglow with candles, hung in their place. Albert, to whom the British Christmas owes its modern form, observed contentedly that 'everything was German and *gemütlich.*' If the lake at Frogmore froze over in a hard winter the Prince, a stylish skater, delighted to give his family an exhibition.

But the family was growing up. In 1857 Vicky, to the Queen's distress, left home. Although the two did not always see eye to eye on politics – Vicky has been called a 'questing liberal' – they were very close and the Queen hated any break in the family circle. But Princess Victoria seemed destined for a brilliant future as the bride of the German Crown Prince Frederick. Albert was still more desolate, for his liberal and intelligent daughter had been a welcome companion at times when her mother was at her most demanding and obtuse. In any case, the Queen soon realized that her distant daughter was an ideal confidante for her voluminous

correspondence. Over the years Berlin found her constant letters often interfering and intrusive, but they had many intimate and revealing touches. Her beloved Osborne featured constantly – we catch glimpses of her reading Jane Eyre to Albert before they adjourn to the piano for their regular evening duets, and of Bertie (the Prince of Wales) with 'a sick head-ache . . . from imprudence.'

The boy himself was proving an almost constant headache as he moved through his teens to what looked likely to be an unnerving maturity. The great favourite at this time was her second son Prince Alfred, 'Affie'. To her great mortification, he too was soon to leave home, on his father's insistence, for a spell at sea with the Royal Navy. As Duke of Edinburgh he was destined to make his career in the service and by his marriage to Marie of Russia to be the father of Marie, Queen of Roumania, whose childbirth experiences were to so interest the old queen in later years.

The Queen's petulance at Affie's departure was only intensified by the fact that Vicky, barely nineteen, was pregnant with her first child far away in Potsdam where her mother could not hope to attend the confinement. Victoria, who always tended to be a little distraught at news of childbirth, gloomily forecast a miscarriage. Vicky's baby emerged with nothing worse than a withered arm. But since he was destined to become Kaiser Wilhelm II there may be those who would consider his grandmother's forebodings not unjustified.

In 1860 Victoria and Albert celebrated their twentieth wedding anniversary. With their children beginning to leave home and to produce grandchildren the dynastic ties between London and other European capitals were beginning to form a network which, in the next century, would link most of the continent's ruling houses. Albert, created Prince Consort in 1857, had established himself as the dominant partner of the royal duet and could look forward to an old age as the elder statesman of Europe. He was as always hard at work, though at times it appeared as if the strain was beginning to affect his health. Even the Queen's ministers were willing to defer to his judgement and it seemed the only person beyond his influence was the one who concerned him most – his son Albert Edward, Prince of Wales.

Since childhood, the Prince had been subject to a strict regimen of study – designed to fit him for the crown, but entirely unsuited to his amiable character. Now in his twentieth year he spent a time at Oxford and then, in 1861, two months with an army regiment based in Ireland. From there he returned for a term at Cambridge and it was while he was there that the

Queen and Albert learnt from Baron Stockmar that their son had made his debut in the world of sex. Albert was heavily burdened with worry. Britain's relations with America were under a severe strain as a result of the outbreak of the Civil War. Palmerston, still prime minister, held neutral only with difficulty – his sympathies were with the southern cause. When, therefore, Federal (Northern) officers boarded the British steamship *Trent* and arrested Confederate officers travelling on her, the British note of protest was so violent in tone as to be tantamount to a declaration of war. Albert, who had hurried up to Cambridge to remonstrate with his son and fulfilled a busy programme of troop reviews in the winter weather, returned to Windsor in mid-November to work at redrafting

Below: Queen Victoria nursing the most famous of her grandchildren, Prince Wilhelm of Prussia, to become the German Kaiser Wilhelm II. The family ties between British and German royals were numerous and complex.

the dispatch for Washington. As reworded by
him the bellicose challenge became a strong but
dignified protest and the danger of war was
averted. It was his last great service to his country.

Weakened by a chill and nervous exhaustion,
the Prince succumbed to typhoid no doubt provoked by the appalling sanitation at Windsor.
After some days of delirium he died in the evening of 14 December in the Blue Room, where
both George IV and William IV had died.

Distraught and forbidden to touch her husband's body for fear of infection, the Queen fled
to Osborne. It was the beginning of a withdrawal from public life that was to last more
than a decade. Much of the time was spent at
Balmoral where her confidant was John Brown,
the Highland ghillie who had been friend and
servant of Albert and herself. When she was at
Windsor, Brown followed and had his bedroom
only a few doors from hers: the scandal mongers
found a new name for the Queen – 'Mrs Brown.'
Her family was appalled by the easy familiarity
with which she treated this blunt, often rude,
and utterly undeferential Scot's peasant's son.
Yet Brown was, undoubtedly, a good friend and
a loyal servant. His overfondness for the whisky
was indulged by the Queen and his relations
found comfortable cottages and secure jobs about the estate at Balmoral. But this was the
limit of his self interest. As court favourite he
could have wielded much more influence had he
wished and the suggestion that they were lovers
– even secretly married – belongs in the world of
fantasy. When told of the rumours the Queen,
with a pleased smile, merely observed: 'I did not
know I was so notorious.'

Far more worrying than the gossip was the Queen's almost total withdrawal from public affairs. Five years went by before she again attended the State Opening of Parliament. For a time her ministers were given audience in a room adjoining the Queen's, who communicated with them through the open door by a nod or shake of the head to their comments.

Even when the consort was alive the more sophisticated courtiers had been wearied by the combination of starchy etiquette and humdrum domesticity which prevailed in the royal palaces. After his death life at court was one of almost unrelieved tedium. Mealtime conversation was conducted in whispers; maids of honour might not entertain a man, even their own brother, in their own rooms; young courtiers of either sex who had the audacity to get engaged were sure to incur royal displeasure. Ministers of State strolling in the Park at Windsor smartly concealed themselves behind a tree when they saw the Queen's pony chair approaching for she objected to being 'stared at.'

And, of course, the family suffered. When the nineteen-year-old Princess Alice got married to Prince Louis of Hesse Darmstadt a year after the death, the 'poor, unhappy marriage' in the Queen's words, seemed 'more like a funeral than a wedding.' If it was so the fault was largely hers. The event might well have been postponed had not the date been fixed by the Consort himself. The gentlemen were dressed in black evening coats, the ladies in half mourning of grey or violet; the bride wore flounces designed by her dead father; and the ceremony, at a temporary altar in the dining room at Osborne, was presided over by a Winterhalter painting of the family dominated by the life-size portrait of the dead Prince. The Archbishop of Canterbury conducted the service with 'tears running down his cheeks;' the Queen's gaze barely shifted from the picture of her dead husband. There was no cake; no confetti. The offspring of these sombre nuptials included Alix, who was to be Empress of Russia by her marriage to Tsar Nicholas II. She was to transmit to her son the Tsarevitch Alexei the dread disease of haemophilia, carried in her genes from her mother.

Palmerston, in all sincerity, described the death of Albert as 'an overwhelming calamity.' But the reaction of the 'Widow of Windsor' was out of all proportion. As year followed year with barely a single public appearance, republicanism, once the preserve of a few radicals, began to seem almost respectable. The Queen received an annual Civil List of £385,000 but what, newspaper articles began to ask, did she do for it all – what, indeed, did she do *with* it all? When the French Emperor Napoleon III was driven from his throne in September 1870, Victoria

grieved for the plight of a friend – many of her subjects rejoiced at the proclamation of the Third Republic. Algernon Swinburne, the avant garde poet of the time, heralded the dawn of a new age with *Songs Before Sunrise*; mass demonstrations were held in Hyde Park and Trafalgar Square; Republican clubs were formed in Birmingham, London and all the major cities; a group of MPs led by Sir Charles Dilke brought the republican cause into the parliamentary arena, and addressed public meetings across the country.

But towards the end of 1871 the Prince of Wales fell dangerously ill with typhoid and a wave of sentiment for the Queen as a mother swept back the faltering tide of republican agitation. Flattered and cajoled by her favourite prime minister Benjamin Disraeli, Victoria emerged once more onto the public stage. In 1876 to her considerable delight, he persuaded Parliament to grant her the title 'Empress of India.'

Opposite above: *The Prince Consort on his deathbed.* Unpopular with the xenophobic British establishment on his first arrival in England, Albert earned respect and even affection by his devotion to his adopted country, and by his manifest talents.
Opposite below: The Queen and her servant John Brown. She was amused, perhaps secretly pleased, by the gossip that whispered around her relationship with this unlikely court favorite.

Below: An official portrait photograph of Victoria in 1876, the year in which Parliament accorded her the title 'Empress of India.'

Right: Part of the procession accompanying the royal carriage on its return from Westminster Abbey after the service of thanksgiving in Victoria's Golden Jubilee year of 1887. In the centre of the photograph can be seen a troop of Indian cavalry, preceding the Queen's carriage with its liveried footmen and postilions. Victoria was not only immensely proud of her title 'Empress of India,' she also had considerable respect and affection for her subjects on the subcontinent. After the death of John Brown in 1883 Abdul Karim, known as 'the Munshi' or 'teacher' became her personal servant. Inevitably, court circles were outraged and, despite their world-wide Empire and Commonwealth no subsequent British monarch has admitted a coloured servant to the higher circles of the household. The Jubilee procession had representatives from all parts of the empire, but for the London crowds the celebrations were for *their* Queen – banners with VR and GOD SAVE THE QUEEN can be seen at some of the windows.

Below right: The Queen and members of her family. Back row, second from left, Prince Henry of Battenberg ('Liko'), fourth from left Princess Beatrice, his wife and next to her George, Duke of York. Princess 'May' Duchess of York sits next to the Queen, Prince Edward of York (future King Edward VIII) on her knee.

Now in her late 60's, Victoria was acquiring a matriarchal aura. Her Golden Jubilee in 1887 was a great European and Imperial occasion. Throughout the programme of receptions, parades, garden parties, firework displays and loyal addresses, the Queen Empress was supported by her youngest daughter, the thirty-year-old Princess Beatrice with her dashing husband, Prince Henry of Battenberg. They had been married two years and had only won her consent

to the match on condition that they continue to live with her and that Beatrice, the mainstay of her mother's old age, continue as her companion.

The two had met and fallen in love at the wedding of Henry's brother, Prince Louis of Battenberg to Princess Victoria, a niece of Beatrice but only six years younger than she. Louis was destined for a distinguished career in the Royal Navy; his grandson is the present Prince Philip, Duke of Edinburgh; while his son (Philip's uncle) was the brilliant Lord Louis Mountbatten, Earl Mountbatten of Burma. The children of the Henry Mountbattens included Ena, who was to be Queen of Spain as wife of King Alphonso XIII.

Enthusiastic, debonair and diplomatic, Prince Henry, always known as 'Liko' in the family, seemed to Victoria 'a bright sunbeam in my home' – his death from malaria while on active service in 1896 was perhaps the greatest grief of her declining years. Heart-broken, but loyal, Princess Beatrice, now honoured with her husband's titles as Governor of the Isle of Wight and of Carisbrooke Castle, remained at her mother's side and, after her death prepared her journals for publication.

As well as the reunion with her ever extending family, the Jubilee Celebrations brought a new theme of interest for Victoria in the persons of two Indian servants. The Queen, entirely free of racial prejudice, welcomed these newcomers

Left: A group taken at Balmoral in 1896 to commemorate the visit of Tsar Nicholas II of Russia to Britain in that year. One year off her Diamond Jubilee, Victoria had been on the throne eleven years longer than her nearest rival in longevity, Emperor Franz Josef II of Austria and her family connexions among Europe's royal houses were far more extensive. Here she is seated with her granddaughter Alix, the wife of the ill-fated Tsar who stands behind. On her knee sits the Grand Duchess Tatiana, destined like the rest of her family, to meet her death in the turmoil following the Bolshevik revolution of October 1917. To the right of the picture stands Victoria's son and heir Edward Prince of Wales.

to her entourage as representatives of her Indian subjects. Astonishingly for a person approaching 70 she began the study of Hindustani under their tuition and of the two Hafiz Abdul Karim, known as the 'Munshi' or 'teacher', soon came to enjoy the honoured friendship once accorded John Brown who had died. Like Brown he soon became the subject of endless scandal and anecdotes though, since he had a wife who lived in her own quarters, the ultimate canard was never run.

The record of her first encounter with the Munshi by the Queen's grand-daughter, Queen Marie of Roumania conveys the sense of unreality that his silent presence brought to the dour precincts of the royal palaces. 'There was a click of a doorhandle and there, on the threshold, stood the Munshi, an Indian idol clothed in gold with a white turban. He remained framed in the doorway ... simply waiting for those things that were to come to pass. Nando (King Ferdinand, her husband) had no idea what was expected of him, and so simply stared at the enigmatic apparition while Grandmama kept hunching her shoulders and smiling as though her smile could make something happen.' Finally, Marie broke the spell and shook the Indian's hand.

The celebration of the Diamond Jubilee in 1897 was on a scale rarely seen before and never

Opposite: The official Diamond Jubilee photograph (1897).

Left: The Queen at Cimiez, Nice, where she took a suite at the Grand Hotel Excelsior Regina. She visited the Riviera more than once and travelled on business as well as pleasure to the last year of her life. In April 1900 she made an Official Visit to Dublin and was delighted by the warmth of the reception she received.
Below: The Queen's funeral cortège passes through the streets of London. At Windsor the long wait had made the horses restive and the gun carriage was hauled by the Naval honour guard.

since. The whole empire was on parade. In the words of one observer 'no sovereign since the fall of Rome could muster so many subjects from so many and so distant countries.' An immense procession escorted her from the Palace to St Paul's where, because the old lady was too infirm to leave her carriage, the clergy and choir had assembled on the steps. Thousands upon thousands of voices joined them in the singing of the hymns of the short service; at the end the Archbishop of Canterbury raised his crozier for silence and then called for 'Three cheers for the Queen.' Deafened by the roars of loyalty and love she wept openly. As ten years before the functions and celebrations went on for days and the 78-year-old Queen attended many in person. At Osborne, in the Durbar room built as her tribute to her interest in her Indian empire, she hosted a state luncheon for the King of Siam come, like the crowned heads of east and west, to do homage.

When it was all over she returned to her sorrows, as friend after friend was taken from her by death, and to her work. She was 'doing her boxes' and reading government papers to within a month of her death. On 14 December 1900 she and the family paid their annual homage at Albert's Mausoleum in Frogmore and then took the royal train for Christmas at Osborne. She died on 22 January 1901 in the arms of her grandson, the German Kaiser. By her wish she was buried in white with her wedding veil. The coffin was conveyed from Cowes to Portsmouth aboard the yacht *Alberta* between a double battle line of battleships to the flat thud of their minute guns.

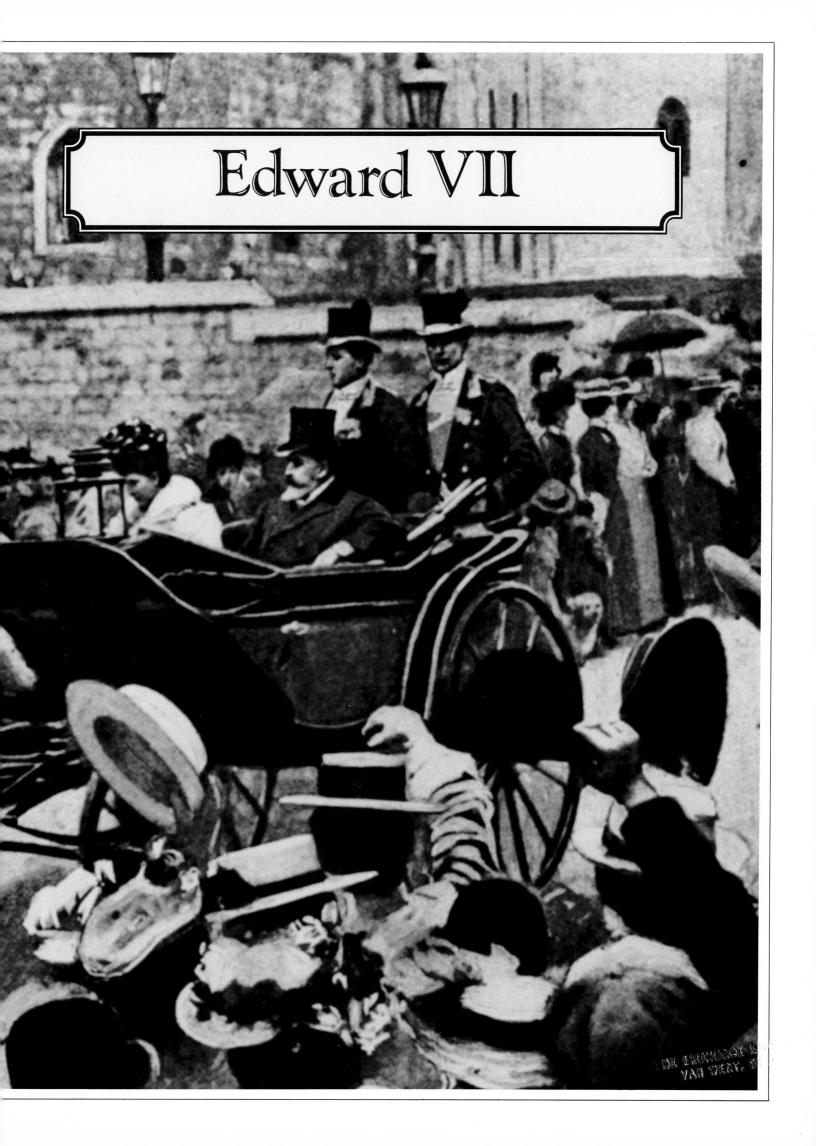

Edward VII

Pages 28-29: King Edward VII and Queen Alexandra leaving Windsor Castle on their way to London after the King's recovery from the severe illness which seemed to threaten his life at the very beginning of his reign.

'I can see no hope for British Jacobitism so long as Queen Victoria lives,' wrote Don Carlos, pretender to the Spanish throne, 'but should her son the Prince of Wales succeed her, his wild ways may make him so distasteful to a Puritan nation that he may be driven out, and then thoughts may turn to the old line.'

The 'old line' to which he referred was the House of Stuart and Jacobitism was the creed of those who believed that the true succession to the British throne lay not with the House of Hanover, but with the descendants of the family of Stuart, to which Britain's last Stuart King, James II, had belonged. Even today, there are people who whimsically claim adherence to this quirk of dynastic loyalism and on the day following Queen Victoria's death a handbill, headed THE ASSERTION – affirming 'Queen Mary IV', a certain Bavarian lady, as true heiress was found fixed to the gates of St James's Palace. It was promptly removed and Edward VII – King of Great Britain and Ireland, and of the Dominions across the Sea, Emperor of India – was duly proclaimed to the general satisfaction of his loyal subjects. The queen-matriarch of Europe was dead: she was succeeded by the 'Uncle of Europe.'

After 60 years as a prince, the tall and portly monarch – with his grizzled beard and twinkling blue eyes – certainly looked avuncular.

And he was, in fact, uncle to the German Kaiser William II; to the Empress of Russia; to the Queen of Spain; and to the Crown Prince of Roumania. Another niece was later to become Queen of Sweden and his daughter was to be the Queen of Norway. The Kings of Denmark and Norway and of Greece were both his brothers-in-law; the Kings of Bulgaria and Portugal his cousins. Further down the royal league, he was also an uncle to the sovereign Grand Duke of Hesse. When he died, Edward VII was the doyen of European monarchy. And yet Don Carlos, if we discount his natural interest in legitimist fantasies, had had a point. The Prince had undoubtedly had his wild ways and many of his sober subjects harboured serious doubts as to his suitability to succeed the old Queen.

At his christening in 1841, the initials of his two names – Albert Edward – were displayed all over a festive London. This cheerful lacework of AE monograms prompted one wit, mindful of the habits of previous Princes of Wales, to remark: 'No doubt he will one day be equally familiar with the other three vowels, IOU.' And he was. Affable and easy-going by nature, Edward was forced to spend his boyhood and youth in a rigid and demanding curriculum of study. Liberated at last by manhood he set a smart pace in the whirl of good living and high society.

His serious-minded father had tried hard to mould him into the ideal of a modern constitutional monarch, well read and mature of judgement. But 'Bertie', despite occasional earnest efforts, was not meant for desk work or study. He was carefully insulated from his age peers during his brief period as a student. At Oxford he lived with his entourage in a private mansion in the town and received private lectures in company with specially selected undergraduates. On the rare occasions that the Prince attended public lectures the other students rose and remained standing until he sat. Edward's brief attendance at Oxford was followed by a still shorter period at Cambridge and from there, aged 20, he was sent to the Army camp at the Curragh in Northern Ireland to sample the training of an army officer.

Again the Prince was set an impossible programme by his father. In ten weeks, it was supposed, he would master and pass exams in the qualifications of all the ranks from ensign to battalion commander. There was no question that he should ever be permitted to see active service. It might have been a reasonable precaution had he been seriously trained for the job his life was being preserved for. As it was, this vigorous and naturally brave young man was thwarted of an experience he longed for and it was to be a cause of humiliation throughout his life. However, a Victorian officers' mess offered

Below: The young Victoria with her first born child, Albert Edward.
Opposite: The young Prince Albert Edward aged seven, in the sailor suit which was more or less standard boyhood dress for the children of royalty. The painting is by the fashionable Winterhalter.

Below: The official wedding photograph of Edward and Alexandra.
Opposite above: Mr Gladstone 'kissing hands' on taking office as Prime Minister. The artist has well caught the Queen's disdain for the statesman. She always undervalued his great qualities just as she did the abilities of her eldest son and his eagerness for real work in the service of the country. Edward's reputation as a roué, which so shocked his mother, did not prejudice Mr Gladstone's respect for his qualities and potential. Anxious to find serious employment for the Prince and confident of his diplomatic abilities, he urged the Queen to appoint him her representative in Ireland – to no avail.
Opposite below: Edward and Alexandra as Prince and Princess of Wales, riding in Windsor Great Park.

other openings and it was here that 'Bertie' first encountered the delights of love – in the arms of the actress Nellie Clifden.

News of the escapade brought Prince Albert hurrying to his son's side. The weather was cold and wet and the Prince Consort took a chill. He never properly recovered. When he died weeks later of typhoid Victoria was convinced that the trip and worry over their son had killed her beloved husband. As for Bertie, his father's death was a tragic end to a frequently unhappy but basically loving relationship. His mother's antipathy lasted for years. She even took steps to prevent his succeeding his father in honorary appointments as president of philanthropic or learned societies.

A new chapter in the relations between mother and son might have opened with the marriage of Prince Edward to Princess Alexandra of Denmark in St George's Chapel, Windsor on 10 March 1863. But Victoria, who observed the ceremony from a gallery, was lugubriously in mourning for Albert and no doubt nursing her resentment of her son. By contrast, the nation was jubilant. The 18-year-old Alexandra was radiantly beautiful, spon-

taneous and graceful. She was to be sorely tried in the years that lay ahead by her husband's philandering, but remained loyal and loving. She also had other more conventional hazards, among them five pregnancies in the first six years of marriage and a hip injury which, before she was 30, left her with a limp for life.

The young couple set up house in London at Marlborough House renovated for them at the vast cost of £60,000 and also acquired the 7000 acre estate of Sandringham in Norfolk for more than £200,000. (Saved from his allowance as prince while he was under age). Here, they were to build the mansion in mock Tudor style which ever since has been one of the royal family's favourite residences. Here it was that Edward loved to indulge his passion for shooting. The objective seems to have been slaughter on the largest possible scale. At the vast house parties Edward and his guests often ended their gunnery practice with a bag of upwards of 6000 birds. The evenings were given over to gargantuan banquets and the nights to bedroom adventures. Discretion was the one unbreakable rule of this glittering and extravagant society. 'Any indiscretion which impaired Society's prestige,' wrote one contemporary, 'invited a sentence of social death which was ruthlessly executed.'

As King, Edward was to spend less time than before at Sandringham but it remained the house for the traditional Christmas. As seen from the windows of York Cottage in the grounds, where his son Prince George lived, it was an intriguing time for the King's grandchildren. Some days before, cohorts of servants arrived to lay the fires in the rooms, prepare mountains of food and adorn the whole house with costly hot-house flowers. The preparations complete, the limousines of the King and Queen and their household lumbered up along the muddy Norfolk roads to be followed in due course by those of their guests – foreign diplomats, society beauties, bankers and politicians in favour.

It was a life-style beloved by both King and Queen but, in their younger days, the old Queen had been shocked. Bertie, in particular, seemed addicted to horse racing (he was to own three Derby winners) and gambling and once, to his mother's profound disgust, he was cited in open court as just one of the co-respondents in a well-publicized divorce case.

On 23 November 1871, following a visit to Scarborough, Bertie contracted typhoid . . . the very disease which had killed his father. At first, it seems, Victoria could not take seriously the idea that her wastrel son was really in danger. After six days she eventually travelled down to Sandringham. Bertie passed the crisis

in his illness on 16 December, and the following February a Service of Thanksgiving for his recovery was held in St Paul's Cathedral. These dramatic – and public events inspired a massive resurgence of popular enthusiasm for the monarchy and from this time forward Victoria's standing with her subjects was never to be seriously in doubt.

To the Prince's frustration, however, his mother continued to refuse him access to the processes of government. Surprisingly, perhaps, the great and serious-minded prime minister, Mr Gladstone, took up the Prince's cause. He suggested that the Prince should be made Viceroy of Ireland. But this idea, and many lesser proposals for giving the Prince worthwhile public scope for his diplomatic nature and genuine keenness to serve, was curtly dismissed by the Queen. She could only look forward with mournful anticipation to the day when her son would be King, and meanwhile guard against inflicting him on the country any earlier than absolutely necessary.

The Prince and his beautiful wife were left to discharge the one function of monarchy which Victoria would not – and could not. She keenly

exercised, often to the irritation of her ministers, the residual rights of the monarchy to advise, to be consulted, and to warn, but her role, as the leader of the courtly world, not unimportant in an aristocratic society, went largely by default. It was filled with charm and stylishness by the Wales's. Victoria even became jealous of their popularity as well as worried by the publicity Edward attracted in his role as leader of London's fashionable set.

Occasionally Queen and Prince attended public functions together, though not, one feels, from choice. Edward was a furious smoker – the day started with one large cigar and two cigarettes before breakfast and thereafter he smoked cigars more or less until bedtime. His mother hated the habit and banned smoking in her palaces. On the rare occasions they attended Covent Garden, the Prince had to indulge his little vice in a special room added at the Queen's instructions behind the royal box, which already had a supper room giving off it. When he became King, Edward used this for immense suppers which required six footmen to prepare them during the afternoon. Hampers of food and gold plate – up to 400 dishes – were brought from the palace kitchens and 30 or 40 guests sat down to cold collations running to ten or twelve courses.

In his 50th year, the Prince was called as a witness in the famous Tranby-Croft case, which concerned one of his gaming partners who had been accused of cheating at baccarrat. Guest at a constant round of country house parties; friend and lover of a galaxy of beautiful women – of whom the actress Lillie Langtry was the most famous; arbiter of fashion and bon vivant, he presided over the 'Edwardian era' years before his mother's death.

Alexandra matched her husband in her taste for the good life, though her notorious unpunctuality and increasing deafness could prove trying. It has been said that she was one of the two women the King ever loved. Adored by the British people, she was frank, courageous and quite unaffected in her spontaneous response to life. Even Queen Victoria, who heartily disapproved her daughter-in-law's frivolous delight in Society, was always captivated by the 'sunny warmth of the princess's actual presence.'

A beauty, though not in the same class as Alexandra, the other true love of the King's life was Mrs George Keppel. Like the Queen she was fearlessly outspoken, but she was also discreet and highly intelligent. Her qualities, rare in a royal mistress, even impressed the King's ministers, one of whom wrote a glowing tribute to her wonderful discretion, and to the excellent influence she always exercised upon the King.

Opposite: Prince Edward and Princess Alexandra with their eldest son Prince Albert-Victor and their daughter Princess Maud. The death of the Prince in 1892 left his brother George as heir presumptive. Princess Maud was to marry King Haakon VII of Norway.
Above: Edward Prince of Wales as man about town, a cartoon by 'Spy' in *Vanity Fair* 1878.
Below: Mrs Alice Keppel, wife of George Keppel, the younger son of the seventh Earl of Albemarle. For years Mrs Keppel was the mistress of King Edward VII. Her intelligence and above all her discretion earned her the respect of the King's ministers.

Above: *The Prince of Wales at Parbutty Hill, Poonah: His first elephant ride.* Edward's tour of India in 1875-6 was a regal event on the grand scale. The royal party disembarked at Bombay. After visiting the cave paintings at Elephanta the Prince went on to Poonah. At Baroda the Gaekwar laid on an elephant combat and an antelope hunt with trained cheetahs. At Madras Edward held a reception for the local princes at a night-time ceremony where 'the illuminations on the rolling surf gave a unique spectacle.' At Calcutta the Maharajahs of Pattiala, Jodhpur, Jaipur and Kashmir and the Begum of Bohpal – 'so thickly veiled that she could not be seen' – were received in audience. Later various Maharajahs, each heralded by a salute of 17 guns, were invested with the Star of India. At Benares the Prince sailed the Ganges in a decorated barge and was welcomed by the Maharajah with processional elephants and fireworks. His arrival at Delhi was marked by a grand levée and in the Punjab the chiefs and princes flocked to do homage. 'The very spirit of chivalry hovered over their martial faces and noble forms' wrote a contemporary.

'She never utilized her knowledge to her own advantage, or to that of her friends; and I never heard her repeat an unkind word about anybody.' The King, who disliked formal audiences with his ministers, formed a circle of seven trusted friends to advise him and act as go betweens. One of them was Mrs Keppel and, we are told, her special position 'was accepted and welcomed by ministers.' The Queen, too, accepted Mrs Keppel – as an improvement on her predecessors and even as a friend. Alexandra considered jealousy a mean passion and refused to let it sour her relations with a husband she adored. But the King's growing attachment to his mistress in his later years pained the Queen and made for inevitable tensions in the family circle.

Well before his accession many people, and not merely the most puritanical, beheld the activities of 'Edward the Caresser' with much unease. Yet he found time from his diversions for quite a full programme of more conventional, official engagements. A tour of India in 1875 took him across 8000 miles of the sub-continent. No doubt, the journey was made less hazardous by lavish entertainment from maharajahs, nizams and princes of various ranks, but it was also a useful royal prelude to his mother's proclamation as Empress of India the following year. At home Edward cheerfully laid his quota of foundation stones, notably that of Tower Bridge; he was closely involved in the organization of his mother's Jubilee celebrations of 1887 and 1897; and, living up to his title, he presided

over the Welsh National Eisteddfod and also became first Chancellor of the University of Wales in 1896.

Shortly before coming to the throne, Edward was initiated into the full status of a latter-day monarch when an anarchist called Sipido took a pot-shot at him in Brussels station, as the Prince's train was pulling out bound for Copenhagan where he was to celebrate Easter. Edward was familiar with many European capitals. In 1890, accompanied by Prince George (later King George V) he made a state visit to Berlin and in 1894 he attended the funeral of Tsar Alexander III in St Petersburg. Apart from these and other official state visits, he annually took the 'cure' at German resorts such as Marienbad and Bad Homburg. Wherever he went his charm and urbanity combined with his exalted social station ensured his popularity with the smart set. One of his closest cronies among these royal playboys was Carlos, Crown Prince and later King of Portugal.

A 'genial, cheery, burly monarch' Carlos was also an enthusiastic sportsman and often a guest at Sandringham – though on one unfortunate occasion, when King, he had been obliged to lunch with Queen Victoria at Buckingham Palace on his way through London for Norfolk. The friendly contacts between the royal cousins were not unimportant since Portugal and Britain were on uneasy terms during the 1880s and 1890s because of rival colonial interests in Africa. At home, however, his English connections brought him unpopularity. The straitlaced Portuguese complained that the King of their Catholic country was being infected with the ideas of Freemasonry for Edward had been inaugurated as Grand Master of the English Masons in 1874. His son and grandsons were to become members of the order in their turn.

King Edward marked his accession to royal power with actions of almost childish pique. Within weeks of his mother's funeral he was moving through the palaces and ordering the removal of pictures and treasured objects which had been in their places for decades. In particular he cleared the room in which the Prince Consort had died forty years previously. This had been kept like a mausoleum, unused – indeed untouched – with all his furniture and personal effects exactly as he had left them. To do this was no doubt healthy and understandable but to sell Osborne House on the Isle of Wight – which his parents had made into a homely retreat for their young family – seemed simply to be taking callow revenge on his unhappy childhood.

On 16 March he bade farewell to Prince George and his wife Princess Mary as they

Left: Edward and Alexandra and their family. Standing, Albert Victor, Duke of Clarence, Princess Maud, later Queen of Norway, Princess Alexandra, princess Louise (who married the Duke of Fife), Prince Edward. Seated are Prince George (later King as George V) and Princess Victoria, George's favorite sister.

Below: The official photograph of King Edward VII and Queen Alexandra at a State Opening of Parliament.

embarked on a tour of Australia, New Zealand and Canada. For Edward, who had a deep affection for his son and heir, it was a bitter leave-taking. But preparations for his own coronation were soon absorbing his attention.

It was to be a magnificent affair, and the questions of protocol and ceremonial it posed were the sort to fascinate the King. Like other modern constitutional monarchs with no real power he was a stickler for formality. At times, one even feels he had a point. A Member of the Royal Victorian Order and a Knight of the Garter both had to be informed by the King of the correct way to wear their decorations. Since these were then the two most prestigious honours in the gift of the British crown it seems the recipients sometimes took their distinctions a little casually. But then King Edward himself sometimes appeared strangely casual. He was wont, we are told, to carry the insignia of the lesser grades of the Royal Victorian Medal around in his pockets 'and hand them out on the spur of the moment to a cook who made him a particularly satisfactory dish, or anybody else who happened to please him.'

The royal martinet was certainly unpredictable. Once, he dispatched an equerry to the orchestra pit in the interval of a performance at Covent Garden – to reprimand a musician who was wearing a black tie instead of a white one. On the other hand it was Edward VII who instituted the Order of Merit, the most highly prized of all British awards because, except in rare instances, it actually is awarded on merit. Its

Above: July 1899 with Mr Montagu (later 2nd Baron Montagu of Beaulieu) at Highcliffe Castle. While the Prince was a guest at the Castle, Mr Montagu was asked to come and show his car, a four-cylinder, twelve-horse-power Daimler. Built on a specially light-weight aluminum body it was capable of the then remarkable speed of 40 mph. As the regular guest of honour at aristocratic country house parties, the Prince had much greater enthusiasm for the delights of high living than the technicalities of motor car design. But motoring was then the fashionable craze and as such claimed the Prince's attention.

distinguished holders have included the poet T. S. Eliot.

Edward's coronation preparations had to be dramatically abandoned with only days to go when the King fell severely ill with an inflamation of the intestine. Dismayed, the nation hourly expected the news of his death. When he made an astonishingly fast recovery the King refused to postpone the ceremony to allow the ranks of impressive dignitaries on the original guest list to reschedule their engagements so as to attend. Instead, he went to his coronation on 9 August 1901, as planned, with few of Europe's royals in attendance ... but to the heartfelt rejoicings of his own people.

Now the King's travels took on a new significance. In April 1903, he made the first visit by a reigning English monarch to Italy, being received by King Victor Emmanuel. His audience with Pope Leo XIII startled public opinion, however. The King was soon to earn the title of 'Edward the Peacemaker' from his admirers (the Italian foreign minister extravagantly dubbed him 'the arbiter of Europe's destiny'). The bridge-building exercise at the Vatican was entirely in character. Of greater importance was his state visit to France, in 1903.

Anglo-French relations had traditionally been antagonistic since the Middle Ages, but they were particularly hostile now because of colonial rivalries in Africa. The French press bloomed with vicious cartoons against England and against Edward personally. The King's cavalcade met with cold indifference from the curious crowds along the Champs Elysées. But Edward the Caresser had his own style of diplomacy. Visiting the Theatre Français that evening, this famous friend of actresses gallantly paid his respects to the renowned Jeanne Granier. In a voice loud enough to carry through the foyer he carefully enunciated in his best French: 'Ah, Mam'selle, I remember how I applauded you in London where you represented all the grace, all the *esprit* of France.' The words were being enthusiastically quoted all round Paris the next day. In his formal speech at the British Embassy he did not forget to mention '*la gloire.*'

The following day, on his way from the Elysée Palace to the Opéra, he found his way blocked by cheering crowds shouting '*Vive Edouard!*' and even '*Vive notre roi!*' The visit which had started so inauspiciously ended, according to the Parisian press, in demonstrations of 'delirious fervour.'

Few doubt Edward's contribution to the improvement of Anglo-French relations. But his

Right: Berlin, February 1909, King Edward rides with the German Kaiser during his state visit. Later the King said: 'My nephew will release the forces of war not as a result of his own initiative, but out of weakness.' As he signed the orders for German mobilization in August 1914, the Kaiser said to his staff officers: 'Gentlemen, you will rue the day that you made me do this.'

forte was not as a diplomat but rather in fostering an atmosphere in which diplomacy might flourish. In 1904 he was with the Kaiser for the regatta at Kiel, no doubt viewed as significant by the Germans who, like other Europeans, had an exaggerated estimate of the King's influence on British policy. In a world where monarchy still bulked large in people's imagination, and above all in Germany where the Kaiser played a not inconsiderable role in affairs, this was understandable.

Yet at home, the King's socializing statesmanship, often undertaken without due liaison with the Foreign Office, was viewed uneasily. To the Germans, the Entente Cordiale between Britain and France seems to have been regarded as the King's personal creation. A German Imperial Chancellor was to declare in the Reichstag: 'King Edward VII believed that his principal task was to isolate Germany. The encirclement begun by the Entente with openly hostile tendencies was drawn closer year by year.' The statement was based on a lofty view of the role of a British monarch in the first decade of the twentieth century. The reality was more accurately reflected in the crisis over the power of the House of Lords which clouded the last months of Edward's reign.

The Liberal government under Prime Minister Asquith wished to push through a series of major social welfare reforms devised by Lloyd George, Chancellor of the Exchequer. But although it could muster a majority in the House of Commons, the government found its legislation blocked by the overwhelmingly right-wing Upper House. The one constitutional way out of the impasse was for the King to create sufficient new peers from among government supporters to overcome the veto power of the Lords. Edward enjoyed dispensing lesser honours among his friends but he was appalled at the prospect of creating hundreds of new noblemen and thus of 'diluting' the aristocracy of England. Perhaps he even reflected wryly that in 1885 the Portuguese administration had legislated to phase out the parliamentary voting rights of hereditary peers and that the monarchy there was on the point of collapse.

In the event, death released him from the decision. Spared to the last of any serious involvement in the sordid arena of politics, Edward VII went to his tomb a symbol of the flamboyant dignity of the last great epoch of monarchy. His grief-stricken subjects mourned the passing of 'our dear Dad:' his cortege was followed by the Kaiser, Crown Prince Franz Ferdinand of the Austro-Hungarian Empire, the Kings of Greece, Spain, Portugal, Denmark, Norway, Belgium and Bulgaria. It was a fitting escort.

Above: A rare and uncharacteristic pose, King Edward VII at his work desk. No glutton for work, the King even reduced formal interviews with his ministers to a bare minimum.
Right: Royal mourners at King Edward's funeral. They include: (left) the King of Denmark, Archduke Ferdinand of Austria and Manoel of Portugal (bottom); (right) the Kings of Norway and Greece, Prince Henry of the Netherlands and Alfonso XIII of Spain (bottom). The German Emperor is to the right of the Dowager Empress of Russia in the bottom row.

George V

Pages 40-41: The Duke and Duchess of York, later King George V and Queen Mary, in their apartments in St James's Palace, 1896. Princess Victoria Mary of Teck had been engaged to George's elder brother, the Duke of Clarence, until his death in 1892. Her marriage to George, arranged for dynastic reasons, was one of the happiest in the history of the royal family.

Below: The young Prince George. The sailor suit was conventional boyhood dress for royalty; in George's case it was apt. Until the untimely death of his brother put him in immediate line for the throne he was making a successful career for himself in the Royal Navy.

'I have lost my best friend and best of fathers.' With these words King George V recorded his deep personal grief at the death of his father. The funeral had been solemnized with all the pomp that royal Europe could muster. But when the ceremonies were over and the crowned heads had departed, the 45-year-old monarch was left to face a troubled political scene in which the ancient prerogatives of kingship would be of little help

The recurrent problem of Ireland was approaching a new crisis; the trade unions were showing new militancy; and the rising naval power of Germany threatened Britain's age old supremacy at sea. But for a King the Liberal government's Parliament Bill presented still more immediate worries. For George V, as for his father, the prospect of ennobling some 500 commoners merely to assist a political programme seemed to strike at the heart of the ancient principal of aristocracy and to sully the 'fount of honour.' Partly because he did not wish to

embroil the apprentice King in immediate controversy, partly because of his own preference for 'wait and see' politics, Prime Minister Asquith arranged an interparty conference on the matter which would give everyone a few months breathing space.

Although without experience, George was not unprepared for kingship. According to biographer Denis Judd, he had been introduced to the mysteries of his statecraft by his father. Determined not to repeat his mother's treatment of him in his dealings with his own heir, King Edward had 'opened all official secrets to his son, and strove to give him confidence and insight.' George was also fortunate in the choice of his private secretary. Sir Arthur Bigge (later Lord Stamfordham) who held the position from 1901 to 1931, was a man of considerable judgement and a good friend. Prince George always acknowledged the debt he owed his father but of Sir Arthur he said 'He taught me how to be a King.' His reign was to prove a tribute to his mentors and also to his own dogged devotion to duty which changed a cheerful, but deferential 'mother's boy' into a sometimes gruff, sometimes shrewd monarch, devoted to the interests of all his people.

Always known as 'Georgie' in the family, Prince George Frederick Ernest Albert, was born in the early hours of 3 June 1865, his parents' second son. Eighteen months earlier Princess Alexandra had given birth to Albert Victor, 'Eddy' to the family, and the brothers were destined for a close relationship in which Georgie was always the leading partner. Their tutor, the Rev. John Dalton, who took charge of their education when George was six, thought the boy lacked 'application, steady application' and went on, 'his sense of self-approbation is almost the only motive power in him.' Proper self esteem is the basis for any happy and successful life and with Georgie it never degenerated into arrogance. He was a bright and outgoing boy where Eddy was listless and backward. When the boys were in their teens a memorandum from Mr Dalton noted that 'Prince Albert Victor requires the stimulus of Prince George's company to work at all.' In consequence – despite their grandmother's view that 'The very rough life to which boys are exposed on shipboard is the very thing not calculated to make a refined and amiable Prince, who in after years is to ascend the throne' – it was decided that Eddy should enrole with his brother with the Royal Navy training ship *Britannia*.

The Navy was considered a fitting career for a second son and Georgie, who was on the active list from 1877 to 1893, early showed his aptitude for the life. Later recalling his cadet years

British forces fighting a rising in South Africa's Transvaal province. The Boer's victory at Majuba Hill led the British government to negotiate and the Princes did not see action. However Prince George did meet Cetewayo, the defeated King of the Zulus who was interned in Cape Town. Later on this voyage he and Eddy visited Japan, to be received by the imperial court, and Greece, where they were guests of their aunt and uncle, Queen Olga and King George I.

Georgie returned having certainly 'seen the world' and something of the realities of empire. He had sampled the strange splendours of an oriental court and experienced the wide connections of his own royal family. Yet throughout his travels thoughts of home were uppermost in his mind. Above all thoughts of his 'Darling Motherdear.' He and Princess Alexandra were bound by ties of deep, almost mawkish affection which, on his side, only began to be broken with his marriage to Princess 'May' of Teck in the Chapel of St James's Palace on 6 July 1893.

The royal partners who for a generation symbolized to their subjects the ideal of married life, had not been intended for each other. The 1880s had been for Prince George a period of rising professional achievement. At the Royal Naval College of Greenwich he gained first class marks in gunnery, torpedo work and seamanship. He rose to lieutenant and then commander in the first-class gunboat HMS *Thrush* with the West Indies and North American squadron in 1890. Meanwhile, the backward Eddy had shown disturbing signs of sowing his wild oats.

he wrote: 'It never did me any good to be a Prince . . . and many was the time I wished I hadn't been. It was a pretty tough place and the other boys . . . made a point of taking it out of us on the grounds that they'd never be able to do it later on. . . . I was awfully small then and I'd get a hiding time and again.' But despite the occasional bloody nose Georgie survived the rigours of bullying and also proved above average in his exams.

From 1879 to 1882 he made three extended cruises on the strength of HMS *Bacchante* with Eddy once again tagging along. Prime Minister Disraeli and his cabinet were appalled that the two sons of the Prince of Wales should together risk the hazards of the sea and Mr Dalton was none too pleased at having to sail as Eddy's tutor. But the elder Prince's education was progressing dismally and only his brother's company inspired him to any effort. Together, the brothers saw the world from South America to Australia and from the Mediterranean to Singapore. In January 1881 they were off the Falkland Islands when *Bacchante* was ordered urgently to Cape Town to render assistance to

Above: Princess Alexandra and her children. The formal studio composition has caught something of the reality of the Wales's family life. Albert Victor, standing behind his mother, was backward and listless as a boy, disturbingly erratic as a young man and always on the edge of the circle. 'Georgie,' his jacket grasped almost possessively by his mother, shared an intense, almost mawkish love with his 'darling mother-dear.'

Right: Prince Albert Victor (known as 'Eddy') and Georgie (standing). Throughout their boyhood, Eddy depended heavily on his confident, lively brother.

Opposite: *The Congratulations after the Wedding Ceremony.* As Princess Alexandra dutifully kisses the old Queen, her husband and his parents, behind her, look on. The marriage of Prince George, Duke of York, and Princess Victoria Mary ('May') of Teck.

Below: The engagement photo. Although, as he admitted to her later, George had not been in love with her at the time of their arranged betrothal, the marriage blossomed into a lifelong romance.
Right: *The Duke of York on the bridge of HMS Thrush.* The loyal cover picture for the royal wedding number of the *Black & White* magazine. George had won a solid naval reputation on his own merits; as future king, he had to abandon his career.

Women at least, stirred him into activity and it may have been thought a wife would help sober him up. In any case, he was approaching 30 and was heir to the throne. In December 1891, while Prince George was at Sandringham convalescing from a dangerous attack of typhoid, the engagement was announced of Eddy to Princess Mary of Teck, a descendant of George III. Barely a month later, her fiancé was dead. Early in January 1892 he contracted influenza, then a potential killer. It developed into pneumonia and on 14 January he died.

The nation and the family mourned. None more so than Prince George, for so long his brother's support and friend. Grief was followed by dismay. From the prospect of a successful and conventional career as a naval officer, earned, be it said, on merit, he found himself heir presumptive to the throne of the world's most powerful empire. In May 1892 he was created Duke of York and in June of that year took his seat in the House of Lords.

For her part, Princess Mary was delicately placed. Born at Kensington Palace in 1867, she had lived most of her life in Britain. At home there and as a princess resigned to the idea of an arranged marriage she was not unduly surprised to find herself formally courted by her dead fiancé's brother. Victoria and Georgie's parents urged the match and the Prince fell in with their wishes. But the Princess seemed 'a little stiff and cold' to one observer while, as George later confessed to her, when he asked her to marry him, he was not very much in love. Yet the wedding in the Chapel Royal, St James's Palace, on 6 July 1893 was a huge success. The crowds outside cheered the bridal pair even more enthusiastically than they did old Queen Victoria, and the guests included the Tsarevitch of all the Russias (later Tsar Nicholas II) who astonished the uninitiated by his resemblance to the bridegroom. And whatever the awkwardnesses of their courtship, the newlyweds were obviously head-over-heels in love.

When they moved into their home Princess Mary may have been a little less euphoric. York Cottage in the grounds of Sandringham was considered by one visitor 'a most undesirable residence, positively a glum little villa.' Their eldest son Edward was to comment 'until you have seen York Cottage, you will never understand my father.' His mother arrived after her wedding to find that it had already been decorated and furnished throughout by an anonymous high class store representative. In the early months of her marriage she was liable to find that 'Motherdear' had been down from the big house in her absence to rearrange the furniture. Yet Georgie was perfectly content there. Even when his father died he left Queen Alexandra in possession of Sandringham House and did not

Right: A wedding group of George and Mary, with sisters and cousins. On Prince George's left stands Princess Victoria, his favourite sister, while at his feet, next to his wife's chair, is his young cousin Ena (Eugenie) of Battenberg who was destined to marry King Alfonso XIII of Spain.

Below: Four Generations, a famous photograph showing Queen Victoria with three future monarchs. On her lap is her great grandson the future Edward VIII, behind her stands her son to be Edward VII and grandson, to be King George V.

move in there until her death in 1925. By royal standards a pokey 'suburban' place, York Cottage provided the childhood home for two future kings. Three children and their nurse shared one small room by day and slept together in another by night.

Princess Mary had pretensions to cultural interests and a certain independence of mind but her devotion and her exalted sense of royal duty carried her through and made her the ideal consort for her adoring husband. Together they faced the skirmishing over names with Grandmama. Victoria wrote it was her wish 'that *Albert* should be his first name.' She was rather put out by the reply, that 'both May and I settled that if it was a boy we should call him Edward after darling *Eddy*,' and responded a little huffily, 'of course if you wish Edward to be the first name I shall not object, only . . . the *real* name of dear Eddy . . . was *Albert Victor*.' In fact the future Edward VIII was known throughout life to the family as David, the last of his seven names.

Early in the morning of 14 December 1895 the Duchess of York gave birth to her second son. The timing could hardly have been worse since this was the very anniversary of Prince Albert's death 24 years before. The Duke recorded the event prosaically enough, noting that the baby weighed 'nearly eight pounds' and that he himself went to bed at 6.45 very tired. The Queen's reaction was awaited nervously. Following his father's suggestion, the Duke this time proposed the name of 'Albert' himself and went on to invite his grandmother to be the child's godmother. A delighted Victoria gladly agreed and assured her 'Darling Georgie' that 'the little one born on that sad anniversary . . . will be especially dear to me' – he was always 'Bertie' to the family.

Such domestic trivialities rated due importance in the world of York Cottage. Frances Donaldson in her superb biography of Edward VIII wrote 'The limitations of King George oppressed even his biographer. During his 17 years as Duke of York, the formative years of his young family, he was "just shooting at Sandringham" and did "nothing at all but kill animals and stick in stamps."' She admits that the Duke was a crack shot and assembled what is today among the world's finest stamp collections (now in the British Museum). But even with these provisos, the assessment is hardly fair.

In 1897 the Duke and Duchess visited Ireland and were so enthusiastically received that the Prime Minister, Lord Salisbury, considered that the visit could have 'a most valuable effect upon public feeling in Ireland.' In April 1900 the Duke was in Berlin for the coming of age celebrations for the Crown Prince. With Europe ringing to accusations of British 'oppression' against the gallant little Boers of South Africa, George found it 'very disagreeable' to have to go to Berlin just now and in fact anywhere abroad as they 'apparently all hate us like poison.' But he did his duty and was rewarded with a small barrage of boos in the Berlin streets.

With his father's accession as King in January 1901, new horizons were opened with a state tour of Australia and New Zealand. The voyage took the Duke and Duchess of York to many parts of the far flung Empire including Malta, Ceylon and Singapore. Everywhere they were the focus of ceremonial and respect. In Australia the Duke opened the first parliament of the newly established Commonwealth and satisfied himself that a 'strong feeling of loyalty to the Crown' existed. The frosty reception of the French Canadians of Quebec may have prompted other thoughts, while the ceremonies of the Maoris of New Zealand introduced him to another culture of Britain's diverse subject peoples. On his return his father created him Prince of Wales as a 'mark of appreciation of the admirable manner in which you carried out the arduous duties in the colonies.'

Four years later, the Yorks embarked on a six month tour of India. Within the traditions of Indian royalty their activities were conventional enough – tiger shoots, meetings with maharajahs, vast banquets. And in the context of the British Raj the Duke attended official briefings and showed himself to the subjects of the King-Emperor. But he also met with the Indian Congress leader Gokhale and assessed the mood of the country as best he could. The outgoing Viceroy Lord Curzon had, by his overbearing

and arbitrary actions sparked off considerable unrest among the Indians. In the Duke's opinion British officialdom in general seemed 'too much inclined to look upon them as a conquered and downtrodden race and the Native, who is becoming more and more educated, realizes this.' This hardly amounts to deep political insight but it reveals a decent, paternalistic, humane concern for people who would one day be his subjects that was entirely characteristic.

Unfortunately, within his family circle the kindly face of paternalism was less apparent. In a rare anticipation of what we today consider 'modern' fatherhood, the king had attended his wife's confinement on one occasion. He noted the birth weight of baby Prince Albert and happily shared the chore of bathing his infant children. Yet, in the words of one biographer he and Princess Mary presided over a family which suffered from 'an almost total inability to com-

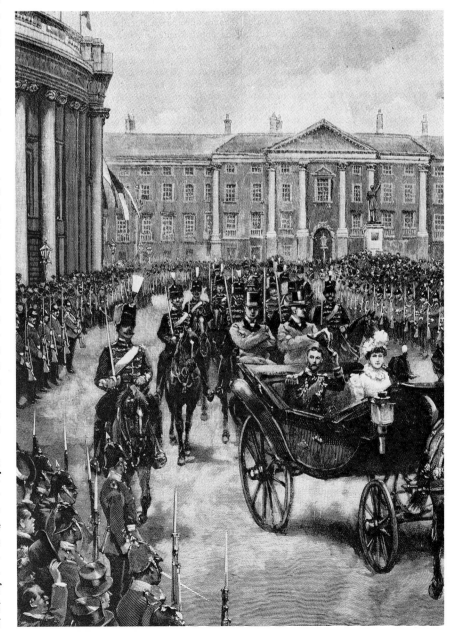

Below: George and Mary, Duke and Duchess of York, during their visit to Dublin in 1897. Somewhat to the surprise of the London government they met with an apparently loyal and certainly enthusiastic reception. Prime Minister Salisbury considered that the visit could have 'a most valuable effect upon public feeling in Ireland.'

municate with one another.' At the time this was in no way unique. Had it been so, J. M. Barrie's story of *Peter Pan* would never have been published. Like Mr Darling, George was a martinet absorbed by his responsibilities and, with his nagging criticisms, a continuing intimidator of his nervous children. His petty complaints dogged them even into manhood. Returning from a triumphantly successful tour of Australia in 1927 Prince Albert, a married man of 30 odd and, moreover the one son of his father who could ride well and so had met the King's highest criterion of public success, was admonished by letter: 'When you kiss Mama, take yr. hat off.'

Even more serious in the childhood years of the young royals was the coldness of their mother who, according to an intimate of the family, 'had nothing of the mother in her at all.' That is a bitter indictment which, today, we cannot assess. Yet Princess, later Queen, Mary was always guided by a paramount sense of royal duty. 'I have always to remember,' she

once remarked, 'that their father is also their King.' The family is a constricting environment and is blamed for many human weaknesses. Yet men and women are, after all, responsible for themselves. Whatever may be the inhibitions among their children we choose to attribute to 'May' and 'Georgie', we should not forget that both, in the words of Frances Donaldson, 'were people of deep natural goodness and noble ideals.'

The King who ascended the British and Imperial throne in 1910 was 'distinguished by no personal magnetism, by no intellectual powers. He was neither a wit ... well read nor well educated.' He was a very ordinary Englishman. To be sure, few ordinary Englishmen (or women) could share a whisky flask with the Archbishop of Canterbury during a deerstalk in the Scottish Highlands. But then the English – who boast Westminster as the 'Mother of Parliaments' – equally expect their King to be a 'real gentleman.' On this, King George would not have disagreed. Like his father he was a pedant

Below: The Duchess of York and her children (1906). Left to right: Prince Henry (born 1900, later Duke of Gloucester); Prince George (born 1902, Duke of Kent); Princess Mary (born 1897, the Princess Royal); Prince Edward (born 1894, Edward VIII); baby Prince John (born 1905, an epileptic, he died tragically at the age of 14); and Prince Albert (born 1895, who was to succeed his brother as George VI). The group was taken at Abergeldie, the little Scottish castle where the family passed many a happy summer holiday.

HAIL, KING!

Left: Britannia hails the new King, George V, in this *Punch* cartoon for 18 May 1910, the second week of the new reign.

Below: Coronation souvenir postcard for 22 June 1911. Portraits of King George and Queen Mary flank Queen Alexandra the Queen Mother (top) and Prince Edward (heir apparent) below; the other royal children surround a view of Westminster Abbey.

was lined with 50,000 troops from all parts of the Empire and hundreds of thousands of cheering people. 'The service in the Abbey . . . was grand, yet simple and most dignified and went without a hitch. I nearly broke down when dear David came to do homage to me, as it reminded me so much of when I did the same thing to beloved Papa. . . .' Three weeks later a very disgruntled David had his own investiture as Prince of Wales, togged out in fancy dress at Caernarvon Castle. But his mother thought he 'looked charming . . . and did his part very well.'

for protocol. Like his son, Edward VIII, he was obsessive about 'correct' or 'fashionable' dress, though the father's and son's views diverged. One morning Edward Prince of Wales attended family breakfast wearing 'cuffs' (trouser turn ups) in what was considered the 'American' fashion (his uncle, Tsar of all the Russias can be seen wearing them in a photo of the 1890s). In his father's world no gentleman turned up his trousers, except, perhaps, to cross a puddle. 'Is it raining in *here?*' roared King George.

The first Labour government was still some years in the future but Lloyd George the Liberal chancellor of the exchequer was proposing welfare programmes and taxation to pay for them which seemed little better than Socialism to most members of the upper classes. The battle over the Parliament Bill, the government's chief instrument for the changes it planned, blew up again in the winter of 1910. The interparty conference had failed and Prime Minister Asquith decided to go to the country. He extracted from the reluctant King a secret promise to create enough new peers to swamp all opposition in the House of Lords should the Liberals win a majority in the Commons. The King was very unhappy with the arrangement. 'I have never in my life done anything I was ashamed to confess, and I have never been accustomed to conceal things.'

Asquith remained prime minister but the Conservatives in the Lords were still undecided on their policy when the King went to his coronation on 22 June 1911.

'May and I left B.P. (Buckingham Palace) in the Coronation coach at 10.30 with 8 cream coloured horses,' ran the King's diary. The route

In August the Parliament Bill passed in the Lords, the majority of the opponents abstaining rather than see the membership flooded with 'upstarts'. King George was much relieved and the royal year ended in magnificence with the King-Emperor and his consort on a state visit to India. A special crown was made for the occasion. At the Durbar held in Delhi on 12 December the King-Emperor's train was carried by maharajahs and the sons of maharajahs; the presentation of the rulers by the Viceroy Lord Hardinge lasted an hour; and the King-Emperor announced reforms in the unpopular measures introduced by Hardinge's predecessor Lord Curzon which, it was hoped, would still the discontent troubling the sub-continent.

The round of receptions and ceremonial was relieved for Queen Mary by culture visits to Agra and the Taj Mahal while her husband went on a tiger shoot. Compared with York Cottage, compared even with Buckingham Palace, the greater Indian princes lived lives of unimaginable luxury. But the King-Emperor came to entertain a somewhat jaundiced view of his fabulous oriental lieges. His father had hobnobbed with the Gaekwar of Baroda at the fashionable German spas in the 1890s and many another maharajah made extensive trips to Europe. In 1935 scores of them thronged to London to celebrate the Jubilee of the King's reign. The monarch was not pleased. 'Why should they come to London at all?' he deman-

ded testily. 'They only spend a lot of money. Tell them to stay in their states and look after their own subjects.'

But if he showed a paternalistic concern for the welfare of his poorer subjects, he detested the disruption of the strikes which the workers saw as their only means of improving it. When he and the Queen returned to England from India in February 1912 the country was in the throes of a coal strike. This was followed by rail and transport stoppages and the next year the leaders of the miners, railwaymen and dockers began to discuss common action.

Opposite: The official photograph of King George and Queen Mary in their coronation robes.
Left: Artist's impression of a pithead scene during the national coal strike of 1912. Industrial unrest was a feature of the early years of the reign. During the brief rail strike of August 1911 the military garrison at Aldershot had been moved to London, so seriously did the government consider the possibility of a revolution. As always, the British establishment supposed the cause of the troubles was political agitation, but between 1900 and 1911 the purchasing power of the pound had fallen by 25 percent and the average weekly wage had risen by barely 2 percent. Legislation had severely limited the power of the unions, but the campaign for the minimum wage was very much in the news. 'Many miners,' runs the caption to this picture, 'regard it as but a stage in a revolution which it is hoped will result in an industrial democracy, and the supremacy of labour.' King George hated the attitudes of class warfare promoted by strikes but he was equally angered by the callous disregard shown by the coal owners to their employees' conditions of work.

Left: George V on a tiger shoot during his state visit to India in 1911-12. The King Emperor shared with his royal Indian lieges the addiction to the hunt in all its forms. Since the days of the Mogul emperors Indian royals had been dealing out slaughter among the animal kingdom on a scale unmatched even by the excesses at Sandringham in the time of his father. While he hunted tiger, Queen Mary visited Agra and the Taj Mahal.

Left: The suffragette Emily Davidson prostrate on the course during the running of the 1913 Derby, after throwing herself under the hooves of the King's horse. She later died of her injuries. Neither King George nor Queen Mary sympathized with such tragic demonstrations in the fight for Votes for Women. Nevertheless, the King was deeply disturbed on reading Mrs Pankhurst's description of what she endured when forcibly fed, and remonstrated with the Home Secretary. The patriarchal image of the King himself contrasted strangely with the troubled times over which he presided.
Right: The Buckingham Palace conference convened by King George to discuss the situation in Ireland, July 1914. Prime Minister Asquith, standing behind the King's right shoulder, was prepared to 'wait and see' but King George distrusted such procrastination. The outbreak of World War I in August in fact meant the postponement of a settlement. When Home Rule was eventually introduced it was under the premiership of Lloyd George, shown here addressing the conference.

Right: A patriotic exhortation to Britain to build up her navy so as to maintain her position as the leading world power.

Worse even than the strikes was the violent agitation of the suffragette militants and the treatment they suffered at the hands of the authorities. When Emily Davidson threw herself under the hoofs of the King's horse in the 1913 Derby and died of her injuries the King was genuinely distressed. The physical assaults made by other women extremists and the planting of a bomb in a house being built for Lloyd George angered him as they did most conventionally minded people. Yet when he heard the gruesome details of the forcible feeding inflicted on Mrs Pankhurst's followers in prison he was shocked and wrote a note of protest to the home secretary.

To the social unrest in Britain itself was added the political agitation and threatening violence in Ireland. Since the time of Gladstone in the 1880s, the more far-sighted of Britain's statesmen had been working for a Home Rule bill hampered by the strong lobby for Ulster Protestants in the House of Commons. In 1913, with Irish pressures building once more, Prime Minister Asquith seemed content to 'wait and see.' King George considered it a policy of drift which might end by compromising him. He proposed a conference be convened. On 21 July 1914 he presided at its opening. But Ireland and Britain's other troubles were about to take second place to events in Europe.

On 4 August, a British ultimatum against Germany over her violation of Belgian neutrality ran out and the two countries were at war. Some six weeks earlier the assassination of the Austrian Archduke Franz Ferdinand at Sarajevo had set in train a seemingly leisurely diplomatic process which ended by embroiling all the great European powers. Even so, few people supposed the conflict would be protracted. When King George and Queen Mary together with the Prince of Wales went out on to the balcony at Buckingham Palace to acknowledge the 'terrific' cheering of the crowds at the outbreak of war, the King's chief hope was that it would all soon be over and that his second son Bertie, then with the North Sea Fleet, would be spared.

OTHERS ARE READY AND WILLING
OUR PLACE IN THE WORLD TO FILL
BRITONS AWAKE, FOR THE OLD LAND'S SAKE
AND SHEW WE ARE BRITONS STILL.

The enthusiasm in London was echoed in every European major capital. All the combatants looked to a quick victory – by Christmas at the latest. When Christmas came a few began to sense the awful future that lay ahead. In Britain, the opening months had been marred by anti-German hysteria. In October the King's cousin Prince Louis of Battenberg, the distinguished First Sea Lord, was forced to yield to public clamour and resign. The family changed its name to Mountbatten. Later, to his personal disgust, the King was obliged to change the name of the dynasty, choosing 'Windsor'. The Kaiser, on hearing the news observed drily, 'I look forward to the next performance of *The Merry Wives of Sachsen-Coburg-Gotha*.'

Necessarily, the King's wartime duties were largely confined to morale, but he provided valuable support for Asquith when, towards the end of 1915, the prime minister decided that conscription would have to be introduced. His cabinet was divided, but sure of the King's backing he was able to override opposition. As 1916 advanced, Asquith's own conduct of the war came increasingly into question and in December Lloyd George displaced him. King George hardly trusted the dynamic Welshman but recognized his qualities. Himself, he continued his duties with unflagging zeal. He visited the trenches of the western front five times and presented no fewer than 50,000 medals for bravery and held some 450 inspections. The King also toured some 300 hospitals and Queen Mary, when not accompanying her husband, had a full official programme of her own.

Of the royal children, Bertie saw active service with the Navy while David spent most of the war doing his utmost to overcome the offical objections to his joining the fighting units at the front. Henry, Duke of Gloucester (born in 1900) and George, Duke of Kent (1902) were too young for any active duties and saw little of their busy parents. John, the youngest child, tragically subject to epileptic fits, lived a reclusive life in a separate house from the rest of the family and died, aged 14, in 1919.

Below: Queen Mary (foreground) and King George (uniformed and with his officer's swaggerstick) on one of their numerous wartime duty visits on the home front. Here they are inspecting a boot repairing factory in London's East End in the summer of 1918, barely six months before the end of the War. The King made several tours of the front line in Europe while Queen Mary attended all sorts of functions and made many visits throughout the country to maintain morale at home.

Above: The signing of the Armistice terms that brought an end to the Great War in Europe in November 1918, was the signal for wild celebrations. Here a crowd of revellers has commandeered an open top omnibus and is driving down a flag-bedecked Fleet Street.

With the signing of the Armistice in November 1918 the nation relaxed in a mood of wildly enthusiastic euphoria. For five days King and Queen drove through the streets of their capital lined with cheering crowds. When he reviewed a parade of thousands of disabled service men in Hyde Park he was nearly pulled off his horse as they pressed forward to shake his hand. Lloyd George fought and won his postwar election on his record as war leader and the promise to create a 'Land fit for Heroes'. But little changed and the discontent of the pre-war years revived. The royal family's advisers felt that a prince was needed to represent the monarchy in the field of industrial relations and the choice fell on Bertie. He became president of the Boys Welfare Society (renamed the Industrial Welfare Society) described by its founders as 'an organization through which industry itself might be responsible for the development of the growing movement for the betterment of working conditions . . . and of proper facilities for the maximum enjoyment in the workers' free time.' Critics naturally viewed it as a spurious exercise in royal public relations but Prince Albert eventually earned praise for his devotion to the work.

Meanwhile, David, the King's eldest son was beginning to exercise his charm on the world. In 1919 he visited Canada and the United States and a year later Australia and New Zealand. Everywhere he was greeted with delight but his 1921 visit to India was a more intimidating prospect. Gandhi was beginning to stir the spirit of nationalism with his campaign of civil disobedience. Ten years later 'the little man with no proper clothes and bare knees', as one courtier described the loin-clothed Mahatma, met the King when he came to London to attend the Round Table Conference on India. The King

ended their meeting with the words: 'Remember, Mr Gandhi, I won't have any attacks on my Empire.' Tense courtiers no doubt heaved a collective sigh of relief when the little saint suavely replied: 'I must not be drawn into a political argument in your Majesty's Palace after receiving your Majesty's hospitality.'

In the immediate post-war years the question of Ireland once again pressed for an answer. The Easter Rising of 1916 in which members of the extremist Irish Volunteer movement had proclaimed an Irish Republic and held the Dublin general post office against the British army, had inflamed tempers on both sides still further. The British considered it an act of wartime treachery, the Irish were incensed by the government's reprisals and executions. With the war over, Lloyd George manoeuvred for a solution to Irish Home Rule and in 1920, in an act of counter terror, sent in the notorious 'Black and Tans', auxiliary troops whose name has become synonymous with brutality.

King George was no supporter of republicanism nor of Sinn Fein, but the Irish people were still his subjects and he memoed the government's chief secretary for Ireland ' . . . is this policy of reprisals to be continued and, if so, to where will it lead Ireland and us all?' He was said to have declared, 'I cannot have my subjects killed in this manner.' In 1922 the 'Irish Free State' became a self-governing Dominion within the Empire, but the problem of the King's other Protestant subjects in the Six Counties remained and Ulster was a time bomb lodged in the foundations of the future.

The other principal pre-war problem, that of woman suffrage, was resolved, eventually, in 1928 when the voting qualifications for women were made the same as those for men. Always the traditionalist, King George hardly approved and was almost dismayed to learn that during all-night sessions MPs stretched out on the benches for a rest. His views were conveyed to Prime Minister Baldwin: 'Members of Parliament now include ladies and such a state of things as you describe seems to His Majesty hardly decorous.'

But there were happier family events in the postwar years. In 1922 the King's only daughter, Princess Mary (later the Princess Royal) married Viscount Lascelles and the wedding rated a special issue of the fashion magazine *Vogue*. Another royal wedding supplement followed in 1923 to commemorate the wedding of the young Duke of York ('Bertie') to Lady Eizabeth Bowes-Lyon. The King was delighted by the union and was to develop a special affection for their first daughter, Princess Elizabeth the present Queen. He had a high opinion of marriage and was increasingly worried by the bachelor state of his eldest son and the gossip surrounding his affairs with women. His constant companion in public and beloved helpmeet in private the Queen, by her majestic and almost austere appearance, was supposed by many people to be the dominant partner in their marriage. The reverse was more likely. When dresses began to shorten in the 1920s, the Queen looked forward to showing off her shapely legs. But first she persuaded one of her ladies to wear the new style at court to test the King's reaction. It was one of crusty disapproval. For the rest of her life Mary wore ankle-length dresses which only added to her dominating presence.

At times, George V played an important role in political affairs. As a young man he had been suspicious of the growing number of Labour MPs, hoping they were 'not all Socialists,' but his feelings of sympathy for the poor and unemployed were genuine. In 1921 he told Prime Minister Lloyd George that men wanted work, not the dole and that, in any case, this unemployment benefit was pitifully small. Then when a Conservative minority government was defeated in January 1924, the King – 'using (my) own judgement' – sent for Ramsay MacDonald the Labour leader and head of the largest party in the house.

This was a truly startling encounter for MacDonald was not only a Socialist, he was also the bastard son of a Scottish peasant farmer. Yet the King came to admire him and was soon on excellent terms with another Labour minister, J.H. Thomas. George V loved a shady joke – his doctors used to bribe him to take his medicine with the promise of a new one – and, though he dropped his aitches, 'Jimmy' Thomas had an inexhaustible supply of doubtful humour.

Labour was thrown out that October in an election dominated by the so-called 'Zinoviev letter', supposedly an intercepted communication from the Kremlin to leading British Socialists. Predictably, it was hailed on the far right as proof of near treason but the King was not convinced of its authenticity and it was, indeed, almost certainly a forgery.

George trusted his people and saw plenty in the state of Britain to justify the anger of the poor. At the time of the General Strike in 1926 Lord Durham – a plutocrat coal owner – told him that the striking miners were 'a damn lot of

Below: Captioned 'The Homecoming of the Prince of Wales, June 1922,' this formal group photograph records the welcome by the family to the Prince of Wales on his return from his Indian tour. It was the kind of royal rigmarole the Prince himself detested and the King his father considered a vital aspect of monarchy. Left to right: Queen Mary, Prince Henry Duke of Gloucester; Edward Prince of Wales; Prince Albert, Duke of York; and the King. On his left stand Viscount Henry Lascelles and Princess Mary, the Princess Royal whom he had married in February. It was the society wedding of the year and, to the King at least, an ideal match. 'Lucky' Lascelles was not only an aristocrat, he was also very rich, a Master of Foxhounds and the owner of his own racing stable. But he was also 14 years older than his bride, inconsiderate and insensitive. On hearing news of the engagement the Prince of Wales had written to his father questioning the suitability of the choice of husband for his shy and retiring sister.

A postcard to celebrate the Jubilee of King George and Queen Mary on 6 May 1935, one of the innumerable souvenirs to commemorate the event. The day itself, solemnized with a service of thanksgiving in St Paul's Cathedral was an idyll – in the King's own words, a 'never to be forgotten day.' The temperature was 75° in the shade and there were, wrote the King in his journal, 'the greatest number of people in the streets that I have ever seen. The enthusiasm was most touching.' The celebrations continued throughout the country for almost a month, with official receptions, loyal addresses in and around London and street parties for the children. The King was astonished by the warmth of public feeling. Aware of his own limitations as a man and quite unaware of how his obvious goodwill towards his subjects and paternal care for their well being had communicated itself to them over the years, he commented 'I'd no idea they felt like that about me.' But the public affection was in part no doubt gratitude that, in the turbulent years of social change, economic depression and international problems of the inter-war years, the country was headed by a man who embodied the straightforward, even old-fashioned virtues which people liked to believe symbolized all that was best in Britain. Jubilee Day closed with a radio broadcast by the King. 'How can I express what is in my heart? I can only say to you my very, very dear people, that the Queen and I thank you from the depths of our hearts for all the loyalty – and may I say so? – the love, with which you have surrounded us. I dedicate myself anew to your service for all the years that may still be given me.' A little more than six months later the nation was plunged into mourning at the news of his death.

revolutionaries.' 'Try living on their wages,' came the gruff royal reply.

After the Strike, Labour came to power again in 1929. Once again they had no overall majority and once again the government was overtaken by disaster. By 1931, Europe's financial structures were teetering on the brink of collapse in the shock waves of the 1929 Wall Street Crash. British financial experts demanded drastic economies to save Sterling, including 10 percent off the dole. So, at 10am, on Sunday 23 August, MacDonald went to Buckingham Palace – where the King had arrived barely two hours earlier off the night train from Balmoral – to warn that Labour would probably have to resign. The King then sought advice from Liberal and Conservative leaders who advised the formation of a national government under MacDonald. Moved by the King's plea that he was 'the man to save the country' the Labour leader eventually concurred although his own cabinet had already resigned. As a result, the Labour Party saw Ramsay MacDonald as a traitor, some even accusing the King of collaboration in a plot to split the Socialist movement.

Certainly, his part in the affair was one of the most decisive interventions made by the monarchy in twentieth-century politics. Yet the royal prerogative had been the one constitutional tool left to deal with the crisis. In urging the Prime Minister to stay on, George had thought to use it in the best interests of the nation.

Throughout his reign George V stolidly aimed to do his duty. Proud to be the King of a 'wonderful people,' he was nonetheless fully aware of his own shortcomings and was astonished at the tumultuous reception he and Queen Mary received during their Silver Jubilee celebrations in 1935. 'I really think they like me for myself,' he commented.

Ordinary almost to a fault, King George embodied the concept of 'an officer and a gentleman' which the conventional wisdom then considered the proper quality of a leader. With his grizzled beard, upright carriage and stern but kindly features, he was the ideal image of the father figure. His gruff, warm voice, heard by millions in his Christmas broadcasts made the image a living reality, which stirred loyalty, affection and pride in country among many of his subjects. They knew him for a good man and the news of his death on 20 January 1936 brought genuine grief into millions of homes.

A procession some two and a half miles long accompanied his coffin from Sandringham to the local station for its journey to London. More than 800,000 people filed past the body as it lay in state in Westminster Hall. During the vigil his four sons silently took up position, dressed in mourning black, between the four uniformed guardsmen round the catafalque. The Kings of Norway, Denmark, Roumania, Bulgaria and Belgium were among the official mourners in the funeral procession. The body was laid to rest at Windsor in the Chapel of St George, home of the Knights of the Garter.

King George died on 20 January 1936, after struggling to put his signature to the proclamation setting up a Council of State. The death bed was surrounded by the Queen and her children, among them the wayward David who had caused his father such uneasiness. 'The boy will ruin himself within 12 months' the old king had prophesied. The events of the new year fully justified his forebodings, but as the solemn obsequies of the dead monarch unfolded in all their pomp few could have guessed the dimensions of the disaster that lay ahead. The King had died at Sandringham and on 23 January the coffin was taken to the local station for the train journey to London. The cortège was accompanied by the new king and his brothers; the Queen and her daughters followed in closed carriages. On reaching London the coffin was taken to Westminster Hall where it lay in state for four days before being taken on to Windsor for the final rites. Left: The royal funeral cortège passing through the streets of Windsor on its way to Windsor Castle for interment in the Chapel of St George.

Edward VIII

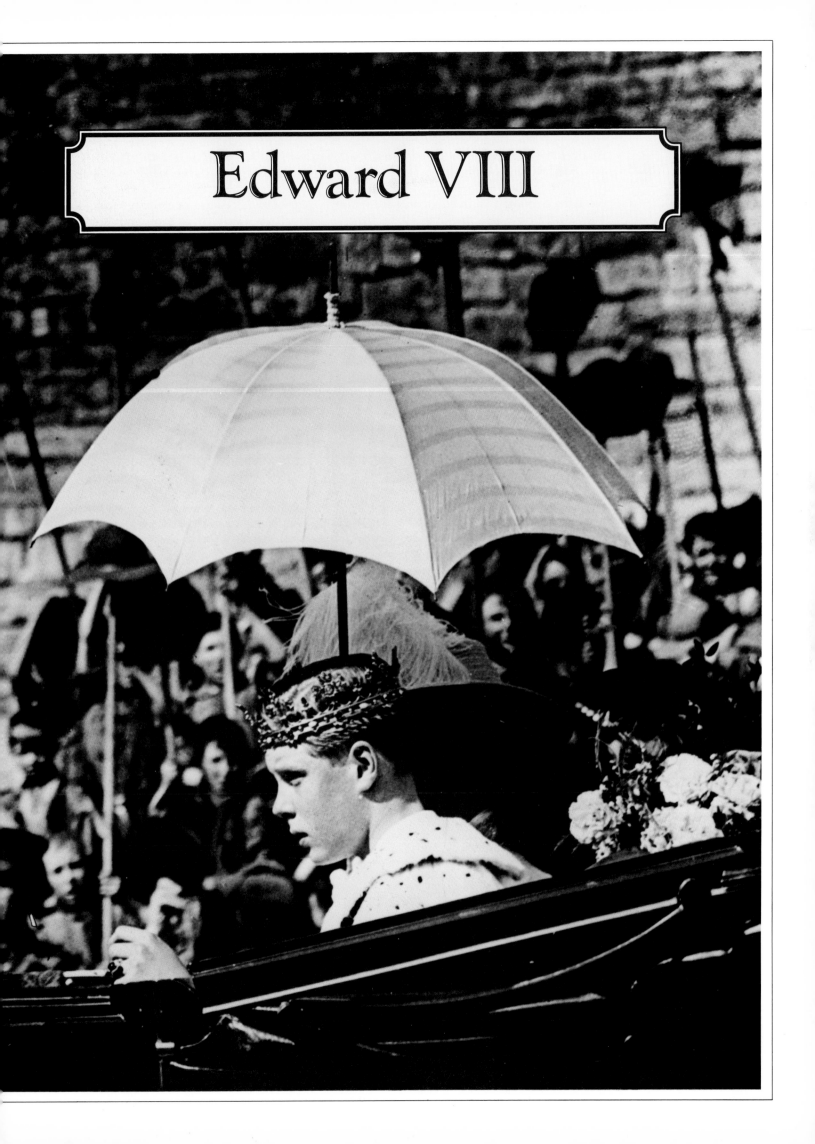

Pages 59-60: The royal party riding in the state landau past the walls of Caernarvon Castle after the investiture of Edward as Prince of Wales in June 1911. The prince was always impatient of the antiquated traditions and conventions surrounding the monarchy; it was his misfortune that even before coming to the throne he was involved in the construction of one. As far as is known, no Prince of Wales in the 600-year history of the title, had ever been invested at Caernarvon. The tradition that King Edward I presented his baby son to the Welsh people here in the year 1284 has no historical justification. Later Princes of Wales were proclaimed at Westminster or some other English town where the king was holding court – few of them ever visited the principality. However, the growth of Welsh nationalistic sentiment in the later nineteenth century, coupled with the fact that a local MP, Lloyd George was the most brilliant and imaginative figure in British politics, combined to suggest that what for centuries had been merely an honorific title for the heir to the British crown, might be exploited for its symbolic value in the political arena. The reign had opened with a major political struggle by the Liberal government, in which Lloyd George was Chancellor of the Exchequer, to force through a budget which coupled tax reforms with measures for social welfare, against the opposition of the House of Lords. Much against his inclination, the new King had been obliged to promise the Prime Minister that he would create as many new Peers as might be needed to vote the budget through. The crisis had passed and now the maverick Chancellor offered a novel piece of pageantry to flatter the palace. the 17-year-old Prince did not relish his part in the charade.

'His face at times wore such a look of beauty as might have lighted the face of a young knight who had caught a glimpse of the Holy Grail.' The 'young knight' in question was the 43-year-old King Edward VIII in his momentous interview with Prime Minister Stanley Baldwin, in November 1936, at which he announced his resolve to marry Mrs Wallis Warfield Simpson. She had received a decree *nisi* of divorce from her husband Mr Ernest Simpson the previous month. Her court appearance had been handled as discreetly as the British establishment knew how. Yet it marked a crucial development in the crisis over the King's love life. Shortly before his death, King George had said: 'The boy will ruin himself within 12 months.' In the history of prophecy few predictions have proved more accurate.

A father figure to his people George V had been an object of awe to his young family. This seemed entirely proper to him. Outside his own family circle, he was considered 'the jolliest and least formal of guests' and 'wonderfully good and disarming with other people's children' at home he expected respect. 'I was always frightened of my father,' he once confided to a friend, 'they must be frightened of me.' Frightened he may have been but he was much loved by his own father who once commented, 'we are more like brothers than father and son.'

George V too had a true affection for his children, but the vital warmth was always absent. When their grandfather came to the throne in 1901, the family acquired a London home at Marlborough House, a country house at Frogmore in Windsor Great Park and the charming little Scottish castle of Abergeldie. There were many happy summer holidays on the Scottish estate, but most of the time they lived still in the cramped quarters of York Cottage at Sandringham. Occasional football with the local children and trips down to buy sweets at the village shop gave them some contact with the ordinary people of England. In the grounds of the estate the children could often be seen bicycling headlong down the drives and pathways, 'David' always in the lead. These were happy and carefree moments but friends of the family already sensed that the high office he was destined for was beginning to weigh on the young prince. In the words of his biographer Frances Donaldson 'he quite early acquired an air of wistfulness, as though something in the view from his elevated position had permanently blighted his hopes.'

David and Bertie's early schooling was in the charge of their tutor, a Mr Hansell, who rigged up a standard schoolroom in one of the rooms at York Cottage. The timetable was rigorous but the teaching uninspiring and conventional. Neither boy was academically inclined but both

Right: Prince Edward aged one year.
Opposite: Aged seven.

were handicapped by their mediocre tutor. From the Sandringham schoolroom David went on to Osborne Naval College, the first member of the royal family to be sent to school alone. It was an abrupt break with the sheltered existence he was used to. The theory was that he was just like other boys and he was subject to a certain amount of ragging from his classmates. However, the fiction was exposed by the visit of Tsar Nicholas II of Russia in 1909. During the visit it fell to the Cadet Prince to escort his 'Uncle Nicky' round the college.

From Osborne he went on to complete his naval training at Dartmouth, where he did his best to shelter his shy younger brother from the rough and tumble.

In August 1911, a few weeks after his father's coronation Edward was invested as Prince of Wales at Caernarvon Castle, its ruins extensively restored for the occasion. It was the first investiture here in the title's 700-year history. Previous princes had been simply proclaimed at Westminster or in some English town. The idea of making the occasion a Welsh pageant originated with Lloyd George. He threw himself into the business of devising the ceremony, taught the prince a couple of phrases in Welsh and

approved the ceremonial costume. Edward contemplated with dismay what his fellow cadets at Dartmouth would have to say about the white satin breeches and the rest of the 'preposterous rig' he was doomed to wear. Queen Mary attempted to calm his angry protests. 'Your friends will understand that as a prince you are obliged to do certain things that may seem a little silly.'

Next spring, accompanied by Mr Hansell and a French tutor, David visited Paris incognito, staying with the Marquis of Breteuil, once one of his grandfather's society friends. On a motor tour of France he also found time for a short cruise with Britain's Mediterranean Fleet off the Cote d'Azur. In the autumn he went up to Magdalen College, Oxford, where he was to stay two years. He showed little enthusiasm for academic business but revelled in the new, informal fashions in clothes and hunted regularly. He would never be a first class horseman but always showed courage and dash. He loved riding, and in later years notched up a respectable tally of wins in point-to-point races.

The Easter and Summer vacations of 1913 were spent in Germany at the castles and palaces of royal relations. These were delightful

Opposite: Edward in full regalia following his investiture as Prince of Wales. Few schoolboys have been required to appear in public in such an outfit. The robe, badge and collar of the Order of the Garter were at least dignified by tradition and might be considered the honourable trappings of an historic order. But beneath them can be glimpsed the ruched breeches of the costume specially designed for the Investiture. When he first saw it the Prince had recoiled in horror from this 'preposterous rig.' The photograph enables us to feel the justice of his censure and to appreciate the dull foreboding with which he anticipated the reactions of his fellow cadets at Dartmouth naval college. Queen Mary, generally considered an unimaginative and austere mother and undoubtedly devoted to the duties of the monarchy, did understand his alarm and attempted to assuage it. 'Your friends,' she urged him, 'will understand that as a prince you are obliged to do certain things that may seem a little silly.'

Left: Embarking for France, April 1912. The ordeal at Caernarvon was followed, the next year, by some pleasant weeks touring France incognito. He was accompanied by two tutors but did not pay undue attention to the educational aspects of the trip. In Paris he was guest of the Marquis of Breteuil, an old friend of his grandfather; he motored in easy stages southward to the Cote d'Azur and there joined the British Fleet for a few days.

Below: Handling a rivetting gun during an official visit to a Clydeside shipyard, March 1918. Like the rest of the family, Prince Edward made many such duty visits across the country to raise wartime morale on the home front. But his one ambition was to see active service. His brother Albert, a second lieutenant in the Royal Navy, went into action with the North Sea Fleet during the brief and indecisive engagement known as the Battle of Jutland. As heir to the throne Edward was denied the chance to fight for his country at a time when the youth of England were flocking in their thousands to volunteer. Even so, as an army officer he got himself attached to British Army HQ in France and although officially there in an observing capacity was constantly up with the forward positions – as close to the enemy and to danger as possible for him.
Below right: Mrs Freda Dudley Ward. The Prince of Wales met her during an air raid in 1918. Both had been partying and took shelter by chance in the same London basement. A romance began which was to last until, 16 years later, the Prince met Mrs Simpson. When in London, he spent almost every afternoon with her and her young children who called him 'Little Prince.' It seems that this happy domesticity, a contrast to his own childhood, was, for him, a vital element in the affair.

months. At Stuttgart the King and Queen of Württemburg (Uncle Willie and Aunt Charlotte) arranged a visit to the Zeppelin works where the Count showed him his latest airship model. At Berlin, the Prince was entertained by his cousin, the Kaiser.

In the summer of 1914, David joined the army, his first priority being further riding lessons, at his father's wish. Early in July he attended his first ball and his diary records that he had had only eight hours sleep in the past seventy-two. With the outbreak of war in August he was determined to join the forces in France.

At the War Office he badgered Lord Kitchener to be sent to the front. 'What does it matter if I'm killed? I have four brothers.' Kitchener explained that the capture of the heir to the throne could cause more problems, even, than his death. Nevertheless, the Prince did get himself attached to British headquarters in France in November. The following year he had a narrow escape when his driver was killed while he was inspecting the trenches. Though never permitted to go into action, he was constantly up with the forward positions and pedalled hundreds of miles on his green, army issue bicycle. His courage became a byword. 'A bad shelling,' it was said, 'will always produce the Prince of Wales.' And always his sharp attention to detail and quest for facts impressed those who heard or read his reports.

The last months of the war were spent with the staff of the Canadian Corps in France. When peace came David had seen much of staff operations in all theatres, but he had also seen, and to some extent shared, the fears and horrors of

that brutal conflict. His fellow officers accepted him as a 'proper chap' and as the years of peace opened out, encouraged by press, politicians and public acclaim, he began to build his dazzling reputation as a modern 'prince charming.'

Prince Edward danced the Charleston like an expert; he had taps fitted to his shoes; he thrilled the debutantes at smart night clubs and society balls and the gossips with rumours of his love life. Whereas his brother Bertie delighted their father with his marriage to Lady Elizabeth Bowes-Lyon, David obstinately remained single – with a penchant for married women. Between 1915 and 1918 he was devoted to the beautiful Lady Coke, some twelve years his senior, until at a party in London during an air raid he met Mrs Dudley Ward.

The relationship, which was to last for the next 16 years, was soon an open secret in London society. They were to be seen together everywhere – at the Embassy night club or on the golf course. The lady had two children and was related to the nobility. Whenever he was in London, the King spent every afternoon at her house, staying to dinner or taking her out. When the Prince set up his own establishment at York House, St James's Palace, Mrs Ward helped him with the furnishings and decor. Old hands at court recalled the 'reign' of Mrs Keppel in the affections of Edward VII. It was no mere sexual liaison but a deep affair of the heart – the Prince's devotion was almost dog-like and he seems to have found with Mrs Ward and her family a vicarious home life of a kind which he had never experienced in his childhood. Whatever the reason, she absorbed his attention apart from the very occasional affair such as his

well-known liaison with Lady Thelma Furness. As Frances Donaldson has written: 'It was for Mrs Simpson that King Edward VIII renounced the crown, but it was because of Mrs Dudley Ward that he was free to do so.'

Immediately after the War the Prince faced a heavy programme of official engagements and was also very busy reorganizing the affairs of the Kennington estate in London of which he was landlord. His concern for the well-being of his poorer tenants earned much admiration. Then in August 1919 the Prince embarked on HMS *Renown* for a visit to Canada.

The tour was a triumphant progress, Prince Edward was well-received even by the French Canadians of Quebec. The Canadian Pacific Railway provided him with a de luxe suite in what amounted to a hotel on wheels. The stopovers were greeted by enthusiastic crowds and for a few days Edward roughed it in camp with Indian guides, eating their food and fishing for trout. The Prince made another innovation of still more interest for the future; whenever possible he insisted on open air 'receptions' for any member of the crowd who could make their way to the little dais. People queued in their thousands so that on more than one occasion he retired of an evening with a seriously bruised right hand. Back home, the King and Queen worried that such public familiarity with ~~r~~ne mystique of monarchy would breed contempt. Today we can perhaps see the Prince's exhausting encounters with the Canadian public as an anticipation of the 'walkabouts' which are now an established part of the royal family's routine.

From Canada, the Prince crossed the border into the United States, celebrating Armistice Day, 11 November 1919, in Washington. Once again his reception was enthusiastic. Wrote the correspondent of the *New York World*: 'Three months ago we wired from St John, New Brunswick, "New York will fall in love with this lad." New York did.' When he returned to England, Prince Edward could look back on the most sensational royal progress in the history of the British monarchy. On a later occasion he irritated his father by assessing one of his own public appearances as a 'propaganda' success. King George did not think in these terms. Nevertheless the Prince of Wales proved one of the most successful public relations officers the royal family has ever known.

And his father kept him at work. The schedules approved by the palace were punishing. In 1920 he was bound for New Zealand and Australia. On the morning of 16 March his cousin Lord Louis 'Dickie' Mountbatten picked him up from Mrs Ward's house to drive him to Victoria for the boat train. The streets were lined with cheering crowds while at Victoria itself the bar-

riers were broken down by the crush of people. When he arrived in Australia the enthusiasm was so great that not even a car provided protection against 'his welcoming hosts, who snatch him out of it and pass him from hand to hand in the streets.' The pressures never let up and on occasion, weary of the constant round, he missed engagements and ignored invitations. A prosperous family in Queensland built an extension to their house for a ball at which the Prince was to be the principal guest. He never turned up . . . 'and hurt a great many feelings in consequence.'

But the Prince too had his feelings. Dickie Mountbatten who accompanied him on the tour learnt that 'despite all the fun that we managed to have, he was a lonely and sad person, always liable to deep depressions.' On his return voyage the Prince, reflecting on the past weeks, looked glumly into a grim future of 'Lonely drives through tumultuous crowds, the almost daily inspections of serried ranks of veterans, the inexhaustible supply of cornerstones to be laid . . .'

Above: In full regalia as 'Chief Morning Star,' during the tour of Canada in 1919. The title, which certainly matched the hopes of many of his British subjects, was conferred on the Prince of Wales at a 'pow wow' of the Stoney Creek Indians of Alberta. For one who had endured the 'preposterous rig' of the Caernarvon investiture some eight years before, the magnificent headdress and manly costume must have seemed truly splendid. In fact, he spent a few days on an Indian 'reservation', fishing and eating with the people.

Above: Driving through
Trafalgar Square on return
from Australia, October 1920.
Below: With the Maharajah
of Patiala in India, 1922.

welcomed in a specially built gilded pavilion by the Viceroy and the sovereign princes of India, presenting a kaleidoscope tableau of shimmering silks and jewelled turbans. From there the brilliant procession wound through crowded steeets – despite Ghandi's call for a nationwide boycott as a protest against British Imperial rule. Over the blaring band music, the Prince and his party could hear the distant crack of rifle fire as troops drove back protestors aiming to break up the crowds.

Three special trains carried the royal tourist, accompanied once again by his favourite cousin Mountbatten, through Northern India. The press went first, equipped with its own travelling post office. The fabulous royal train followed, with luxurious accommodation for a 100-strong retinue. Bringing up the rear was a mixed passenger and freight train, carrying an army of servants, flat trucks for the landaus to be used in the formal entries to the cities on the route, and closed vans for the Prince's horses.

The royal progress rolled majestically on through a whirl of polo matches and banquets, tiger shoots and receptions. It visited Nepal and Burma, and then returned to Delhi in mid-February. Here the Viceroy was his host at a banquet whose guest list included 150 princes.

1921 and it must be India. In November, the battlecruiser HMS *Renown*, all flags flying, steamed into Bombay to the thunder of artillery salvos. Aboard was the Prince of Wales. He was

Outside the old city on a building site some five square miles in extent, work was in progress on the new Imperial capital of New Delhi. To the designs of the architect Sir Edwin Lutyens, majestic facades of half built mansions and state buildings were rising among mounds of building materials. It was a grandiose gesture against the swelling tide of Indian nationalism.

From India, the royal party journeyed eastwards through Ceylon, Malaya and Hong Kong to Japan. Here they were lavishly entertained by Crown Prince Hirohito and discreetly steered away from a tour of the shipyards where a powerful new Japanese warship was under construction. *Renown* sailed for home via the Philippines, the Indian Ocean and the Red Sea. The Prince left the ship at the Suez Canal, entraining for Cairo where he paid his respects to King Fuad of Egypt. He reached England again eight months after his departure to universal acclaim in the British press. Everywhere he had gone the public response had been euphoric and he had brought a new brilliance to the image of the monarchy. But there were signs that the Prince was being spoiled by his success. More than once he failed to turn up at functions and receptions. As yet, foreign criticism remained muted and there was not a hint of it in the British news coverage.

The moodiness of the Prince must have been deepened by the stream of hectoring complaints from his father. Back in England, Edward gravitated naturally to the family of Mrs Dudley Ward. Almost daily telephone calls and visits endeared him to her children who always called him 'Little Prince.' He in turn adored them and in response to any proposal for a game or an outing would reply 'anything to please.' In his sunny moods this willingness to please extended to the world at large and was the principal secret of his popularity.

In the depressed conditions of British industry and economy of the 1920s the extravagant life-style of the smart set offered a stark contrast to the poverty and misery of the unemployed. Yet the Prince earned popular admiration with his visits to the depressed areas and comradely visits to working men's clubs.

While in Canada, the Prince had bought himself a ranch and in 1924 he planned another visit to the country to his property there. However, he broke his journey in America to attend the international polo match between Britian and the States on Long Island. Once again, he was a riotous success with the public at large although he earned some ill will among society by giving the miss to some of the functions, which he considered somewhat starchy. He seems to have felt himself more at his ease dancing with the short-skirted flappers or sam-

pling bootleg gin in the speakeasies. Back at Buckingham Palace, it is reported, an eavesdropping flunky had once heard the quarterdeck voice of King George lambasting his heir: 'You dress like a cad. You act like a cad. You *are* a cad. Get out!' By the end of the 1924 tour, there were some American hostesses who might have sighed a heart-felt 'Hear! Hear!'

For his part, the Prince felt 'chained to the banquetting table.' At the age of 21 he had complained: 'It is sad to say, but I have no real job except that of being Prince of Wales.' After his adventures in America he was back on the job

Below: The future Edward VIII and his father King George V (on the Prince's return from his world tour of 1922). A haunting, almost archetypal image of 'Father and Son' quite unexpected in its power from the archives of royalty. The King's earnest sense of duty, almost mask-like, overbears his son's anguished horror at his pointless role in the pageant of life and his marked apprehension of the unknown future.

Right: The Prince of Wales outside the ranch house of his EP Ranch near Pekisko, Alberta, in October 1924. The Prince had bought the ranch on his first visit to Canada in 1922 and the principal reason for his '24 trip to North America was to make another visit to his Pekisko estate. However, he broke his journey in the United States to attend the international polo match, played on Long Island, between Britain and the United States. He was guest at an almost unbroken round of parties and receptions. He revelled in the illicit excitements of America during the Prohibition years. His habit of slipping away from balls and banquets mounted at fabulous cost in his honour to visit night clubs and speakeasies, angered more than one society hostess.

Below: On tour in Africa, 1925, the Prince inspects Swazi warriors at Mbabane after their ceremonial dance in his honour.

with a tour down the west coast of Africa to South Africa. Here, the famed charm even worked its effects on the Afrikaaner population - when a commando of Boer farmers turned out in his honour, Edward mounted a horse and rode into town at their head. It was a typical, and brilliant, gesture. On the voyage home he put in at Buenos Aires on a courtesy visit to the President of the Argentine. Here too, unfortunately, he ruffled feathers by cancelling a visit to a local school without notice. For a vigorous,

fun-loving man in his 30's such functions are hardly a ball; but they were all part of the job.

He was back in North America the following year, this time accompanied by his brother Prince George and the prime minister Stanley Baldwin, to attend the Diamond Jubilee of the Confederation of Canada. In 1928 came a holiday in the form of a semi-official safari tour in East Africa. Casual affairs with various ladies appear to have provided the principal diversion between the endless rounds of golf and expeditions after big game. The tour was abruptly cut short by news of King George's illness. A light cruiser made the voyage from Dar-es-Salaam to Brindisi in Italy in eight days. He was met by Mussolini's special train and whirled up Europe. Landing at Folkestone he motored straight to Buckingham Palace. Accounts of the meeting differ, but the Old King's recovery is dated from this time and the Prince seemed to take his official functions more seriously. Wearing his 'dentist smile,' to use the somewhat catty phrase of the society diarist 'Chips' Channon, Edward assisted his mother at Court receptions and sometimes received ambassadors presenting their credentials.

The King still refused him access to all important State Papers – a frustration of his interest and sense of duty that seems difficult to justify. Yet perhaps the King knew his son too well. When Edward did become King, government ministers heard with dismay that the 'red boxes' of ministerial papers, were left lying about at

Fort Belvedere, open to casual inspection by the weeekend guests.

The Fort 'a child's idea of a fort,' was an eighteenth-century royal folly, enlarged for George IV with battlements, near Virginia Water outside Windsor. Prince Edward discovered the place in 1930 and Mrs Dudley Ward helped with the decor. Lady Furness became a frequent visitor; sometime late in 1930 she introduced one of her friends, the American Mrs Ernest Simpson, to the Prince. Early in 1932 he sent the Simpsons an invitation to the Fort. Ernest Simpson found himself at work in the garden with the Prince, clearing away undergrowth. Soon the Prince was visiting the Simpsons at their London house and Ernest developed the habit of being out when he called. In the early months of 1934 Lady Furness was away in America; she returned to find herself displaced in 'David's' affections by Wallis Simpson. In May of the same year his almost daily telephone calls to

Left: Lord and Lady Furness outside the Tote office at Doncaster Races, on the First Day, in September 1935. In the early 1930s Lady Furness, in the view of some society observers, seemed to have displaced Mrs Dudley Ward in the Prince's affections. More recent biographers consider that his liaison with her was merely a passing affair – certainly he continued his almost daily phone calls to Mrs Ward and her children throughout. Nevertheless, Lady Furness may have loosened the ties that bound the Prince to Mrs Ward. She was a frequent visitor to the Prince's home at Fort Belvedere and she it was who introduced Mrs Wallis Simpson to the Prince. Early in 1934 Lady Furness paid a visit to the United States and rumor linked her name with the Aga Khan; on her return to England she found herself displaced in 'David's' affections by Mrs Simpson.

Left: Mrs Ernest Simpson, a 'camera portrait' of Wallis as the vivacious society woman who captivated Prince Edward.

Right: The Prince of Wales and Mrs Simpson at Ascot, 1935. By this time David's friendship with this married woman, already once divorced, was known to everyone in London society and very worrying for his parents. Many people thought, and King George certainly hoped, that David would eventually leave Wallis as he had all his other mistresses. But when the Prince insisted on formally presenting her at Court and publicly flaunted their friendship at society occasions such as Ascot, the King realized this was no ordinary infatuation.

Below: HRH the Prince of Wales, a portrait (1925) by John St Helier Lander.

Mrs Dudley Ward stopped without explanation, after a period of nearly 17 years. Society quickly realized Wallis as the new favourite.

Wallis Warfield Simpson had been born in 1896 into a leading Baltimore family. Unfortunately, her father died leaving her and her mother in a state of genteel poverty from which they were only rescued by Aunt Bessie Merryman. Always a success with the boys if a little 'fast', the 20-year-old Wallis Warfield was married in 1916 to Earl Winfield Spencer Jr., an American Army flyer. When he became an alcoholic Wallis, to the horror of both sides of her family, got a divorce. That year (1927) she met Ernest Simpson, a British American in a prosperous family business and formerly a lieutenant in the Grenadier Guards. He too was in the process of divorce and in July 1928 the two married.

Simpson was not only well off he was also in Wallis's phrase 'a cosmopolitan mind' and well

educated. With him she toured Europe and then found herself established in their apartment in London's Mayfair. She was possessed by the idea of entering London society – Ernest Simpson provided the wherewithal and the entrée.

Stylish if not beautiful, sharp if not witty, Wallis Simpson was, by all accounts, fascinating to men. She bewitched Prince Edward whom she mothered almost bossily to his obvious delight. At the Fort her censorious finger detected dust on the mantlepiece; at the theatre he was forbidden to smoke. The Prince was, in the words of his biographer, 'exceptionally domestic;' a graphologist detected in Mrs Simpson's writing a 'male and dominating streak.'

David's former friends were cold-shouldered while society gossiped that this 'jolly, unprepossessing American . . . is madly anxious to storm society so that when he leaves her (as he leaves everybody in time) she will be secure.' In the summer of 1934 the Prince took a house at Biarritz and invited the Simpsons as guests. Ernest found he had to be in the US 'on business' and Aunt Bessie Merryman came as chaperone. Other guests included the Prince's equerries and secretary. A cruise along the French Riviera followed, during which, according to the Duchess of Windsor's memoirs she and 'David' crossed the boundary between friendship and love.

King George and Queen Mary had stoically accepted the rumours of his previous love affairs – always with married women. Ruefully, perhaps they recognized that such licence was traditonally allowed the heir to the crown. More worrying for them was his increasingly relaxed attitude to the duties of monarchy, which provided the guiding principles for their own lives.

They hoped for a day when he would see his obligations in the same light as they did. But the King suspected that Wallis was something more than a passing infatuation. Their son was moving into middle age and his father's doubts were strengthened when, in the autum of 1934, David formally presented Wallis at court.

The following February the two were off to Kitzbuhl for the winter sports – Mr Simpson being again away on business. On their return to England they entertained at the Fort American style. The swimming pool was the centre of things, lunch self-service and the Prince mixed the cockails (though as always he drank far less than his guests). Later in the summer of 1936 they were again cruising in the Med and touring in Budapest and Vienna.

On Thursday 16 January 1936 Prince Edward was shooting in Windsor Great Park when a letter arrived from his mother suggesting he come to Sandringham for the weekend as his father's health was failing. He flew there in his private plane on the Friday. On Sunday he motored to London to inform Prime Minister Baldwin of his father's approaching death.

On Monday night, after hearing the BBC's famous bulletin 'The King's life is drawing peacefully to its close' on his radio, the Sandringham clockmaker received a telephone instruction from the Prince to come up to the house at once to begin work on setting right the clocks – kept thirty minutes fast for the past twenty-five years on orders of the dying king. 'By the time I arrived (getting on for midnight) by taxi . . . the King had died.' Yet despite his extraordinary and apparently heartless order, observers described the Prince's grief at his father's death as 'frantic and unreasonable' and far in excess of his mother and his brothers.

Days later, as his sons followed King George's body on its jolting gun carriage, the jewelled Maltese cross on the royal crown atop the coffin shook loose and rolled into the gutter, to be discreetly pocketed by the company sergeant major of the honor guard. 'Christ!' King Edward VIII was heard to remark, 'What will happen next?'

Many looked to the new King to democratize the monarchy, even to revive the atrophying royal prerogative in the cause of social justice. As the pending crisis over the Simpson affair burgeoned, political romantics hypothesized an 'Establishment plot' to oust the 'people's king' before he should topple it from the controlling heights of the economy. It is true that King Edward VIII conducted his business from home – at Fort Belvedere - that he pruned some inessentials from court expenditure and introduced a contemporary style – he it was who founded the King's Flight. It is true, also, that a

highly placed German agent in England believed that 'the King is resolved to concentrate the business of government in himself.' Chips Channon even mused that he might aim 'at making himself a mild dictator.'

Chips was nearer the mark when he abandoned such political fancies with the observation 'the King is insane about Wallis, insane.'

Above: News sellers in Fleet Street at about 11 pm on 20 January 1936, an hour before King George V died.

Below: King Edward VIII as Admiral of the Fleet and as Sovereign of the Order of the Garter.

Above: The King and Mrs Simpson pictured at Trau on the Dalmatian coast, Yugoslavia, during their 1936 summer cruise on the yacht *Nahlin*. Pictures like this were the nearest the British public got to the gossip and scandal about the *Nahlin* that was fascinating newspaper readers the world over. A British expatriate wrote anonymously to London protesting that foreign press coverage was giving Britain the image of a 'dizzy Balkan musical comedy.'

Right: Headline from the New York *Daily Mirror*, 26 October 1936. The story claimed that 'King Edward's most intimate friends state that he is deeply enamored of Mrs Simpson and that almost immediately after the coronation he will take her as his consort.' Nearly two months before the British public knew about the King's infatuation the American press was reporting a solution to his dilemma that some of the King's friends undoubtedly proposed.

Whatever his contempt for the hidebound British system, whatever his sentimental sympathy with the sufferings of his underprivileged subjects, the King had only one person in mind. As he docked the salaries of loyal palace servants in pursuit of penny pinching economies, he showered Wallis with presents until she was 'dripping with emeralds.' Her influence ruled at Fort Belvedere. She distracted him from the simplest public chores of his royal job.

In August 1936 he invited her to Balmoral. Her train arrived on a day when the King was scheduled to attend a hospital fete at Aberdeen Infirmary. He cancelled the engagement on the pretext that 'the King is still in Court mourning for his father.' Instead, he drove to the station in holiday style at the wheel of his own car, to pick up his guest.

Later that month, the King and Mrs Simpson chartered the yacht *Nahlin* for a cruise in the eastern Mediterranean. The tour also took in Istanbul and various Balkan capitals where Edward met presidents and kings and, it must be admitted, did much for Britain's image in the area by his personal diplomacy. More newsworthy was the holiday behaviour of the happy couple.

The carefree King was photographed dressed only in his 'spick-and-span little shorts and binoculars'; in the sea with Mrs Simpson; out of the sea holding hands with Mrs Simpson; acknowledging shouts of 'Long live love' from the crowds of tourists and bystanders. While the British press made demure references to the King on holiday as 'the younger English tourist to the life,' the foreign media gorged their readers on a rich diet of gossip and pictures.

That summer, London found itself bombarded with letters from British residents abroad protesting the King's behaviour had 'transformed Great Britain as envisaged abroad into a dizzy Balkan musical comedy.' Baldwin seemed obsessed with the King's business: Foreign Minister Anthony Eden thought there were more pressing matters. It was, after all, the year which saw Hitler's armies reoccupy the Rhineland and the start of the Spanish Civil War. But at an interview in October Baldwin told him: 'I hope you will try not to trouble me too much with foreign affairs just now.'

With Mrs Simpson's decree nisi at Ipswich on the 26th October the drama intensified. Yet still, in Britain, knowledge of the 'King's business' was confined to courtiers, press barons and London society. While the world's press (even the Chinese vernacular papers) carried headlines like 'Mrs Simpson – Queen of Love' and 'King will wed Wally,' the British media maintained a gentleman's agreement of silence.

On 3 November the King performed the State Opening of Parliament, though he disappointed

DAILY ☀ MIRROR PAYOFF EDITION

KING TO MARRY 'WALLY'

WEDDING NEXT JUNE

LONDON.—Within a few days Mrs. Ernest Simpson of Baltimore, Md., U. S. A., will obtain her divorce decree in England, and some eight months thereafter she will be married to Edward VIII, King of England.

King Edward's most intimate friends state with the utmost positiveness that he is very deeply and sincerely enamored of Mrs. Simpson, that his love is a righteous affection, and that almost immediately after the coronation he will take her as his consort.   *(Continued on Page 10)*

(See later editions for detailed story and photographs)

the crowds by cancelling the traditional pageantry and driving to Westminster in a closed car, because of the torrential rain. Yet nine days later he was demonstrating the old magic on a visit to the fleet at Southampton, 'he seemed to know personally every officer and seaman.' He returned to Fort Belvedere that night, the cheers still ringing in his ears, to find a letter from his Private Secretary, Major Alexander Hardinge. Dated 13 November, it informed him that the silence of the British press could not be maintained much longer, that the resignation of his government was becoming a possibility, and begged him to send Mrs Simpson abroad without delay. To Edward this statement of the facts seemed a 'challenge.'

On 16 November the King told his Prime Minister of his decision to abdicate, if need be, to marry. Need almost certainly it would be for, in the immortal words of Chips Channon, 'The country, or much of it, would not accept Queen Wallis with two live husbands scattered about.' That she was an American and a commoner might have irritated die-hard traditionalists but would have been accepted. The English upper classes had been marrying American wives for decades. But a divorcee of whatever nationality simply could not be Queen of England. The monarch is supreme Governor of the Church of England and the Church did not permit marriage between divorced persons. No priest in England would have presided over the wedding of Edward and Wallis; if he delayed the coronation until after a civil marriage, the Archbishop of Canterbury could not crown him; and Edward honourably refused the suggestion of a devious friend that he be crowned first and then marry by civil law. He would not take the coronation oath which pledged him to uphold the Church knowing he meant to break it.

He kept his official programme with an arduous tour of the depressed mining areas of South Wales on 19 November. He was clearly genuinely moved by the hardship he saw and promised – 'You may be sure that all I can do for you I will.' Yet only three days before he had told his prime minister and also his mother and brothers of his intention to abdicate. He must have realized, even as he spoke, that he would never be in a position to implement the promise.

Events were hurrying to their climax. In a last desperate throw, friends about the King suggested the idea of a morganatic marriage: Mrs Simpson would become his wife but not the Queen, and any children they might have would be debarred the succession. The formula was used in Europe to facilitate marriage between royalty and commoners but was unknown to English law.

Baldwin proposed that before any final decision be taken to enact the necessary legislation, the Dominion governments be consulted for their advice. The King agreed. Having asked the advice of his ministers he would be constitutionally bound to accept it. The outcome could not, in fact, be in doubt. De Valera of Catholic Ireland responded that others might do as they pleased but married, even morganatically, to a divorcee Edward would not be acknowledged as King by Dublin. The prime ministers of Australia, New Zealand, South Africa and Canada, refused to countenance the morganatic proposal – as did the British Attorney General and the Labour Party leadership.

Edward's friends, Winston Churchill among them, now urged the formation of a King's Party which could appeal to the country over the heads of his ministers. A few demonstrators, mostly women, paraded banners supporting the King, though even he noted they were not overnumerous or enthusiastic. Honourably, and wisely too, he refused to sanction such divisive politicking. MPs touring their constituencies that weekend found the overwhelming majority opinion against the marriage. The press had broken its silence only days before but, though momentarily stunned, public attitudes hardened almost at once against the King.

Shaken, Edward had recognized the mood: 'They do not want me,' he sighed to a friend. Both he and Mrs Simpson it seems had supposed that his charisma as Prince would survive the crisis. But Edward had not merely breached

Below: A Fleet Street news vendor on Tuesday 8 December 1936. Up to the last moment, it seems, both the King and Mrs Simpson believed that somehow or other he would be able to retain the crown and marry her. King Edward had never contemplated the suggestion (reported by the press – see opposite page) that he should go to his coronation and then marry the lady. Yet he hoped that the charisma that had surrounded him as Prince of Wales would carry public opinion with him to his marriage with the woman he loved. By mid November he had at last recognized that neither the London government nor any government in the Empire would entertain the idea of Mrs Simpson as Queen-Empress, or as the King's Consort under any formula. On 16 November he told Prime Minister Baldwin he intended to abdicate, if need be, so as to be able to marry Mrs Simpson when her divorce became absolute. With public opinion mounting against her, Wallis left England for Cannes at the beginning of December.On Monday 7 December Mrs Simpson announced from Cannes her willingness 'to withdraw from a situation that was both unhappy and untenable.' The next day it was headline news.

Right: King Edward VIII's
Instrument of Abdication
dated 10 December 1936,
whereby he renounced the
throne. It was signed at Fort
Belvedere and witnessed by
his brothers Albert, who
succeeded as King George VI,
Henry, Duke of Gloucester
and George, Duke of Kent.

INSTRUMENT OF ABDICATION

I, Edward the Eighth, of Great
Britain, Ireland, and the British Dominions
beyond the Seas, King, Emperor of India, do
hereby declare My irrevocable determination
to renounce the Throne for Myself and for
My descendants, and My desire that effect
should be given to this Instrument of
Abdication immediately.

In token whereof I have hereunto set
My hand this tenth day of December, nineteen
hundred and thirty six, in the presence of
the witnesses whose signatures are subscribed.

SIGNED AT
FORT BELVEDERE
IN THE PRESENCE
OF

Edward RI

Albert

Henry

George

Opposite: Edward Prince of
Wales as a young officer in
World War I. This portrait by
R G Eves, now hanging in the
National Portrait Gallery,
London, is perhaps a little
idealized, as official portraits
often are. Nevertheless, the
image of a serious and
idealistic young man was
undoubtedly true to an
important aspect of Edward's
character. Even during his
'playboy' years of the 1920s
and 1930s he won almost
universal affection with a
strong undercurrent of
respect. Where his
grandfather, King Edward
VII, had gained an
unenviable reputation as a
royal roué during his long
years in waiting as heir
apparent, David was always
'Prince Charming' in the
public mind. He was thought
to be talented and democratic
in his attitudes. His war
record justified both
judgements. He had made
every possible effort to be
assigned to active service
during the war and when
confined to staff duties
exhibited qualities of
observation, judgement and
courage that impressed men
and officers alike. After the
war he longed for a 'real' job
and, frustrated in this aim,
broke free of the routine of
official appearances as a star
of high-life society. The high
hopes placed on him were
tragically disappointed, in
the public mind, by the
Abdication crisis.
Right: Crowds listening to
Prince Edward's Abdication
broadcast on BBC radio
receivers installed 'by special
permission' outside the offices
of the HMV company in
Clerkenwell Road, in
London's East End.

conventional morality; he had deserted one lover, the nation, for another. To many it seemed a deep betrayal. When, on the afternoon of Monday 7 December, Churchill tried one more appeal in the House of Commons, he was shouted down. That evening Wallis, who with the King's reluctant consent had left the country the week before, announced from Cannes her willingness 'to withdraw from a situation that was both unhappy and untenable.' If she intended to free the King it was too late. And in fact, over the past few days, there had been almost constant calls between Cannes and Fort Belvedere. The King had seemed 'besotted', 'the crown was only valuable to him if it would interest her.'

On Thursday 10 December 1936, King Edward VIII signed the instrument of his Abdication. The Bill of Abdication became law next day, signed – like all British Acts of Parliament – by the King himself in old Norman-French *'Le roy le veult'*, 'the King wills it.' That evening 'His Royal Highness Prince Edward' made a touching and dignified farewell broadcast to the nation from Windsor Castle.' . . . I have found it impossible to carry the heavy burden of responsibility and to discharge my duties as King as I would wish to do without the help and support of the woman I love. . . . And now we all have a new King. . . . God bless you all. God save the King.'

After the broadcast Edward, now 'Duke of Windsor,' returned to Royal Lodge, Windsor, to say goodbye to his family. About midnight he left for Portsmouth where HMS *Fury* was waiting to carry him to the Continent. His destination, settled only hours before, was Schloss

Enzesfeld, the Austrian castle of his friend Baron Eugene de Rothschild. David's lawyers had insisted that he lived apart from Wallis while the decree absolute for divorce was pending – to avoid any possible charge of collusion.

Within a week of his departure, the party of the King's Friends evaporated like a morning mist on the Channel while the country at large, having lost their Prince Charming, rallied to support their new King and his family. For his part, the Duke confidently expected to be recalled, after a short exile, to some responsible position under the Crown. It seemed, indeed, he saw himself as a continuing power behind the crown. He regularly phoned his brother King George with advice (often conflicting with that

Right: One of the wedding photographs of Edward Duke of Windsor and Wallis Simpson, Duchess of Windsor. They were married on 3 June 1937 at the Château de Candé, near Tours in France, owned by the French-born American industrialist Charles Bedaux. There were messages of congratulations from the British royal family, though no member was present, and the ceremony was conducted by an English clergyman who was disowned by his bishop. The glum expressions of bride and groom are certainly remarkable for a wedding photograph. Years later, when interviewed for the film 'A King's Story,' both affirmed they had, by mutual consent, never once mentioned the events of the Abdication. Yet from this photograph we may be forgiven for doubting that the matter never crossed their minds.

of the King's ministers). One evening late in January 1937 the Palace informed him that the King was too busy to phone him back at the time he had requested. 'It was pathetic,' wrote Major 'Fruity' Metcalfe a loyal friend of years' standing who followed him into exile, 'to see HRH's face. . . . He has been so used to having everything done as he wishes.'

The once 'democratic' Prince began to stand on dignity – insisting on wearing all his orders and decorations. He also became embarrassingly tight about money – though it has been estimated that cash and assets in excess of a million pounds were settled on him by the family. Such generosity did not extend to their treatment of his wife, who was refused the title of Her Royal Highness. In the 1970s, the legality of this ruling was questioned in the pages of Burke's Peerage, for in the traditions of British aristocracy it was the settled rule that a wife take the status of her husband. The treatment of his Duchess was a cause of bitterness throughout the Duke's life.

The two lovers were finally married on 3 June 1937 at the Chateau de Candé, near Tours in France. Constance Spry arranged the flowers; Cecil Beaton took the photographs; 'Fruity' Metcalfe was best man; and the marriage was celebrated by the Rev. J. A. Jardine, who had offered his services. He was disowned by his bishop. Telegrams arrived from the King and Queen and also from Queen Mary.

The chateau had been loaned for the occasion by Charles Bedaux, a French-born American industrialist with large interests in Germany. At his suggestion, the Duke embarked that autumn on a tour of Germany 'to study labour conditions.' The Duke's attitude to and relations with the Nazi leaders have been a matter of controversy ever since. In October 1937 the New York Times commented: 'The Duke's gestures and remarks during the last two weeks have demonstrated that the Abdication did rob Germany of a firm friend on the British throne.' Certainly the Duke expressed admiration for the German regime and met on seemingly friendly terms with Hitler.

In 1938-39 the Windsors were living in France, entertaining close friends at their villa near Antibes and Parisian society at their residence on the Boulevard Suchet. When War broke out on 3 September 1939, they were at Antibes. After 'cloak and dagger' arrangements with the British government they motored north to Cherbourg where Lord Louis Mountbatten was waiting with his destroyer HMS *Kelly* to carry them back to England. The Duke, still a Field Marshal, was posted to the British military mission at Vincennes near Paris. He and the Duchess, accompanied as always by the faithful Major Metcalfe, returned to Paris. In

mid-May 1940 the Duchess left for a hotel in Biarritz, for the collapse of France was appearing daily more imminent. The Duke continued his tours of inspection until, on 28 May without a word to the ever loyal Metcalfe, he too went to Biarritz.

The situation there now seemed precarious and the Windsors made a difficult journey to the Spanish frontier where a phone call to the British embassy in Madrid procured them a visa. From Madrid they found their way to Estoril in Portugal. Prime Minister Churchill and the London government wanted them back in Britain. There were rumours of a German kidnap attempt while the Germans, it is now known, entertained the possibility that the Duke might be reestablished as 'King' of a puppet regime. Through June-July the Duke bargained his return to England against an HRH for Wallis. At length he accepted posting as Governor of Bermuda. But still he delayed his departure and it was not until the beginning of August 1940 that he and the Duchess finally sailed from Lisbon.

Above: The Duke and Duchess of Windsor pose for a New Year photograph, 1939, at their Riviera home the Villa La Croce, Cap d'Antibes. This picture comes from the first photo call they held in the house but they were not destined to enjoy their new home for long. They were at Antibes on the outbreak of World War II on 3 September 1939 and hurriedly made their way through France to the Channel coast where they were carried to England by a specially commissioned warship.

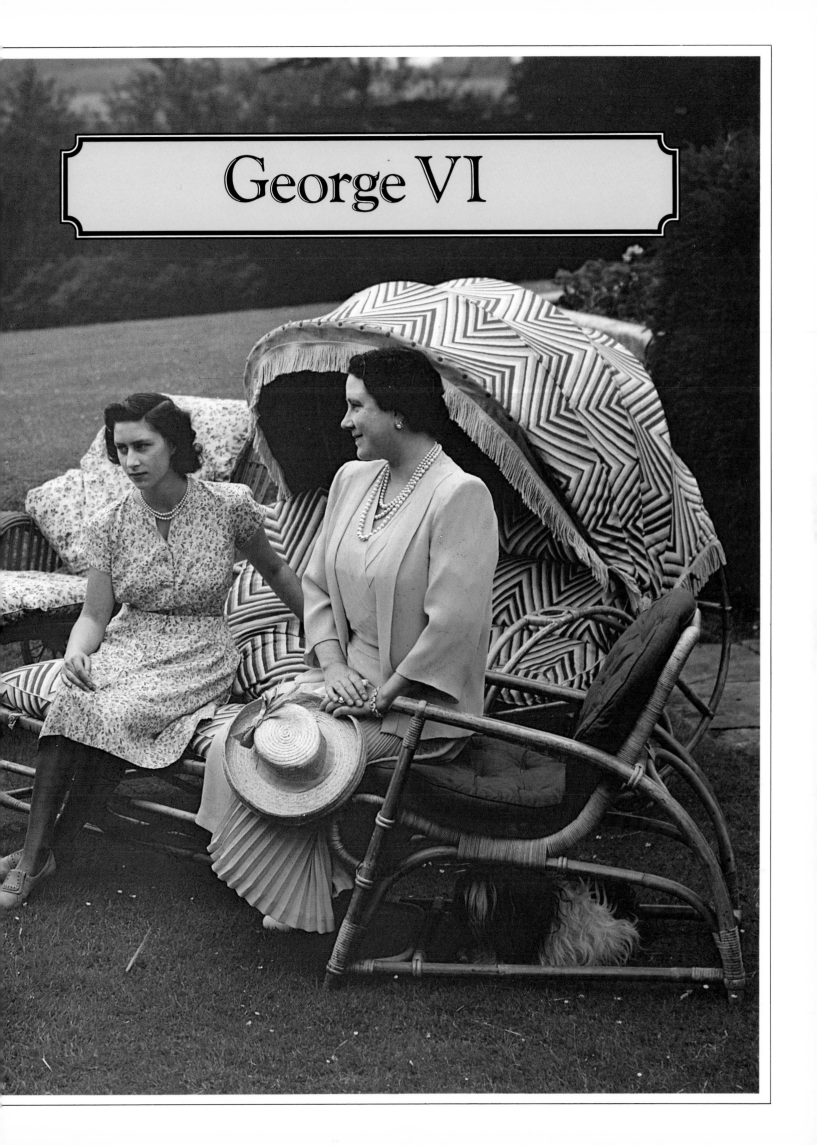

George VI

Pages 78-79: King George VI and Queen Elizabeth and their daughters, photographed in the gardens of Royal Lodge, Windsor in July 1946. Princess Elizabeth, now Queen Elizabeth II, sits next to her father, Princess Margaret next to her mother. The Duke and Duchess of York, as they then were, had received Royal Lodge as a country home from King George V in 1930, the year of Princess Margaret's birth. The place was somewhat dilapidated but the young couple set about the business of renovation with a will. As one biographer commented: 'No two people, not even Victoria and Albert, could have been happier in their home making.' This happy family life was a vital element in the success of George and Elizabeth, thrust into the limelight of monarchy after the scandals of Edward VIII's Abdication. Opposite: Prince Albert George, 'Bertie' as he was always known in the family, at the age of ten. The sailor suit anticipates Bertie's brief career in the Royal Navy, a traditional one for royal princes. He was not destined to distinguish himself in the service, leaving the Dartmouth Naval College with very mediocre grades, unlike his father George V who made a respectable career as a naval officer. But then, unlike his son, George V never saw active service. In May 1916 Bertie known to the Navy as sub-lieutenant Johnson, as one of the gun crew in 'A' turret on HMS *Collingwood*, went into action with the British Fleet at the Battle of Jutland. The brief and indecisive encounter was nevertheless the only major engagement between the German and British fleets throughout the war; Bertie discharged his duties creditably.

On the first night of his reign King George VI was at Fort Belvedere with his cousin Lord Louis Mountbatten waiting as his brother, ex-King Edward was completing his packing. George turned to his cousin with the words: 'Dickie, this is absolutely terrible. I'm quite unprepared for it. David has been trained for this all his life. I've never even seen a state paper. I'm a Naval Officer, it's the only thing I know about.' George V had addressed virtually the same words to Mountbatten's father back in 1895 on the news of his elder brother's death. 'I will give you the answer my father gave yours,' said 'Dickie' Mountbatten. 'A King could not have a better training than the Navy.'

Born on 14 December 1895, Prince Albert Frederick Arthur George was some 18 months younger than his brother. He once mused ruefully on how much difference 18 months could make. For where Edward was to become dashing and debonair, Bertie was a repressed and worried child, liable to break out from his natural shyness in fierce childish tantrums of frustration. At first, the royal nursery was ruled by a domineering head nurse who pampered Edward but neglected him. She was dismissed when he was just two, but by then Bertie, starved of affection and physically undernourished, had developed a chronic gastric weakness that was to recur in later years.

The sickly baby grew up to be a gawky boy. He was forced to wear splints to cure his knock knees and, although left-handed, he was dragooned into writing with his right. About the age of seven, he began to show signs of a stutter, which soon developed into an appalling stammer. His dismal record continued as he began his naval schooling at Osborne and then went on to the naval academy at Dartmouth. 'Mr Johnson,' as he was called, was treated with almost exaggerated disregard for his status, and was prominent only at the bottom of the table of exam results. But Dartmouth introduced him to tennis of which he became a skilled player, while the masters there encouraged his self-confidence by permitting him to use his left hand.

His cadet training ended with a tour of duty on the cruiser *Cumberland*, which he joined in January 1913. On board, he discharged the full duties expected of a naval rating, even the filthy job of coaling. Ashore, he found himself enthusiastically feted as prince from Tenerife to the West Indies where his natural reticence was actually heightened by the enthusiasm of the crowds. More than once he had a friend of similar height and build stand in for him at his non-speaking engagements. He made use of the same evasive tactics when possible when the tour took him to Canada. But on his return to England that summer, his mind filled with memories of Jamaica, the St Lawrence, Montreal, the Great Lakes and Niagara he was obviously maturing into manhood.

Right: David (King Edward VIII; centre) with Bertie and Mary (the Princess Royal).

Recurrently plagued by his old gastric complaint, the Prince nevertheless saw action during the First World War. On 31 May 1916, sublieutenant Johnson was part of the crew of 'A' turret on HMS *Collingwood* in the Battle of Jutland, but ill-health soon put an end to his naval career. After convalescing from an operation for an ulcer, he joined the Royal Naval Air Service at Cranwell, where he was put in charge of the boy cadets. With characteristic thoroughness he decided that he should know how to fly. Although he did not enjoy it, he doggedly pushed ahead with the course and qualified as pilot. In the last month of the war he joined air staff HQ in France and spent the first year of peace as an undergraduate at Cambridge.

Created Duke of York in 1920, he found his public functions beginning to increase and with them the dread duties of speech making. In July 1920 he held his first Investiture at Buckingham Palace on behalf of his father and the following year was in Belgium to present decorations to Belgian citizens who had distinguished themselves during the War. 1922 saw him discharging a family duty when he stood as chief sponsor at the wedding of Alexander, King of

Above: The 18-year-old Prince Albert with his sister Princess Mary and a friend, disembarking from a steam launch at the Cowes Regatta, August 1913. Plagued by an embarassing stammer since childhood and always dreadfully shy in his public appearances Bertie was rarely at his ease outside the family circle. There seems to be something apprehensive in his expression even on this relaxed social occasion.

Right: Prince Albert leaving Downing Street after a meeting with the prime minister in March 1920. The year saw the beginning of his working life as a royal. His appointment as President of the Industrial Welfare Society earned him the nickname of 'the foreman' in the family. His father had created him Duke of York, the title he himself had borne and in July 1920 the new duke held his first investiture at Buckingham Palace on behalf of his father.

the Serbs, to Princess Marie of Roumania. Even this, for the shy prince, was somewhat irksome. But his sense of duty made him anxious to take his share of royal chores.

With the coming of peace it had been felt that a prince of the blood was needed to represent the royal family in the field of industrial relations – the choice fell on Bertie. As President of the Industrial Welfare Society, he advocated partnership between management and workforce and himself developed a warm personal relationship with the mineworkers' leader, Frank Hodges. Where his glamorous brother made occasional but much publicized visits into the blighted industrial areas of Britain, the Duke of York, known to the family now as 'the foreman,' was actively at work, mostly concerned with welfare of young workers, for 15 years from 1920 to 1935. In July 1921, he presided over the launch of the Duke of York's Camp, which he came to regard as his own 'private enterprise.'

Many organizations had promoted holiday camps for working class boys before this. The Duke of York's was the first to mix the social classes. Of the 400 boys who assembled that July day for the inaugural lunch at the Royal Mews, Buckingham Palace, half came from working class districts, half from public schools. The atmosphere was frosty and embarrassed among the boys – apprehensive among the organizers. Fraternization across the social frontiers looked unlikely. One of the organizers reckoned that some of the boys would have 'deserted' at once if they could have summoned up the courage. But when the campers arrived at the site at New Romney on the Kent coast matters began to improve. The boys changed into the standard uniforms and were split up into 20 'teams' of 20, in which the social mix was enforced.

With unexpected imagination, the organizers, at the Duke's suggestion, had devised new team games so that the public school boys should not have an unfair advantage. The teams were soon working with enthusiasm and camaraderie so that when the Duke paid his visit to the camp on the fourth day of the week the enterprise, which many had criticized as a contrived exercise in social engineering, was flourishing. Applications for the next year's camp were overbooked and in 1930 the camp had to be cancelled because the site had become so heavily congested with 'royalty gazers.' The following year the camp was re-opened at Southwold Common in Suffolk. No one supposed that the camps could transform English society, but the participants had fun and were introduced, if only briefly, to the novel idea of friendly cooperation across the barriers of class. The Duke himself sometimes joined in the games as well as the campfire songs and his

Above: HRH the Duke of York from the painting by John St Helier Lander for the special wedding number of the Illustrated London News of April 1923.

Below: Prince Albert Duke of York and his aide Major Sir Louis Grieg in full flying gear standing in front of a Handley Page 0/400 bomber. Having been discharged from the Navy on health grounds during the war, he joined the Royal Naval Air Service at its college at Cranwell, where he was put in charge of the boy cadets. Although he did not relish the prospect, he decided that he should learn how to fly and became the first member of the royal family to hold a qualified pilot's licence.

Right: An engagement photograph of the Duke of York and Lady Elizabeth Bowes-Lyon, on Wolverton Station on their visit to the King and Queen at Sandringham in January 1923. The two first met as children and as a young man Prince Albert set his heart on marrying the beautiful and vivacious Lady Elizabeth. It was a challenge as she was apprehensive about committing herself to the constraining formalities of the royal life style. Queen Mary reckoned her son would be lucky to win this fascinating young woman, one of the stars of fashionable society.

Below: The Duke and Duchess of York returning from Westminster Abbey after their wedding in April 1923.

personal enthusiasm and determination were principal factors in the scheme's success.

Bertie brought similar determination to his courtship of the Lady Elizabeth Bowes-Lyon, pressing his suit despite early refusals. Their marriage in April 1923 was the best thing that ever happened to him. Lady Elizabeth was beautiful, sparkling and quick-witted, and she had a warmth and approachability that would compensate in their public life for his diffidence.

In October 1923 Prince Albert (accompanied by his new wife) found himself once again in the Balkans as sponsor at yet another marriage among his distant royal cousins. It proved more than a merely social event. Balkan aggresssion by Mussolini's Italy earlier in the year had succeeded despite protests from Britain. The Foreign Office saw the royal visit to Serbia as a welcome opportunity to reaffirm Britain's interest in the region and refurbish, a little, their tarnished image. While the politicians were pleased with the diplomatic impact of the young couple, Bertie was delighted to show off his beautiful bride.

In July 1924 the Yorks paid an official visit to Northern Ireland where they were ecstatically received by the Loyalist Protestant community. That winter saw them on tour in Kenya which enchanted them with the beauties of its landscape and the thrills of the six-week safari laid on for them. Yet the Duke still itched for the chance of a major imperial tour. This came in July 1926 when Buckingham Palace received a request from the Australian prime minister Stanley Bruce for a senior prince to open the new parliament building in Canberra, scheduled for 9 May the following year.

The Yorks faced the long-awaited opportunity with mingled feelings. Their first-born, baby Elizabeth, had arrived on 21 April and it seemed hard to have to leave her so soon. And now he was facing the full implications of a major tour, Bertie was suddenly apprehensive. Despite treatment by numerous specialists, his stammer was no better. His speech at the closing ceremony of the 1925 Empire Exhibition at Wembley had been marred by long unnatural pauses and 'agonizing silences.' According to his official biographer he was falling into 'the inconsolable despair of the chronic stammerer, and the secret dread that the hidden root of the affliction lay in the mind rather than the body.'

Among the Wembley crowds who heard the Duke speak was one man who knew he could help. Lionel Logue had established a reputation in his native Australia in some remarkable speech therapy with shell-shocked soldiers. Now he was beginning to make a name in London. Dreading another failure, Bertie yielded with reluctance to the urgings of his Duchess to visit Logue's Harley Street consulting rooms. The therapist insisted his patients come to him and, in the case of the Duke, he stipulated they should meet as equals. He saw 'a slim, quiet man with tired eyes and all the outward symptoms of one upon whom the habitual speech has begun to set the sign.' But that first October meeting inspired the Duke with the belief that success was possible. A month later he wrote to his father of 'a great improvement in talking and also in making speeches.' Logue's system depended on building confidence in part by psychological means but also by a programme of breathing exercises. The Yorks were due to leave for Australia and New Zealand in a little more than three months. The Duchess pleaded with Logue to accompany them. He refused. Over dependence on the teacher was no cure and though he continued to work with his patient for the next 20 years he always insisted that he rely on himself.

On 22 February 1927 the battle cruiser HMS *Renown* with the royal couple aboard, anchored off Auckland, New Zealand. Surrounded by en-

thusiastic, if respectful, crowds wherever they went, they were an immediate success. Some two months later *Renown* entered Sydney harbour. Australia was ecstatic about the visitors. They were charming, unpompous and delighted with everything they saw. The Duchess met with spontaneous affection everywhere, while the Duke came across as 'a really genuine young man with decided opinions of his own – which is what we like here in Australia.' His speech on Anzac Day moved the most hardened veterans while in opening the New Parliament building in Canberra and in his delivery of the formal Speech from the Throne, he behaved with dignity and assurance. 'I have so much confidence in myself now,' he wrote home, 'which I am sure comes from being able to speak properly at last.'

It seemed obvious that with the Yorks the British monarchy had acquired a workmanlike and dedicated new team. Unfortunately King George did not see things that way. Bertie and his wife were never sent on another tour by his father.

In late 1928, when the King seemed to be at death's door and Prince Edward was hurrying home from East Africa, Bertie wrote him a letter in which he mentioned 'a lovely story' going about 'that the reason for your rushing home is that in the event of anything happening to Papa I am going to bag the throne in your absence! Just like the Middle Ages.'

'Bagging the throne' was the last thing Bertie could have thought of. At this time, as always in the future, the Yorks' happiness lay in their home. The birth of their second daughter

Left: Prince Albert, Duke of York, competing in the men's doubles at the Wimbledon championships of 1926. He was partnered by his aide Major Sir Louis Greig. During his childhood, his left-handedness had been a considerable handicap. It was still considered to carry a social stigma and the unhappy boy was disciplined into learning to write with his right hand. The psychological pressure, coupled to his natural timidity, no doubt contributed to the boyhood stutter which developed into an appalling stammer. These pressures eased during his schooling at the Dartmouth Naval College. There his teachers permitted him to use his left hand and it was here that he first became interested in tennis. He developed his game to reach top amateur status, at a time when the professional game was virtually unknown. Wimbledon was still a sporting event, rather than a commercial circus, and one of the dates on the social calendar. Standards on court were certainly high, and the Duke's achievement in reaching the championships, though he and his partner were knocked out in the early rounds, a real one. But tennis had not yet become a form of warfare carried on by other means and, like most competitors in those distant days, he was satisfied to have competed and not unduly cast down by defeat. Bertie was also a keen and competent golfer and two years before his Wimbledon appearance had taken part in an exhibition match on a miner's golf course in the Rhondda Valley against Frank Hodges, leader of the National Union of Miners.

Margaret Rose, on 21 August 1930, brought further enrichment to their joy in the family circle. King George gave them Royal Lodge, Windsor, as a country house and the Duchess set about transforming the inconvenient and dilapidated residence into a real home. 'No two people,' observed a biographer, 'not even Victoria and Albert – could have been happier in their home making.' And the close-knit family unit basked in the affection the old king showed for his grand-daughter Elizabeth whom he always called 'Lilibet,' from her first childish attempts to pronounce her name.

While the Duchess busied herself with the decor of Royal Lodge, the Duke devoted himself to the garden. Like his father he was a keen philatelist and he was also a crack shot, but gardening became a passion which he developed into an expertise admired by professionals.

Behind this family idyll lay a strength of personality which King George, for one, came to recognize. 'Bertie,' he once said, 'has more guts than the rest of his brothers put together.' The King's death in January 1936 set in train events that were to test Bertie's resilience to the utmost. As the year advanced, rumour concerning King Edward VIII's intentions mounted – his brother, next in line to the succession, could only watch apprehensively.

Late in October, when Mrs Simpson got her divorce *nisi*, the Duke received a visit from the King's private secretary to inform him that abdication must now be considered as a possibility. Like most people, he could hardly entertain the idea that David would really go to such lengths. When, on the morning of 17 November the King told his brothers that, if need be, he would abdicate to marry, Bertie, 'literally dumbfounded by what this meant for his own life and that of his daughter Elizabeth, could not say anything at all.'

He had a deep admiration for his brother. David had been coached for kingship since boyhood while he had been insulated from affairs of state. Now, in a matter of weeks it appeared, he was to be catapulted from comfortable domesticity as *pater familias* at Royal Lodge and their London house at 145 Piccadilly, to a pinnacle in world affairs as King-Emperor. Closer home, great danger seemed to threaten his beloved

Below: The family photographed in the grounds of Windsor in June 1936. Six months later, their idyllic home life was overshadowed by the Abdication crisis which was to drag the Duke from the comfortable role of *pater familias* of second ranking royalty to the Palace. While the Princesses play with the royal dogs, their mother holds her favourite, Chu Chu.

country and the whole royal family. A few days after the bombshell announcement he told his own private secretary: 'if the worst happens and I have to take over . . . I will do my best to clear up the inevitable mess, if the whole fabric does not crumble under the shock and strain of it all.'

His resolution was never in question: his ability to handle the monarchy's greatest modern crisis may have been. Court gossip spoke of the possibility of passing him over in favour of his 'apparently more able brother,' George, Duke of Kent. Prone to debilitating fits of depression, and even drug taking, in his younger years, the Duke had found new stability after his marriage to Princess Marina of Greece in 1927. Theirs had been the society wedding of the year; they had a son, a potential Prince of Wales; and the Duke had a forthright bearing more suited to kingship, it seemed, than Bertie's modest diffidence. Where Bertie had been tongue-tied in the face of David's talk of Abdication, Kent had reacted furiously. He emerged from the meeting fuming, 'He is besotted on the woman . . . One can't get a sensible word out of him.'

Yet it is hard to credit that the 'Kent' option was ever seriously considered if, indeed, it was ever suggested. To follow the abdication of a king with the open admission that his natural successor was incapable would, indeed, have caused 'the whole fabric' to 'crumble.' Old King George would certainly have had no truck with such nonsense. According to Lady Airlie he said shortly before he died: 'I pray to God that my eldest son will never marry and have children, and that nothing will come between Bertie and Lilibet and the throne.'

Yet as the crisis unfolded Bertie found himself excluded from his brother's councils. A meeting arranged for Thursday 3 December was abruptly postponed by the King for the following day, when it was again put off. On Saturday, Prime Minister Baldwin learnt of the King's final decision to abdicate but his brother and now successor was not informed until the following Monday, 7 December. On Wednesday the brothers met again, the Duke hoping to persuade the King to reconsider – the Abdication papers were signed the next day.

From the outset of his reign the new King faced a seemingly trivial but in fact important question – what title should the ex-King bear? Edward was to broadcast on 11 December and Sir John Reith, director of the BBC, was intending to introduce him as 'Mr Edward Windsor.' Senior courtiers were at a loss: the King was not. 'He cannot be Mr E.W. as he was born the son of a duke,' he pointed out. But mere 'Lord Edward Windsor,' the standard courtesy title for sons of the peerage would make him eligible to stand for election to and vote in the House of Commons. As 'Duke of Windsor' he could sit and vote in the House of Lords. Neither prospect appealed to the worried advisers. However, as 'H.R.H. the Duke of Windsor,' a royal duke, both possibilities were excluded while the ex-King could still retain his courtesy ranks in the armed forces.

The King's decision on his own title was of equal interest to his subjects. On Abdication Day the London *Evening News* noted the choice was between 'Albert I' and 'George VI.' By choosing George proclaimed continuity with the pattern and style of his father's reign. Prime Minister Baldwin noted that he more closely resembled his father in character and mind than any of his brothers and considered this would 'endear him to his people.' During the early months Queen Mary was a tower of strength and a further reassuring symbol of continuity

The King looked to the future with apprehensiveness. His first sight of the government document boxes quite unnerved him by the sheer bulk of the papers they contained. Nor did he or the Queen entirely discount the possibility

Below: King George VI as Sovereign of the Order of the Garter by Sir Gerald Kelly. One of the numerous official portrait sittings which was one of the chores that fell to the new King's lot. Even the loyal skill of the court artist has not been able to mask entirely the dogged sense of obligation that drove the reluctant monarch to the conscientious discharge of his royal duties'. The painting hangs in the National Portrait Gallery, London.

Above: The official photograph of King George VI and Queen Elizabeth, with their daughters, after the coronation in Westminster Abbey in May 1937. Every face wears an expression of heavy seriousness which contrasts with the happy family group on page 86. The King had gone to his coronation on the day fixed for that of his brother, Edward VIII. Following the dramas of the Abdication he had reason to be apprehensive, yet during the five months since his accession his calm dedication to his duty and the reassuring presence of a loving and devoted family surrounding the throne, had done much to re-establish the monarchy in the affections and respect of the British public.

King had successfully completed the complicated Declaration, he flashed his mentor a look of modest triumph.

The whole route of the coronation procession was lined with crowds cheering despite the rain; the royal progress through the East End of London the next day met the same ovation. Over the following weeks the royal pair visited cities all over the kingdom and with a confident speech at the State Opening of Parliament in October the reign was truly launched.

But if Britain's monarchy was once more securely based, the peace of Europe was not. After the coronation, Stanley Baldwin had resigned to be followed as prime minister by Neville Chamberlain. Self-contained and strong minded, he was, like the vast majority of his compatriots, for peace at almost any price. Men and women still recalled the holocaust of 1914-1918 – the 'war to end wars.' The Jeremiads of Winston Churchill, an outcast from the Conservative Party and further discredited by his advocacy of Edward VIII during the Abdication Crisis, were generally discounted. Chamberlain's policy of appeasement, based on the (as it turned out absurd) assumption that Germany's leaders were rational statesmen like himself, seemed to be bringing results. The Munich agreement of 1938 had apparently secured peace in Europe, for which the fate of Czechoslovakia, though bitter, seemed an acceptable price. When, too late, Chamberlain realized the realities behind Hitler's manoeuvrings, he proclaimed Britain's guarantee to Poland and with France issued an ultimatum; it ran out on 3 September and the two countries were at war with Germany.

At the time, neither was under attack or even immediately threatened by Germany. There were those who thought the ultimatum a mistake. Joseph Kennedy (father of the future President), American ambassador in London and a firm advocate of appeasement, dismayed King George in a private audience by decrying Britain's 'folly' in pursuing a war which might cripple her financially (which it did) and, apart from high sounding talk of principle, seemed to have as its only cause the territorial integrity of Eastern Europe.

The King had come, slowly, to realize the point which Kennedy could not see. At some stage principle had to be asserted. Like most ordinary, decent-minded people, he had hoped that appeasement would ensure peace. When it had obviously failed he, like the bulk of the British nation, prepared for war.

King George had already made a contribution to foster goodwill between the allies who were to battle the Third Reich. In the summer of 1938, while German pressure mounted against

of a Windsor 'comeback.' After all, no prince had ever been more popular than Edward. One worry they did not have. Republicanism, so strong in the middle decades of the nineteenth century, was dead. An amendment to the Commons debate on the Abdication Bill calling for the abolition of the monarchy, was lost by 403 votes to 5.

George VI went to his coronation on the day originally set for his brother. The omens were alternately worrying and absurd. In preparation for the trendy Edward, souvenir manufacturers had prepared a startling range of oddities such as women's corsets embellished on the hip with a crown flanked by lion and unicorn. New designs were in production within hours of the Abdication speech. On the morning of the coronation itself the King and Queen were awakened at 3.00am by the noise of loudspeakers being tested along Constitution Hill. During the ceremony the supporting bishops could not find the text of the King's oath while the Archbishop of Canterbury in offering his own copy at first obscured some of the words with his thumb. The night before, the King had been working with Lionel Logue on the oath and the Accession Declaration. The therapist, wearing the insignia of the Royal Victorian Order bestowed on him the previous evening, had a special seat reserved in the Abbey and when the

Czechoslovakia for the 'return' of the Sudetenland, the King and Queen made a state visit to France. Diplomatically it was opportune, in personal terms it was a triumph. As they drove down the Champs Elysées, 'roofs, windows and pavements roared with exultant crowds.' In May 1939, the Royal couple arrived in Canada to a still more enthusiastic reception. On 9 June they crossed the border into the United States.

It was the first time a reigning British monarch had set foot there. The three-day trip was dogged by an army of reporters, while in Washington the streets were 'jammed with citizens and soldiery, thundering salutes and applause.' Queen Elizabeth almost stole the show, but the King, too, charmed the Americans with his informality, obvious good nature and unexpected youthfulness of manner. When they arrived at President Roosevelt's Hyde Park residence the cocktails were waiting. Offering them, the President laughingly observed, 'My mother thinks you should have a cup of tea; she doesn't approve of cocktails.' 'Neither does my mother,' the King observed as he took one.

Informality was the keynote at Hyde Park. King and President took a dip in the pool; relaxing in open-necked shirt, the King-Emperor dined off hot-dogs and beer and, in the words of *Time* 'Squire Roosevelt whizzed the Royal pair around in his Ford . . . giving Scotland Yard palpitations.' But there were also serious discussions centring on American attitudes to the prospect of War. King George took careful notes and reported back to his government on his return. If the Roosevelts developed a 'father-motherly feeling towards this nice young couple,' there were also the beginnings of a deeper respect. 'The North American tour,' it has been said, 'was a climacteric in the King's life. . . . It marked the end of his apprenticeship as a monarch.'

Back in England, King George offered, as Head of State, to appeal directly to the Axis leaders: the government rejected the idea, fearing he would meet with a rebuff. Nevertheless, the King played a part in behind-the-scenes diplomacy, he maintained correspondence with President Roosevelt throughout the war years his letters to Tsar Boris of the Bulgars may have helped delay the inevitable capitulation of Bulgaria to German pressures for an alliance. The King was kept fully informed on the highest secrets of state – he was one of only four men in England to know the full details of the atom bomb project. American chiefs of staff were astonished by his grasp of affairs and occasionally, as in the reorganization of the Allied High Command in the Mediterranean, following the Casablanca Conference of January 1943, his recommendations contributed to shaping policy.

The career of Prime Minister Chamberlain was ended on 8 May 1940 by an historic debate in the House of Commons. His conduct of the war seemed ineffectual, even humiliating. The debate climaxed as the distinguished Conservative Leo Amery hurled against his own prime minister Oliver Cromwell's words when dismissing the Long Parliament back in 1655: 'You have sat here too long for any good you have been doing. Depart, I say, and let us have done with you. In the name of God, Go!' Two days later, Chamberlain tendered his resignation. The King 'knew there was only one person that I could send for to form a Government, who had the confidence of the country, and that was Winston.' Yet he deplored what he considered the Conservative rebels disloyalty to Chamberlain and was unsure how he and Churchill, one-time supporter of his brother, would get on. In fact, the partnership began to build with the first of their formal audiences and in September these gave place to relaxed working lunches at which the monarch and his first minister served themselves from a buffet.

The war continued to go badly. By January 1942, Rommel had driven back the British forces in North Africa and the following month came the capitulation of Britain's island fortress of Singapore to the Japanese. Churchill

Above: The King and Queen on board the liner the *Empress of Australia* en route for their tour of Canada and the United States in May 1939. With the worsening situation in Europe (World War II was only four months away) royal advisers had been genuinely apprehensive about allowing the visit to go ahead. Some, it seems, even feared the possibility of a rogue German U-boat attack. The decision to release an official photograph of the royal couple wearing life-jackets during lifeboat drill may have been intended to reassure public opinion. The fears proved groundless and the tour proved a triumphant success.

faced a vote of confidence in the Commons. He weathered it triumphantly, but King George put his finger on the underlying trouble when he wrote: 'The House wants Winston to lead them; but he ... likes getting his way with no interference from anybody and nobody will stand for that sort of treatment in this country.'

In these dark days British morale remained high thanks as much to the inspiring example of the King and Queen as to the stirring rhetoric of the prime minister's broadcasts. King George continued the traditional Christmas broadcasts begun by his father and the occasional pauses, mute echoes of the old stammer, served only to lend dignity to the simple words. More important still, was the presence of King and Queen at Buckingham Palace, where they commuted daily from Windsor. There had been plans to shift the seat of government from the bomb-torn capital. The King would have none of them. He and the Queen lived through the Blitz with the rest of the country, visiting the bombed areas of the capital and many other cities. Once, after a raid on the East End of London, a survivor called out: 'Thank God for a good King.' Emotionally, the King responded, 'And thank God for a good people.' Ironically, a daring *Luftwaffe* pilot cemented the bond of loyalty between King and people. Flying low down the length of the Mall, he roared close over the roofs of Buckingham Palace and unloaded a cluster of bombs. One

stick fell directly outside the window where the King was working and others wrecked the chapel. He and the Queen welcomed their baptism by fire. 'It makes me feel,' commented Queen Elizabeth, 'that I can look the East End in the face.'

During the course of the war they travelled some 50,000 miles through the length and breadth of their realm by special train. Secrecy was necessary for there were real fears of assassination or abduction by enemy agents. When

Opposite: Princess Elizabeth looks on as her father works on his official documents: the famous 'red boxes' in which State papers are delivered to the monarch, can be seen in the foreground.
Above: Accompanied by Mr Churchill, the King and Queen examine bomb damage at Buckingham Palace in September 1940. The royal couple were conscientious in visiting bomb-damaged areas throughout the country and often visited London's East End and Dockland during the Blitz.
Left: The King and Queen with senior officers at Buckingham Palace; the Queen's elegant costume is in powder blue, one of her favourite colors. She dressed as elegantly on her visits to the East End, thinking it would be insulting to people to 'dress down' to them. Neither she nor the King once considered leaving the country for the safety of Canada or the United States and, since they would not dream of being separated from their children, the Princesses stayed in England – many well-to-do English families did send their children to friends and relations overseas. As late as 1941 the threat of a German invasion of Britain seemed a possibility and both King and Queen practised pistol shooting in the grounds of their palaces. Throughout the war the King was thoroughly briefed by the prime minister and his military chiefs on the military situation.

Above: The royal family, with Prime Minister Churchill, on the balcony of Buckingham Palace, VE Day, 8 May 1945. Five years before, the King had been apprehensive about Churchill's appointment and when (1942) he faced a Commons vote of censure, shrewedly noted: 'Winston likes getting his way with no interference from anybody and nobody will stand for that sort of treatment in this country,' but the two men worked in closest amity throughout the war.
Below: With General Smuts on the South African tour of 1947.

King George travelled by car a sten gun lay on the seat beside him and the chauffeur had strict instructions to drive on, in case of attack, while the King shot it out.

George VI made several tours of his forces overseas. In June 1943 he made a hazardous flight to visit the Allied armies in North Africa and from there he sailed to Malta. A slim figure in white naval uniform, his hand at the salute, he entered the Grand Harbour, Valetta, on the bridge of the cruiser *Aurora*. It was 'a lovely sunny day' and the people 'cheering at every vantage point . . . brought a lump to my throat, knowing what they had suffered from six months constant bombing.' The heroic endur-

ance of the Maltese during those months had already been honoured with the presentation of the George Cross, inaugurated and designed by the King 'For Gallantry,' as an award for civilians. At the Teheran Conference late in 1943, Churchill made a presentation on the King's behalf to Marshal Stalin. This was the Stalingrad sword inscribed: 'To the steel-hearted citizens of Stalingrad. The gift of King George VI, in token of the homage of the British people.'

In June 1944 the King visited the Normandy beach-head just ten days after D-Day, both he and Churchill having reluctantly agreed not to accompany the assault force itself. In July he was with the troops in Italy and that autumn with Montgomery's 21st Army Group in the Low Countries. The King's relations with Churchill became ever closer as the war progressed. The prime minister, he noted, 'told me more than people imagine and only when the time was ripe did he air his plans and policies to his colleagues and chiefs of staff.' When victory in Europe came in May 1945, Churchill joined the royal family on the balcony at Buckingham Palace on VE Day 8 May to receive the ovations of the crowds.

The landslide defeat of the Conservatives at the July election and Churchill's resignation saddened the King whose relations with the Labour prime minister, Clement Attlee, were never to be so close. A traditionalist as well as a monarch, George VI hardly approved of socialism even though he appreciated the need for social reforms But, as always, he conscientiously discharged his constitutional duties and the Labour ministers developed considerable respect for his grasp of affairs, his 'good judgement and sure instinct for what was really vital.' When Attlee surprised the pundits by appoint-

ing Ernest Bevin to the Foreign Office, it was partly in deference to the King's shrewd advice. The Potsdam Conference of the Allied Powers to settle the affairs of postwar Europe was in session and it may be that the King saw in the solid and reliable figure of Bevin a steadying influence and a tough negotiator. Certainly, he had admired his work as Minister of Labour during the war.

The Royal Family shared in the austerity years of postwar Britain and the King felt uneasy when a state visit to South Africa took them to the sun during the hard winter of 1946-47. The family travelled thousands of miles throughout the country where Afrikaaner Nationalism was beginning to threaten the traditional ties with the Empire, and also visited the colony of Southern Rhodesia.

The King returned exhausted and with the worries of Indian independence to face. At his urging, Lord Mountbatten had accepted appointment as Viceroy, to supervise the transition. The King-Emperor could not easily reconcile himself to relinquishing Britain's position in the sub-continent though he found Jawaharlal Nehru's commitment to continuing membership of the Commonwealth heartening. The new title of 'Head of the Commonwealth' made continuing allegiance possible to India and many other newly independent countries, though Burmah severed all ties with Britain at this time. As Attlee later wrote it was King George's fate 'to reign in times of great tension. He could never look round and see a clear sky.'

The 600th-year celebrations of the founding of the Order of the Garter in 1948 were among the King's happier functions at this time, though the marriage of his daughter Elizabeth to Prince Philip of Greece the previous November had broken the happy family circle which had so long been his mainstay. Moreover, his health was beginning to fail and in March 1949 came an operation to relieve a thrombosis in his leg. It was suggested he go into hospital. 'I never heard of a King going into hospital before,' was his only comment and a fully equipped operating theatre was rigged in a room at Buckingham Palace. In May 1951 he and the Queen presided at a service of dedication in St Paul's Cathedral for the Festival of Britain, a kind of centenary of the Great Exhibition of 1851 and, despite the hostile comments of the Tory press, a huge and much enjoyed success which lightened the gloom of the national and world situation. The Korean War was claiming its terrible toll among British servicemen, while the Labour government, its majority shattered by elections the previous year, was in disarray.

The King's health was once again giving cause for alarm. In Setember 1951, tests having

revealed a malignant growth, his left lung was removed. King George smoked on average 25 cigarettes a day, but at the time any connection between this and his illness was underplayed. The King never knew the true nature of his complaint and the family continued its normal schedule of engagements. In fact, the King seemed to be recovering and early in December 1951 there was a day of national thanksgiving. On 30 January he went with the family to see a performance of *South Pacific* at Drury Lane theatre and the next day drove to London Airport to bid farewell to Princess Elizabeth and the Duke of Edinburgh leaving for their Commonwealth Tour. On 5 February he spent the day at Sandringham. The following morning his valet found him dead. He had died in his sleep of a coronary thrombosis.

The country mourned him as a great and good man; the tributes from overseas were heartfelt for all their formal phrasing; among the wreaths was one bearing the name of Churchill since 1951 once again prime minister. It took the form of a George Cross and bore the motto of the award: 'For Gallantry.'

Above: With his grandson, Charles, Prince of Wales on his third birthday in 1951. Within months of the jubilant VE celebrations of May '45 Winston Churchill had been turned out of office by a Labour landslide. The King was dismayed by the fate of his old friend and uneasy about many of the policies of the new socialist government. He and Prime Minister Attlee shared a mutual, if wary, respect, but for the King the haven of his home life became ever more important. He was loath to let his daughter Elizabeth marry, but soon found the family circle enriched as he and the Queen moved into the role of grandparents.

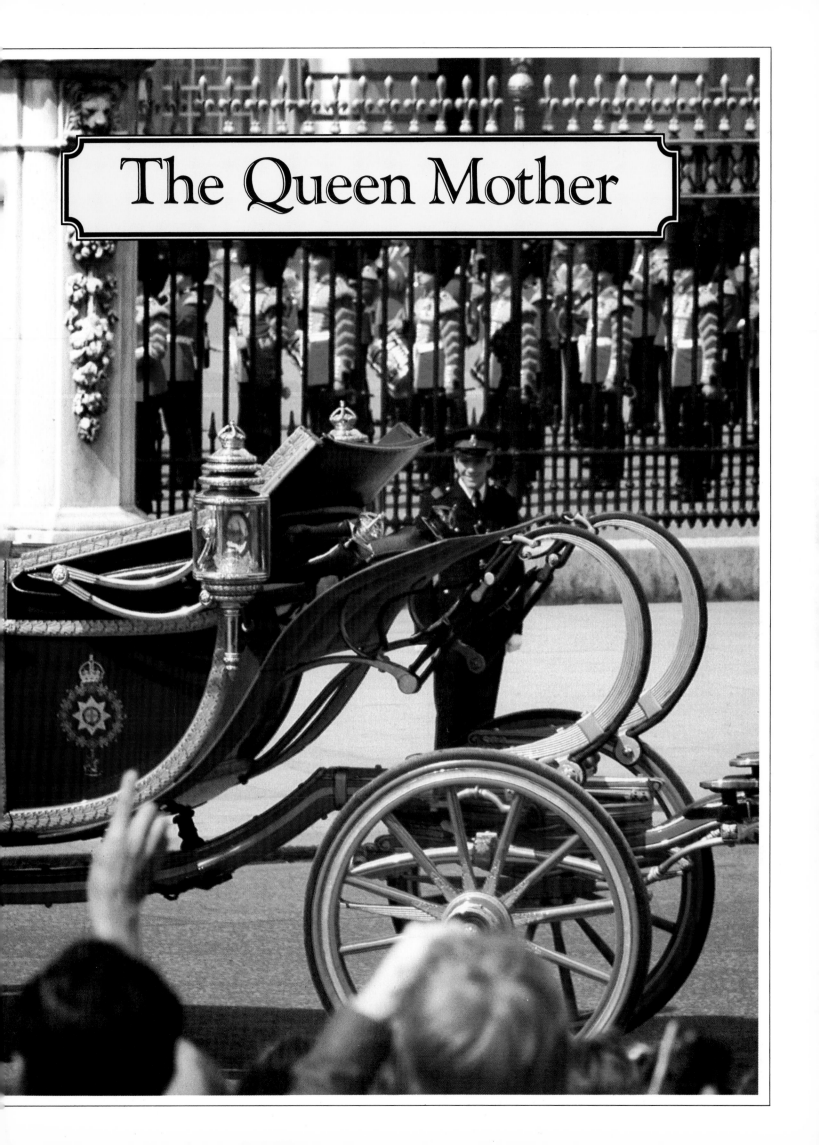

The Queen Mother

Pages 94-95: Queen Elizabeth the Queen Mother returns in triumph to Buckingham Palace after her progress through London's streets during the celebrations of her 80th birthday in the summer of 1980.

Below: The nine-year-old Lady Elizabeth Bowes-Lyon and her brother, in fancy dress; taken at the family home of Glamis Castle.

To her husband 'the most marvellous person in the world,' for a generation of admirers throughout the English speaking world quite simply the 'Queen Mum,' Queen Elizabeth the Queen Mother now in the autumn of her life enjoys an affectionate popular esteem unexcelled by any member of the royal family. Perhaps her greatest fan is her grandson Charles, Prince of Wales. 'I am,' he admits, 'hopelessly biased . . . Ever since I can remember my grandmother has been the most wonderful example of fun, laughter, warmth and infinite security . . .' The warm smile, the regal bearing combined with an outgoing ease of manner and the apparently genuine interest in everything she confronts during her still busy round of public engagements, seems today one of the most se-

cure traditions of the modern British royal scene. But behind this imperturbable geniality lies an act of personal courage which is typical of the woman but largely unsung.

The death of her husband unlocked a flood of grief and sense of personal loss throughout the nation. A survey of public opinion at the time found an overwhelming majority expressing sorrow for the king himself, a few commiserating with the plight of the new young queen, but very few indeed giving thought to the suffering of the widow. It was partly an expression of gratitude to King George for his devotion to the country during the war years. 'He never wanted to be King.' Said one worker, 'I think if anybody died for his country it was the King.' But it was also part of the nature of things in a monarchy. 'The King is dead. Long live the King.' It is said that King Charles II first knew of his father's execution when the courtier bringing the news addressed him as 'Your Majesty.' It was a constitutional convention rooted deep in public consciousness. In February 1952 a headmaster in the south of England told his school 'I have assembled you here in order to send on your behalf and in the name of the school a message of condolence to the Queen.' He meant, of course, Elizabeth II and the assembly ended with the head boy giving the loyal salutation 'Long Live the Queen!'

Few even of those close to the royal family 'realized how desolate and drained the Queen Mother had been by the death of her husband.' Apart from her immediate family circle she was left to contend almost alone with her grief. Among those who did think of her at this time was her friend the poet Dame Edith Sitwell, who sent her a copy of a recently published anthology of English literature. In a heartfelt letter of thanks Elizabeth mentioned a poem in the collection by the 17th-century poet George Herbert which had led her to reflect 'How small and selfish is sorrow,' and yet, she went on, 'It bangs one about until one is senseless.' Where Queen Victoria had allowed the 'small and selfish' emotion to shackle her spirit and had for years withdrawn, senseless to her royal duty and her own family's feelings, Elizabeth was to emerge triumphantly on the other side of grief after only months of deeply felt but personal mourning. It was typical of her gallant and cheerful nature.

Queen Elizabeth the Queen Mother was born at St Paul's Walden Bury in Hertfordshire, on 4 August 1900. She was the ninth child of Lord and Lady Glamis (of the Strathmore family) and descended on her mother's side from the medieval kings of England, on her father's from the royal line of Scotland. The family name of Bowes-Lyon derives from the ancient Scottish

family of Lyon – Sir John Lyon having married the daughter of King Robert of Scotland back in 1372 – and from Eleanor Bowes, daughter of a Durham industrialist who married the ninth Earl of Strathmore in the 1760s.

She spent a secure and happy childhood in the bosom of a large, united and somewhat old-fashioned family between their homes in Hertfordshire, Glamis Castle in Scotland and their London town house. Here, when she was a little girl of five, she first met Prince Albert, the ten-year-old son of the then Duke of York at a children's party. Fourteen when World War I broke out, Elizabeth Angela Marguerite spent the later war years helping as a nursing auxiliary in the convalescent home for wounded soldiers her father had set up in Glamis Castle. Eighteen when the war ended the Lady Elizabeth, 'a girl of striking beauty . . . with a slim attractive figure . . . and very beautiful violet-blue eyes' was surrounded by admirers. One of them was to recall: ' . . . the magic gripped us all. I fell *madly* in love. They all did.'

On a visit to Balmoral in the autumn of 1920 her childhood friend, the diffident Prince Albert, now himself Duke of York, went over to Glamis Castle and soon joined the ranks of the love-struck swains paying court to the beautiful, sparkling and quick-witted Lady Elizabeth. In that lively and extrovert company the chances of the stammering duke seemed slim. When he told his father he intended to propose marriage to her the King wished him well with the comment 'You'll be lucky if she accepts.' Bertie duly proposed the following year – to be refused. Elizabeth was not keen to marry into the royal family, fearing she would 'never again be free to think, speak or act as I really feel. . . .' Her mother, sympathetic with the disappointed young man, wrote 'I like him so much, and he is a man who will be made or marred by his wife.' The duke pursued his courting doggedly and, at the third time of asking, was accepted in January 1923.

The two had been increasingly in each other's company over the past year. In February 1922 the Lady Elizabeth had been a bridesmaid at the first royal wedding of the new reign when Princess Mary, the Princess Royal was married to Viscount Henry 'Lucky' Lascelles. Bluff and insensitive, he was hardly the natural soul mate of his shy and retiring young bride, 14 years his junior. But he already had an immense private fortune, was a Master of Foxhounds, owned a racing stable and was heir to the Earl of Harewood. To King George V these were ideal qualifications for a prospective son-in-law. The match was made and Mary prepared to do her duty. The age of the arranged marriage was by no means dead in upper class

society, though Mary's brother David, sensitive as always in the affairs of the heart, let his parents know that he was 'not at all happy' with the arrangement.

Above: Another charming girlhood portrait.
Below: The wedding photo of Viscount Lascelles and Princess Mary.

At just after 11.00am in the morning of 26 April 1923 Lady Elizabeth Bowes-Lyon, accompanied by her father Lord Strathmore, left her family's new London house at 17 Bruton Street for Westminster. Punctuality was never her strongest point, but she did get to the church on time – only forgetting her little handbag which was left on the seat of the carriage. Hers was the wedding of the year – *Vogue* commissioned articles from Osbert Sitwell on Royal Journeys and from Aldous Huxley on Royal Banquets – the wedding breakfast in Buckingham Palace was an eight course affair. The Prince of Wales accompanied the couple on their drive to Waterloo Station for the first stage of their honeymoon.

In June, perhaps reluctantly, the newly weds moved into White Lodge, Richmond Park, given by the king and decorated to the directions of Queen Mary. Towards the end of the month, Elizabeth entertained her in-laws to lunch. Queen Mary enjoyed the plain cooking – all the Yorks' cook was capable of – while King George

Opposite: A girlhood portrait, by Mabel Hankey, in the Royal Collection. 'A recent study of the bride', April 1923. The year before, Lady Elizabeth Bowes-Lyon had been a bridesmaid at the wedding of Viscount Lascelles and Princess Mary (see picture page 97, bottom). Left: In 1923, hers was the wedding of the year. In the caption to this picture readers of the Illustrated London News wedding number are assured that she will be a very popular society hostess.

Below: Lady Elizabeth, accompanied by her father Lord Strathmore, leaving the London family's house at 17 Bruton Street for her wedding in Westminster Abbey.

Above: A commemorative postcard of the wedding of the Duke and Duchess, the bride and groom surrounded by bridesmaids. For some time after the wedding the Duchess spent much time at her parents' house in Bruton Street (her first daughter Elizabeth was born there). However, from June 1923, their official home was White Lodge, Richmond given them by the King.

Below: Removing the Duchess of York's items of furniture from Bruton Street, May 1923.

thought they had made the house 'so nice with all their presents.' He was delighted with the new addition to the royal family, 'attractive, attentive and . . . unafraid of her father-in-law.' Bertie was delighted with himself. And with reason. His wife had a warmth and approachability that was a constant support to him, and the ideal foil in their public life for his diffidence.

It was to be some time before they found a house to suit them. White Lodge was unfriendly, overlarge and expensive to run and the Duchess longed for a place in London. Her first daughter was born at her parents' Bruton Street

house. Later, the Yorks established themselves in London at 145 Piccadilly and then, after a good deal of restoration and decoration, at the Royal Lodge, Windsor, in January 1932. This was to be the real family home. The Duchess had the grand saloon restored to its full magnificence and two additional wings were added. Her own bedroom was decorated in a pretty scheme of white apple wood, lemon and blue-grey, her favourite colour. The children's rooms were light and airy, while the gardens offered a world of adventure and fun.

The arrival of Elizabeth Alexandra Mary in the early hours of Wednesday 21 April 1926 had been greeted with relief and then delight by an anxious father. After a difficult labour the baby had been delivered by caesarian section but the Duke was delighted that his first born should be a girl. The mother breast-fed her baby before handing over to the charge of a nurse. But then, all too soon, the call of duty took the Duke and Duchess away from home in January for the tour of Australia. The Duchess was to cherish a tender memory of the farewell at Victoria Station – 'the baby . . . so sweet playing with the buttons on Bertie's coat . . . it quite broke me up.'

Three years later another baby was expected. Wishing to have her confinement at Glamis Castle, Elizabeth travelled north with the family. Born in the evening of 21 August 1930 the new daughter was thus the first royal child to be born in Scotland since the early seventeenth century. She was to have been christened Ann Margaret but because King George did not like the choice she was named Margaret Rose.

Left: The village fete, like foundation stone laying, was an essential part of the duties of royalty and the upper gentry. When her engagement to the Duke of York was announced, Lady Elizabeth's sister had assured the press that she had 'a healthy taste for outdoor life in the countryside' and that she also shared 'the Duke's interest in more serious matters, such as social questions.' Here, with the Duke standing just behind her, she combines the two – trying her hand at the Fresh Air Fund Outing to raise money for the charity, in July 1923.

While their mother and father were often travelling on official duties, the two little princesses were left in the care of their nurse 'Allah' Clara Cooper Knight, who had been nanny to the Duchess and Nurse Margaret MacDonald. For little Elizabeth this was the beginning of a friendship for a life. Miss MacDonald RVO, still known to her mistress by the nursery name of 'Bobo,' became dresser to Elizabeth as Queen, with her own suite of rooms at Buckingham Palace.

Family life when the parents were at home was quietly domestic. At 145 Piccadilly, family board games were a favourite diversion with an occasional visit to the picture palace at Marble Arch, or visits from Aunt Mary or Uncle David. With the country retreat at Royal Lodge, summer holidays at Balmoral and Christmas at Sandringham, the years passed pleasantly. Even her official engagements as a member of the royal team were less intimidating than the Duchess had feared. Then, shortly after the move to Royal Lodge a governess joined the household to help with the education of Princess Elizabeth. This was the 23-year-old Scottish girl Miss Marion Crawford. A great success with both the children, 'Crawfie' stayed with the family until the late 1940s. When she left, she made a public name for herself with her book *The Little Princesses* – and earned the royal family's ill will with her disclosures of the private life she had been a part of for so long.

The family schoolroom's schedule with Crawfie and a French governess was hardly overtaxing – just some ten hours a week, excluding dancing, drawing and music lessons. Queen

Mary, 'Gan Gan,' took far more interest in the progress of her grandchildren than she had in that of her own family. She took them round the sights of London at a smart trot, introduced them to 'genealogies, historic and dynastic,' and wearied them with overpacked tours of art galleries. Queen Elizabeth also did her stint on the gallery circuit and made tentative gestures to

Left: Leaving her parents' house in Bruton Street in May 1926, for the christening ceremony of baby Elizabeth. Behind her, the nurse bears the future queen of England in her arms.

introducing them to other children with carefully arranged parties and supervised meetings of Brownies and Girl Guides. The princesses were, apparently, fascinated by other children who seemed like 'beings from another world,' but such contacts were never allowed to become close. When, with his brother's abdication, their father became King, Queen Elizabeth decided that her elder daughter should have the horizons of her education extended. After consultation, she arranged for the vice-provost of Eton to give her bi-weekly tutorials in history and constitutional theory.

1936, the year of three kings, had been an increasingly bitter time for the Duchess. Uncle David had always been a favourite friend with her family, but as his affair with Mrs Simpson became increasingly open to scandal and gossip, so the feelings of the Duchess towards him became increasingly cool. In September the King spent a couple of weeks at Balmoral. Seeing this scheduled on the calendar, Queen Mary may have been heartened by an apparent return to the traditional ways. When it appeared that Mrs Simpson and friends were included in a guest list conventionally confined to members of the royal family and political dignitaries, and when the King left brother Bertie to preside at the formal opening of the Aberdeen Infirmary on the very day that he drove down to the station to meet his guests, gratification turned to dismay. The Yorks, staying at nearby Birkhall were also invited to Balmoral and the Duchess was not best pleased to find the King's married divorcee friend playing hostess there.

As 1936 advanced the feelings of the Duchess became increasingly cool. David's disregard for the constitutional position and personal sentiments of her husband brought her close to open hostility. Because, by the terms of Edward VII's will Sandringham and Balmoral were the personal possessions of the sovereign, Edward VIII was bought out to the tune of one million pounds so as to secure these two properties for the new royal family. Rumour also had it that among the jewels he showered on Mrs Simpson were the magnificent emeralds formerly owned by his and Bertie's grandmother, Queen Alexandra.

When, after the abdication, the possibility of the ex-King's return was under discussion, George VI seems to have been willing to entertain the idea – Queen Elizabeth, according to one close witness, was not. Walter Monkton, a friend of the Duke of Windsor believed that she 'thought that she must be on her guard because the Duke ..., to whom the other brothers had always looked up, might be a rallying point for any who might be critical of the new King who was less superficially endowed with the arts and graces that please.'

Opposite: An early official portrait (c. 1938) of Queen Elizabeth, shown wearing the sash and insignia of the Order of the Garter and other decorations.
Left: Police hold back crowds of excited women as the Duchess of York and her children, Princess Margaret Rose in the lead, leave their official limousine on a summer's day in 1935.

There may have been an element of protectiveness in the Queen's attitude. None knew better than she the diffidence and modesty of her husband. She stood at his side as he manfully mastered the public role of a royal duke. Now

Below: The Yorks and their daughters attending the wedding at St Margaret's, Westminster, of the Hon. Jean Elphinstone, a niece of the Duchess.

Above: The Duchess of York with her daughter Princess Elizabeth, in the garden of the Yorks' London home at 145 Piccadilly in July 1936. Since becoming Queen, the younger Elizabeth has become renowned for her love of corgi dogs: the enthusiasm seems to go back a long way. Life at the Piccadilly house was simple but happy. Family board games or an occasional visit to the cinema being the principal entertainments and visits from Aunt Mary (the Princess Royal) and Uncle David, the Prince of Wales, being delightful diversions.

Right: George and Elizabeth, now King and Queen in the Royal Box at a variety matinée in November 1937.

he was thrust into an infinitely more demanding position and in the most inauspicious circumstances possible. It is said that she believed the strain of kingship shortened her husband's life – certainly she never seems to have forgiven the once admired brother-in-law who had thrust it upon him. The coolness was mutual. David never forgave the denial of the title 'Her Royal Highness' to his wife. This was authenticated by King George under the Great Seal on 27 May 1937, almost certainly on the insistence of his political advisers. But the Duke always believed that the Queen was behind it.

After the War, when David paid occasional visits to England to see his brother, the Queen always failed, on some pretext, to meet him. Even when he attended the King's funeral in 1952 she barely spoke to him. Years later, when the Duke was again in England, this time for specialist eye surgery, accompanied by the Duchess, there was something of a reconciliation among the family. Even Queen Elizabeth II visited the Windsors – the Queen Mother did not.

Bertie's accession to the throne as King George VI meant a revolution in the family life style. Not the least among their discomforts was the move from the cheerful home in Piccadilly to the draughty corridors and echoing rooms of Buckingham Palace. Queen Elizabeth set about making a home there too, in a suite within the warren of rooms that make up the place . . . and had a rabbit hutch built in the gardens for the children.

According to the royal photographer, Arundel Herald, Dermot Morrah, the new Queen also insisted that the 'unbending' must be left to her and that the crowned and anointed King should not be too ready to step down from his pedestal. It suited the King's retiring and traditionalist temperament; it also suited the mood of the public, unnerved by the heady excitements of a modern-style monarchy under David, which had run so soon out of control.

As we saw in the last chapter, the new royals were able to win hearts with a relaxed 'modern' style all their own. The Canadian tour of May 1939 was a triumph for them both, especially perhaps Elizabeth, who was later to confess that it 'made' her. With the clouds of war in Europe looming on the horizon, some of their advisers were apprehensive about the venture. But the royals were determined and the visit would certainly be a fine chance to sound out likely Commonwealth reactions in the event of war breaking out. The Atlantic crossing did prove hazardous, though the dangers were from fog and icebergs rather than surprise U-boat attacks.

The ecstatic reception accorded the King and Queen proclaimed that nostalgic, patriotic love

of the 'mother' country was still very much alive in the self-governing Dominion of Canada. Elizabeth played a vital role. Lord Tweedsmuir (formerly John Buchan, the novelist) the Governor General considered she had 'a perfect genius for the right kind of publicity.' Her secret was less a matter of calculation than of natural spontaneity. At a ceremony attended by 10,000 Canadian veterans, she expressed the wish 'to get a little nearer to them.' When Tweedsmuir suggested they went down among the crowd Elizabeth and the King cheerfully agreed. The official party was 'simply swallowed up.' The Scotland Yard detectives were dismayed and the American correspondents following the tour 'staggered.' They said that no American President would have dared do that.

When they entered the United States on 9 June, those same American correspondents wanted more of this democratic monarchy. 'Would the Queen do something human, like going shopping.' Nonplussed, the British ambassador had to confess that 'if shopping should become necessary' Her Majesty would probably send her maid. Nevertheless, the general American opinion was that 'Elizabeth was the perfect Queen: eyes a snapping blue,

chin tilted confidently . . . fingers raised in a greeting as girlish as it was regal.' Her long-handled, lace-trimmed parasol 'seemed out of a story book' and set a fashion that year among the ladies of Long Island society.

On 2 September 1939, the very eve of war, the royal family was at Balmoral. Queen Elizabeth returned with the King to London, leaving the children in Scotland. The parents phoned daily and a week before Christmas gave orders for their daughters to join them for Christmas at Sandringham. In February 1940 they were established at Royal Lodge, Windsor and a few months later when German bombing began in earnest, they were moved to the Castle. The castle grounds were cut with slit trenches and an armoured car was permanently stationed there. Air raid shelters were prepared in the basements. More than 300 bombs fell in the grounds of Windsor during the war and Sir Hill Child, Master of the Household, was officially responsible for the princesses' safety when their parents were not there. To his dismay, Princess Elizabeth liked to dress properly rather than dash for cover in her night clothes. When the all clear was sounded Sir Hill would bow to her with the words 'You may now go to bed ma'am.'

Above: Princess Margaret, having her ankle strapped up, and Princess Elizabeth, securing a sling for a broken arm, practicising their first aid drill with the Girl Guides at Frogmore, June 1942. The royal children led quite sheltered lives with what may be called 'limited access' to ordinary families.

Above: 'Their Majesties the
King and Queen visit bomb-
damaged London, South
Western District,' 19
September 1940. The clipped
English of the official caption
writer purposely restricts
information in the blanket
interests of national security.
As usual, the King is in
uniform and the Queen
elegantly turned out: 'If the
people came to visit me,' she
used to say, 'they would put
on their best clothes.' Both of
them toured the country
throughout the war often
arriving unexpectedly, the
details of their schedules
being so well guarded that not
even their hosts knew of the
impending visit until the last
moment.

Opposite: a delightful
wartime study of the Queen
entitled 'Syringa (lilac) time
at Windsor Castle, July 1941.'

Throughout the war years Queen Elizabeth
was indefatigable. She organized a twice weekly working party to make surgical dressings for
the troops; sent thousands of letters of thanks to
families which took in refugees and visited
many bombed cities. Like the King she practised revolver shooting in the grounds of Buckingham Palace and agreed with him that 'one of
the main jobs in my life is to help others when I
can be useful to them.' On her visits to the
stricken cities she gave much thought to the
way she should dress – choosing unflamboyant
shades of dusty blue and pink, but always in
immaculate style. 'If the people came to visit
me,' she observed, 'they would put on their best
clothes.' For security reasons the visits were
often unannounced and, as a result, often poorly
attended. A shipping clerk in Liverpool recorded, 'a friend told me that they were visiting
Lancaster yesterday, but as nobody was expecting them, very few people were congregated
about. Last night the wireless announced that
the crowds were so great that their car had to go
at walking pace. One of us is wrong.'

Inevitably, the propaganda machine made

the most of their visits and there was a genuine
response of affection and sympathy for the royal
family when they too suffered loss. The death of
the Duke of Kent in a plane crash thrilled many
people with a genuine sense of horror that such
a fate should have befallen a member of the
royal family. A common response to the bombing of Buckingham Palace was – 'what a wicked
thing to do.' And yet the English remained level
headed about the monarchy. 'I should think
they're quite nice people,' remarked one man
interviewed by the Mass Observation team in
July 1940, 'quite harmless, but redundant . . .
unnecessary.' The view seemed to be empha-
sized by a soldier interviewed for the same survey: 'When a man like me's fighting for his
country, as they say, it's not the King and
Queen he's fighting for, it's England . . . they
only *represent* what we're really fighting for,
which is our country.'

But in a real way the royals did represent the
mood of the country. Even the most sceptical
discounted the rumour that they had sent the
princesses to Canada. 'I can't believe they'd do
such a thing,' commented one woman. She was

quite right. The remark is a telling tribute to the King and Queen at a time when hundreds of wealthy families were sending their children to safety across the Atlantic. George and Elizabeth just did not see it as an option. As the Queen said: 'The children cannot go without me and I will not leave the King; and the King of course will not go.'

The wartime Christmases offered the parents new delights in their children in the field of amateur theatricals. Elizabeth was 'absolutely amazed' at the talents revealed by the princesses. But her own talent for mimicry has always been a family delight and both daughters, notably Margaret, inherited it. The family shows were launched with a nativity play *The Christmas Child*. It was followed by a series of pantomimes devised and written by the household,

Right: Princess Margaret looking like a cross between a Pre-Raphaelite princess and Alice in Wonderland, but in fact dressed for her role in Old Mother Red Riding Boots, the Windsor Castle Panto for December 1944. With the Waterloo Room as their auditorium and the empty frames of ancestor pictures (stowed in wartime storage) to carry their posters, the sisters, helped by nursery staff and friends put on regular Christmas entertainments throughout the war years ranging from pantomimes to a nativity play, 'The Christmas Child.' One Christmas, Prince Philip of Greece, on leave from the Royal Navy, was among the audience. Princess Margaret has a natural genius for mimicry and it is said her sister is not far behind. The Windsor family's love of and talent for amateur theatricals has blossomed on more public stages in the university revue sketches of Prince Charles and Prince Edward.

from *Cinderella* to *Old Mother Red Riding Boots*. Princess Margaret found the empty frames of the portraits, removed for safe keeping, ideally suited for posters. 'How do you like my ancestors?' King George asked his guests. It was possibly in 1943, when *Aladdin* was on the programme, that Lieutenant Philip of Greece, RN, was in the audience, to the wide-eyed delight of the seventeen-year-old Princess Elizabeth.

By this time the Princess thought she should be doing more for the war effort than merely sharing the Blitz with the Londoners, or living in the comparative safety of Windsor. Eventually, in 1945, after constant urging, her father allowed her to do her National Service and Second Lieutenant Elizabeth Windsor – of the Auxiliary Transport Service, Mechanical Transport Training Centre No. 1 – was soon to be photographed wielding a spanner. She was a competent driver, capable of changing a wheel and full of her expertise with spark plugs.

Life in general was austere for the palace as for the rest of the population. In October 1942 Mrs Eleanor Roosevelt paid a visit to the King and Queen. The President had written asking that they tell her 'everything in regard to the problems of our troops in England which she might not get from the . . . authorities. You and I know that it is the little things which count but which are not always set out in official reports.' But the First Lady was still more intrigued by the conditions at Buckingham Palace. The baths were marked by the King with a waterline five inches from the bottom; the palace was still battle scarred from its bombing and the Queen's bedroom, where Eleanor was lodged, had no glass in the windows. The family were observing national economies in fuel and both King and Queen were suffering from colds. 'I do not see how they keep the dampness out,' wrote Mrs Roosevelt. She was equally astonished to be served unappetizing if nutritious meals, based on the standard rations of any English family, on gold and silver plate.

At last, on 8 May 1945, the long ordeal came to an end. That evening the Queen, King and their family were the focus of the VE Day celebrations in London. The crowds outside the palace called them back to the famous balcony no fewer than eight times. When the crowds at last began to thin in search of the celebrations in town, the princesses pleaded to be allowed to go out into the streets. King George at length agreed, with the proviso that Piccadilly Circus should be out of bounds. The two, accompanied by a governess and a Major of the guards jogging along as escort, ran gaily down St James's Street. When they got back to the palace they found that hundreds of people were still there.

Left: Princess Elizabeth changes a wheel on a service vehicle, during her training in the wartime Auxiliary Transport Service, at a training centre in southern England, April 1945. It was only after months of urging by his teenage daughter that King George finally allowed her auxilliary military training. As Second Lieutenant Elizabeth Windsor at the Mechanical Transport Training Centre No 1, she threw herself into the work with a will and was soon boasting of her expertise with spark plugs and other details of engine maintenance. This particular picture is one of the best known from her teenage years.

Happily the girls joined in the chanting – 'We want the King, We want the Queen.'

With the ending of the war the business of 'the firm,' as King George liked to call the family, returned to something more like normal. In 1947 they were on tour in South Africa where, according to a friend, it was Queen Elizabeth 'in her towering, flowery sumptuous hats,' with her winning smile and ready wit, made the tour the success it was, despite the political undercurrents. At one point, the King, exasperated by the attitude of the extreme Nationalists, burst out 'I would like to shoot them all.' Such fits of temper behind the scenes, known to the family as the King's 'gnashes,' were not uncommon. The young Princess Margaret was often able to jolly him out of them. Queen Elizabeth adopted a more reliable, more soothing, approach. 'But dear,' she observed on this occasion, 'You couldn't shoot them *all*!'

She used her charm rather more diplomatically in her own encounter with a disgruntled old timer with bitter thoughts about the Boer War some 50 years earlier. After a polite greeting he went on, 'But we still feel sometimes that we can't forgive the English for conquering us.' Smiling warmly the Queen replied: 'I can quite understand that. We feel very much the same in Scotland.'

It was in South Africa that their eldest daughter celebrated her 21st birthday, and that Princess Margaret made her first acquaintance with Group Captain Peter Townsend. As its younger

members grew up so the firm began to show signs of future change. But it was still a close-knit team when King George died in Febuary 1952. As we have seen, Queen Elizabeth remained something of a background figure in the period of national mourning which followed. A photograph of the three queens, herself, her mother-in-law and her daughter, now Queen Elizabeth II, provided a dramatic symbol of the national mood of grief. On 17 February the widow issued a long formal statement to the nation, letting it be known that in future she wished to be known as Queen Elizabeth the Queen Mother. King George had always seen her as the chief mentor of their eldest daughter. As though to symbolize the ending of her charge, the statement contained these words: 'I commend to you our dear daughter: give her your loyalty and devotion: in the great and lonely station to which she has been called she will need your protection and love . . .'

After the funeral the Queen Mother retired for a time from public life, staying with a friend at a house in the north of Scotland. Out driving one day between Thurso and John o'Groats she caught sight of an old castle perched on the cliffs of the Pentland Firth. Long unoccupied it was a dilapidated ruin standing in two acres of wilderness. To the mourning queen its desolate isolation may have seemed an ideal retreat. But the place also offered an invigorating challenge for her energies. Her admiring husband had once said, 'Elizabeth could make a home anywhere;'

Opposite: Queen Elizabeth the Queen Mother, on the occasion of her eightieth birthday.
Right: The Queen Mother has been Colonel-in-Chief to a number of British regiments and is said to be as at ease, and as popular, with the men as with the officers. Official photo calls like this are, of course, an unavoidable part of the royal routine, but Queen Elizabeth is unfailingly good natured and interested.

Below: With Princess Anne, Princess Margaret and Lord Snowdon at the Investiture of Prince Charles as Prince of Wales at Caernarvon in July 1969. As Constable of Caernarvon Castle, Lord Snowdon had been principally responsible for the organization of the event along with the Duke of Norfolk, Earl Marshal of England. It is to be hoped that Queen Elizabeth approved of the arrangements since, as is recognized by the family, Charles has always been her favorite grandchild.

at Barrogill, which she renamed the Castle of Mey, she triumphantly vindicated his faith. Along with the estate she bought the shooting rights over the adjacent moorland. The castle was entirely renovated and decorated throughout, with carefully chosen antiques, local landscape paintings and commissioned adornments.

Work at the castle progressed so fast that in August 1955 it was fit to be floodlit in honour of Princess Anne's fifth birthday. At the time, Princess Margaret was reaching the climax of her sad love affair with Peter Townsend and sought refuge from the press in Scotland, staying for a time at Castle Mey. When her mother had first been informed of the romance with the divorced RAF war pilot she wept. Echoes of 1936 were still, no doubt, vibrant in her memory and she must have seen only tragedy ahead for her high-spirited second daughter. Today, the Castle still provides a

Right: Queen Mother as grandmother; Queen Elizabeth with Prince Charles and Princess Anne at Royal Lodge Windsor, 1954. After the coronation in the summer of 1953 the Queen and Prince Philip went on a world tour of several months, leaving Queen Elizabeth in charge of her grandchildren. After the accession, the Queen and her family had moved out of Clarence House to Buckingham Palace and Clarence House became the home of the Queen Mother with Royal Lodge as her country house near London. After the return of her daughter and son-in-law in 1954, the Queen Mother herself went on a tour of Canada and the United States. It was a great success and it may be at this time that her affectionate nickname 'the Queen Mum' first came into general use.

summer retreat for the Queen Mother and her many guests and friends.

While in London, Queen Elizabeth lives in Clarence House. Designed by John Nash and built in 1820 for William Duke of Clarence (later King William IV) it was the first home of Princess Elizabeth and Prince Philip. They had been happy there, but Buckingham Palace is the residence of the monarch so mother and daughter changed homes. Princess Margaret accompanied her mother to the new house. Royal Lodge remained a weekend retreat for the widowed Queen. Here she kept King George's desk as it had been in his lifetime with its furniture and photographs in their accustomed places.

In the early years of her widowhood she saw much of her grandson Charles and during the world tour of the Queen and Prince Philip in 1953-54 she had charge of both Charles and his baby sister Anne. In 1954, the Queen Mum herself visited Canada and the United States, travelling on the liner the *Queen Elizabeth* which she herself had launched back in 1938. In Quebec she was hailed with shouts of '*Vive la reine;*' in America she renewed her friendship with Eleanor Roosevelt, and received an honor-

ary doctorate of law from Columbia University. The old magic still worked; indeed it is said that her affectionate soubriquet was first coined at about this time in the States.

As one of the councillors of state, Queen Elizabeth helps deputize for the Queen when she is out of Britain. Among many other official appointments, she is commandant-in-chief of Britain's women's armed services, Colonel in Chief of the Black Watch, her family regiment as well as numerous other regiments in Britain, Canada and Australia and Grand Master of the Royal Victorian Order. She has been of course patron of many organizations, of which she has taken a special interest in the King's Lynn Festival and the Royal Schools of Music. For 25 years she was Chancellor of London University, relinquishing the position in 1980 to be followed by Princess Anne.

Around her official engagements she fits a fully active private life and her special passion which is racing. Her steeple chasers run under the Strathmore colours of her grandfather and over the years she has had some 400 winners over the jumps and on the flat. In 1956 her horse Devon Loch came within an ace of winning the Grand National. Lengths ahead of the field and

Left: Queen Elizabeth, during her inauguration as Lord Warden of the Cinque Ports in 1978. Her appointment to this ancient honour was something of a break with tradition, insofar as the post had never been held by a woman in the whole of its 800 years history. The office originated in the reign of William the Conqueror when the warden was charged with seeing that a group of south coast ports, chief among them Hastings and Dover, supplied ships to the King in time of war. King Richard I added two more ports to the original five. But changing patterns of war and a retreating coast line meant that by the sixteenth century the office of Warden had lost its military significance. Yet, as such things do in England, it continued to exist as an honorific title with Dover Castle as the official seat of the Lord Warden.

with only 50 yards to go, he fell, his jockey Dick Francis, still in the saddle. The fall, one of the most celebrated mysteries of the racecourse, was never adequately explained. Queen Elizabeth took her misfortune phlegmatically, but her immediate concern was for rider and horse.

In 1978 she received remarkable official recognition, so to speak, of the special place she had so long held in the affections of the public. In that year, in a quite unprecedented breach with tradition, she became the first woman in history to be made Lord Warden of the Cinque Ports. Among her famous predecessors in a post which dates back to the days of William the Conqueror, was Sir Winston Churchill. The 'Cinque' or 'five' ports in question lie along the south coast of England. Hastings and Dover are the best known of the original five; King Richard I added Rye and Winchelsea to the group – thus making seven 'cinque' ports. A retreating sealine over the centuries means that neither now has a water front. In the middle ages, the towns enjoyed privileges in exchange for supplying ships in time of war - then the Lord Warden had real powers and responsibilities. For at least three centuries, the ports have had no military function and the Lord Wardenship became a bastion not of national defence but of male privilege.

In 1980 the nation celebrated with her the 80th birthday of this grand old lady. The ceremonies were preluded with a garden party at Buckingham Palace and this was followed with a service of thanksgiving, on 15 July, in St Paul's Cathedral. The whole of the royal family, except for her three-year-old great-grandson Master Peter Phillips, was present. The car-

riage procession rolled through London's cheering Streets with the state landau carrying the Queen Mother and Prince Charles occupying the place of honour in the rear by special order of the Queen. In the cathedral hung a great banner bearing the golden legend: 'All shall be well, and all manner of things shall be well.' The words, a source of comfort to Queen Elizabeth ever since the death of her husband, came from the writings of the great medieval English mystic Julian of Norwich.

After the service there was a celebration lunch for the family at the Palace. Clarence House was already deluged with cards, flowers, telegrams and presents, and on the day itself 4 August, crowds thronged the streets outside chanting 'Happy Birthday' and 'For She's a Jolly Good Fellow.' The birthday lunch was followed by a gala performance at Covent Garden of the ballet *Rhapsody*, specially created by choreographer Sir Frederick Ashton.

In his address at the St Paul's Service of Thanksgiving, Archbishop Runcie had proclaimed what might be taken as a motto for modern monarchy. 'Royalty,' he said, 'puts a human face on the operations of government.' At the beginning of her husband's reign, Queen Elizabeth had decided that the 'unbending' share of the royal role should be her province in the business of the 'firm.' For 50 years she has shown that 'human' face, the genuine expression of a very human personality, with charm and good humour. But behind it there has always been a rugged sense of duty, epitomized by King George. In the person of their daughter Queen Elizabeth II, the two qualities have become fused to perfection.

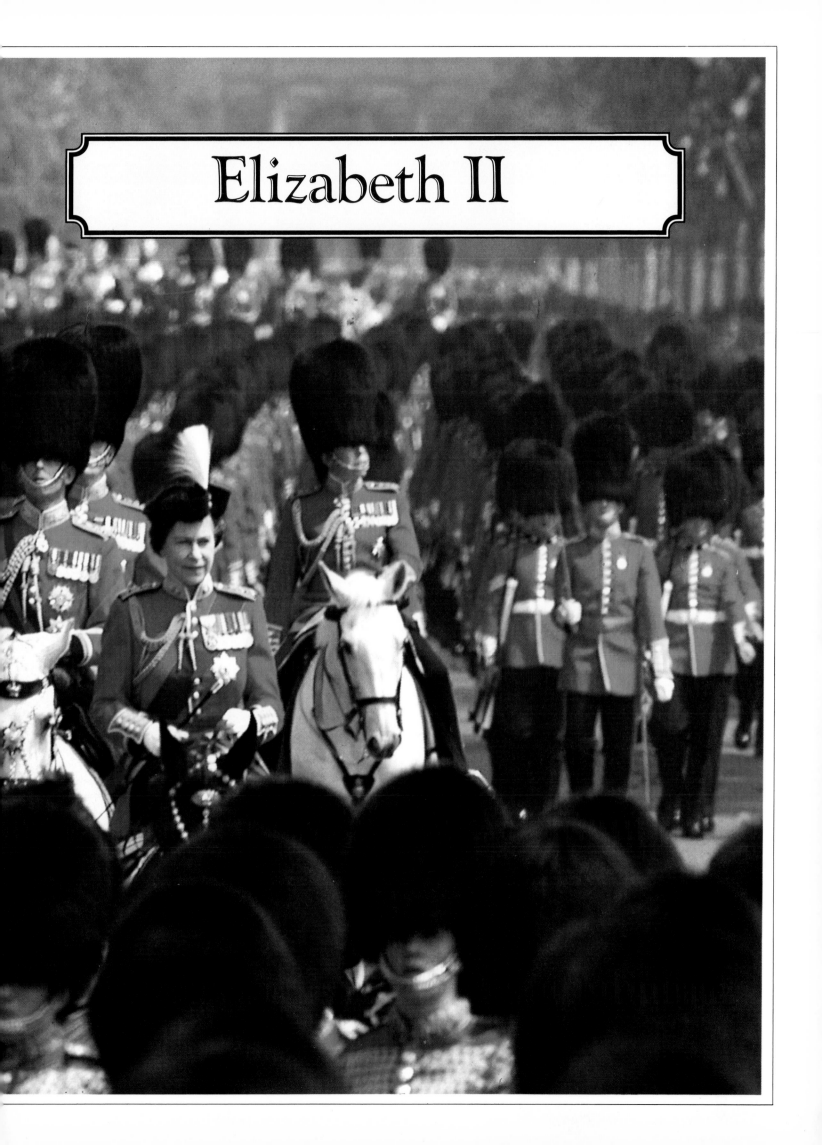

Elizabeth II

Pages 114-115: The Queen with her Guards riding down the Mall after the Trooping the Colour ceremony, June 1978. Out of the picture, to the right of Admiralty Arch, which can be seen in the background, lies Horse Guards Parade where this annual celebration of the Queen's official birthday is held. Although a great state occasion, Trooping the Colour honours the birthday of an individual; although a military spectacular it displays none of the fearsome weaponry of modern warfare. An old-style parade ground pageant, it avoids the macho excesses of May Day in Red Square, Moscow, or of Bastille Day in Paris.

Queen of the United Kingdom, Head of the Commonwealth and bearer of many another high-sounding title, Queen Elizabeth II is also the successful mother of a happy family and the loving wife of the man who was her first and only love. She is also the first British monarch in generations to look back on a childhood of unalloyed happiness and security. Queen Marie of Roumania, a cousin of King George V, once wrote: 'My English family was terribly exclusive, and only grudgingly opened its doors to strangers.' What may have been true of an earlier generation did not hold within the charmed circle of the Yorks' household, where the little newcomer Princess Elizabeth was surrounded by love. 'We always wanted a child to make our happiness complete,' wrote her father. 'Now that it has happened it seems so wonderful and strange.'

From the first, Elizabeth shaped up to become a lively and practical little girl. One Christmas a present of a housemaid's set released a 'passion for housework,' characteristic of a devotion to tidiness and order that has stood her in good stead. As Queen, she is, according to the recollection of a member of her staff, a marvel of concentration and accuracy. Like many girls of her class she also developed an engrossing enthusiasm for pony riding and is today an outstanding horsewoman.

The sense of responsibility, so strong a buttress in her work as monarch, sometimes expressed itself in childhood with a degree of primness towards her vivacious and mischievous sister who tended to be a little spoilt by an indulgent father. When the great day of their parents' coronation was approaching she mused pensively about Margaret: 'She's very young for a coronation, isn't she?' Uncle David's Abdication was the first cloud on the edge of Elizabeth's life. It revolutionized the position of her family and reshaped her future, but she faced it phlegmatically enough. A note she wrote that day was dated simply 'Abdication Day.' From now on, her young life was increasingly shaped by her destiny and she, more fully than any of her predecessors was prepared for the work that lay ahead, her father introducing her to the business of monarchy as she advanced through her teenage years.

By the terms of the Regency Act the Princess became a councillor of state at the age of eighteen; if her father should die before her twenty-first birthday she would come to the throne without need of a regency council. Some thought that having attained her royal majority and as heir to the throne she should be created Princess of Wales. But her father, a stickler for royal convention and tradition, rejected the idea on the grounds that the title was exclusively the entitlement of the wife of a Prince of Wales. For her part, his daughter was contemplating a much more important, and far more significant change of status.

The beginnings of her romance with Prince Philip of Greece are often dated to 1939 when she was thirteen and he was eighteen. The occasion was a visit by King George VI and his family to the Royal Naval College at Dartmouth, in a nostalgic gesture to his young days as a cadet there. Prince Philip had entered the College just a few weeks earlier and his Uncle 'Dickie' Mountbatten was with the royal visitors as the King's aide-de-camp. It seems to have been at his suggestion that Philip was deputed to entertain the young Princesses during their parents' official engagements on the two day visit. Those close to the Princess at the time believed that she was decidedly interested in the tall and handsome cadet. Two years later Chips Channon, the diarist, was describing Philip as the 'man who is to be our Prince Consort.' In 1941 that must have been an inspired guess but Elizabeth's affections were definitely engaged. The romance became an increasingly discussed matter so that, in 1946, Queen Mary was writing 'They have been in love for the last eighteen months – in fact longer I think . . . But the King and Queen feel she is too young to be engaged.'

Below: The baby Princess Elizabeth of York, not quite one year old, 17 March 1927.

Prince Philip was born on 10 June 1921, the son of Prince Andrew of Greece and Princess Alice of Battenberg. His grandfather on his father's side had been Prince William of the Danish house of Schleswig-Holstein-Sonderburg-Glucksburg who, accepting an invitation by the Greek parliament, became King of the Hellenes as George I in 1862. After the long reign of 51 years King George was assassinated in 1913. The troubled annals of the Greek monarchy, ever since its foundation in the 1830s, hardly concern us here, but they did impinge on Philip's childhood. A wit once remarked, 'he who would be king of Greece should keep his bags packed.' Philip's uncle King Constantine I was forced into exile twice; on the second occasion because of Greece's humiliating defeat in her war with Turkey. Philip's father Prince Andrew had been a lieutenant general and was involved in the reprisals which followed. Five politicians and one general lost their lives. In October Prince Andrew was arrested and his wife left their home at the palace of Mon Repos on Corfu to plead for his life in Athens. The new King was then far too insecure on his throne to offer assistance so Princess Alice wrote to her royal relations, chief among them King George V.

A British agent was dispatched to plead the Prince's case. But on 2 December the Prince stood before a court in the Athens Chamber of Deputies. The trial ended at midnight with the sentence of death. But King George had done more than send an agent. In an almost certainly unconstitutional exercise of his powers he had put a call through to the Admiralty in London and ordered a ship be sent at once to the rescue of his relations. Thus it was that the Royal Navy's light cruiser HMS *Calypso* arrived in Phaleron Bay on the morning of 3 December. Under the threat of her guns the sentence on Prince Andrew was commuted. The Prince was stripped of his Greek nationality and condemned to exile for life. With this new verdict confirmed, Prince Andrew was driven down to the port by the Greek revolutionary leader General Pangalos and embarked. *Calypso* steamed to Corfu to pick up Andrew's family and the eighteen-month-old Philip was packed aboard in a carry cot hastily improvised from a padded orange box.

From England, the refugee family settled in France and Philip attended his first school, at the age of six, there. On visits to Britain he stayed mostly with his uncle George Mountbatten, second Marquess of Milford Haven and

Above: The 16-year-old Princess Elizabeth in her Girl Guide uniform, at Frogmore in June 1942. Her pensive, dreamy expression in this charming study reveals her in typical teenage mood. But of course, as heir to the throne, she was no ordinary teenager and her youthful seriousness, noted by many friends and observers, had deeper causes, perhaps, than that of her age peers. Some two years after this picture was taken, on her 18th birthday she was to become a Councillor of State and officially of age. From that moment on she would be considered old enough to reign in her own right, should her father die, without the need for a regency council.

at nine entered preparatory school at Cheam. He spent his holidays either at Linden Manor with Uncle George, at home in Paris or with various relations in Europe. This early cosmopolitan background gave the young prince an enviable breadth of experience – the fact that his four sisters married members of the German nobility was less in his favour after the war.

When he was 12 he himself was sent to school in Germany at Salem, formerly a family castle of the Margraves of Baden, where the progressive educationalist Kurt Hahn had founded a school in 1920. It was a natural and enlightened choice. Philip's sister was married to the Margrave and Hahn's educational principles, based on the development of the whole personality and combining tough physical and intellectual discipline with a view to self reliance and independence of judgement, were a world away from the conventional and often constricting educational ideas of the time. With the advent of Nazism, however, Hahn fled Germany to set up a new school at Gordonstoun in Scotland. Here, the young Philip completed his education. It was still a small establishment and the boys were enlisted in work on the buildings and in the grounds – feeling themselves pioneers as much as schoolboys. Philip became head boy ('Guardian') and captain of cricket. Too much should not, perhaps, be made of the fact that he also excelled at the high jump and the high dive. The headmaster was much impressed by his sense of service. He also thought that the young prince would make his mark in any profession 'where he will have to prove himself in a full trial of strength.'

At Gordonstoun he began his love affair with the sea – inspired in part by his great ancestor, First Sea Lord Louis of Battenberg. He chose the Royal Navy as his career. In 1938 with the death of Uncle George, he spent more and more time with the family of his other uncle Lord Louis Mountbatten – a distinguished naval

man himself and one of the chief influences on the teenage prince.

Philip completed his training at Dartmouth with moderate distinction and early in 1940 found himself on minor convoy duties with the Navy. But he wanted to see real action and in October he was transferred to the battleship *Valiant*; March of the following year found the *Valiant* engaged in the Battle of Cape Matapan and Prince Philip mentioned in despatches. He was to serve in various other theatres of war; rose to the rank of lieutenant and, during rare visits to Britain saw Princess Elizabeth from time to time. Asked many years later when he had fallen in love with her he said, 'I suppose I began to think seriously about it . . . when I got back in 1946 and went to Balmoral.'

Elizabeth had certainly been set on the marriage before that, as we know from Queen Mary's remark. King George was reluctant to entertain the idea that his dear daughter had at last reached the age when she could be expected to leave home. Queen Elizabeth urged that the announcement of the engagement be postponed

Opposite: Princess Elizabeth aged 14, photographed at Windsor Castle by Lisa Sheridan in June 1940. The year before she had first encountered Prince Philip of Greece when King George VI took his family on a visit to Dartmouth Naval College. She was clearly enchanted with him.

Left: Prince Philip aged one, July 1922. Just seven months before he and his family had been forced to flee their home, *Mon Repos* on Corfu. Philip's father, Prince Andrew, a lieutenant general in the Greek army, had been arrested in the reprisals following the defeat of Greece by Turkey. Philip and his family were brought to England by a Royal Navy cruiser, the baby travelling in a make-shift, orange-box carry cot.
Below: The 17-year old Prince dressed for his part in the Gordonstoun school production of *Macbeth*.

Above: 'Princess Elizabeth and Lieutenant Philip Mountbatten, on whom the King yesterday conferred the title of Duke of Edinburgh . . . with the King and Queen and members of the royal family at Buckingham Palace, on their return from Westminster Abbey.' The royal wedding photo on 20 November 1947. The dry words of the agency caption give no hint of the opposition to the match voiced here and there among the old established families at court and in some sections of the press. The Beaverbrook papers were simply hostile to the Mountbatten family and some courtiers considered them upstarts. Such petty minded carping cut no ice with the king; he was simply unhappy that his beloved daughter was marrying at all and leaving home. But her obvious happiness stilled all doubts and he cheerfully welcomed Philip onto the family team.

Opposite: An informal photo.

until after the family's tour of South Africa. There, the princess achieved the age of 21; there too she made her famous broadcast of self-dedication to the Commonwealth. But aware though she may have been of the duties that lay ahead she would no longer delay her marriage. Prince Philip's naturalization as a British subject had come through in February 1947 and in July the announcement of the engagement came from Buckingham Palace.

The wedding took place on 20 November that year. Although less grand than some other royal weddings, it had sufficient pomp and splendour to make a glittering display in the austerity of postwar Britain. Costly presents flooded in from all parts of the world, but among the most treasured by the young couple was a simple table mat. This was the gift of Mahatma Gandhi, who had spun the thread on his own spinning wheel and had it woven up to his own design.

The couple began their honeymoon at 'Dickie' Mountbatten's country estate of Broadlands. But it was unhappily disturbed by press intrusions and busloads of sightseers, ferried out from London. Prince and Princess travelled north to the royal estate of Birkhall near Balmoral. For the next four years, the young couple had to fight a running battle with press and

protocol to live something approaching a normal life. Prince Philip was dourly determined to live his own life and to continue his career as a naval officer before the dreaded descent of what he called 'the royal rigmarole.' Suitably accoutred with royal titles – His Royal Highness, Baron Greenwich, Earl of Merioneth, Duke of Edinburgh and Knight of the Garter (eight days his wife's junior in the Order) – Philip also received a taxed salary of £10,000 from Parliament to fit him as far as possible for the ceremonial life. Probably more important to the 26-year-old junior officer, was the order from his superiors to take the Naval Staff course at Greenwich – necessary if he was to receive a senior commission.

In 1949 he and his wife moved into their London home of Clarence House. For a time, Philip was on naval half pay to allow time for official duties – such as the Presidency of the National Playing Fields Association, which he took over from Uncle Dickie. But he returned to full pay in October and remained on the active list until July 1951 having achieved the rank of lieutenant-commander and receiving his own ship the frigate HMS *Magpie* in September 1950.

Philip and Elizabeth had followed their Scottish honeymoon with a trip to Paris – their first visit abroad together. It began rather stiffly,

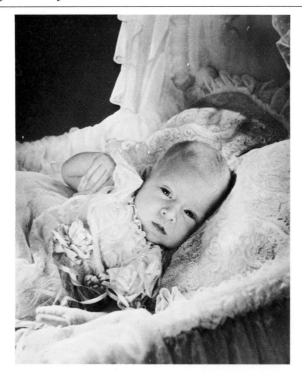

Opposite: The one-year old Prince Charles with his mother, early in 1949.
Right: One month old: an official photograph by Cecil Beaton. The Prince's birth had been celebrated with guns, bells, bonfires and fountains which streamed blue for a boy for the next week. This, the first official photograph, was released for publication on Sunday 2 January 1948, no doubt as a cheerful welcome to the new year. Any form of cheer must have been welcome to the British people at that time. Post-war austerities and rationing were still severe while the winter of 1947-48 was one of the hardest on record.

hedged about with protocol, but ended with the Parisian public in raptures with the English princess. These must have been fairy-tale months for her and then, shortly before their first wedding anniversary, came their first baby. Prince Charles Philip Arthur George was born at Buckingham Palace at 9.14pm on 14 November 1948. The capital celebrated the birth of the next heir to the crown with guns, bells, bonfires and fountains which streamed blue for a boy for the next week. But there was a cloud on the horizon – King George's doctors had discovered the beginnings of arterio-

sclerosis and for a time his right leg, seemed in danger.

The King weathered the danger and on Waterloo Day, 18 June, 1949 threw a splendid ball at Windsor. 'The Edinburghs' wrote Chips Channon, 'looked divine . . . characters out of a fairy tale.' That Christmas, leaving baby Charles in the care of his grandparents, they were off to Malta where Philip had been attached to the First Cruiser Squadron, commanded from his flagship HMS *Chequers* by his Uncle Dickie, now Earl Mountbatten of Burma. Elizabeth, beautiful and in love, was naturally guest of honour at any function they attended, and she enjoyed to the full her position as a young bride in the world of privilege.

Those Mediterranean months were indeed a happy time for the princess and her entourage, which included Philip's cousin Pamela Mountbatten who was later to marry the designer David Hicks. When Philip got his command in HMS *Magpie* he provided one of the escort vessels accompanying his wife in HMS *Surprise*. The radio traffic and signalling between the two ships fizzed with private jokes and the highlight of the cruise was the visit to King Paul and Queen Frederika of Greece, the cousins of Prince Philip.

By this time the married couple had established their London home at Clarence House and it was here, at 11.50am on 15 August 1950 that Elizabeth gave birth to her second child, Princess Anne Elizabeth Alice Louise. 'Anne'

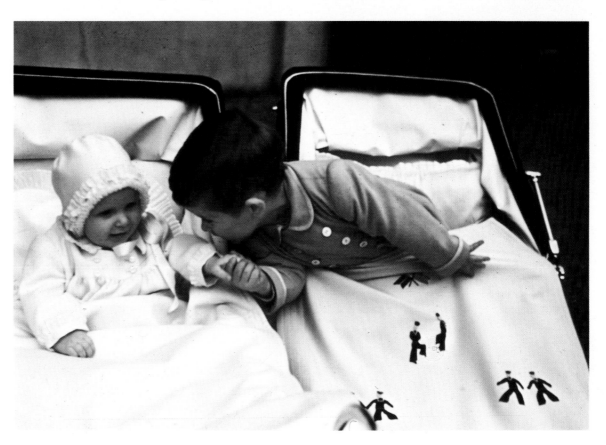

Right: The three-year-old Prince Charles with his baby sister, Princess Anne.

had long been a favoured family name, apart from the disapproval of King George V who had vetoed it in the case of Elizabeth's sister. 'Alice' was chosen in honour of Philip's beloved mother. King George and Queen Elizabeth were delighted with their new granddaughter and the following year 'Granny,' so called to distinguish her from 'Gan Gan' Mary, found herself in *loco parentis* for the two babies as their parents departed for a tour of Canada and the United States in October 1951.

Barely a fortnight earlier King George had had a lung removed and there were fears for his life. At Philip's insistence the young couple flew the Atlantic to save time and Elizabeth had a sealed envelope in her baggage containing her Accession documents. Wherever they went, even French Quebec, they were received with real enthusiasm by vast crowds. In Washington too the crowds turned out in force. In January 1952 this much travelled couple were off once again.

This time they boarded a flight for Nairobi, Kenya, on the first leg of a Commonwealth tour which was to take them on to Australia and New Zealand. On Wednesday 5 February they checked in at the Treetop hotel which was less a hotel than a small suite of rooms built in amongst the branches of a huge wild fig tree overlooking a waterhole in the Kenyan forest. They and their party were enchanted by the situation and after an adventurous day were entertained by the trumpeting of elephants and the gambolling of baboons.

The following day, as Mombasa was putting out the bunting in preparation for the arrival of the Princess who was to take her departure there on the next leg of the tour, news came through of the death of King George. After its confirmation Prince Philip was informed and he it was who had the heavy charge of telling 'the lady we must now call Queen,' in the words of her private secretary. Immediately there was business to attend to – letters and telegrams to explain the cancellation of the rest of the tour; the opening of the sealed Accession documents; and even the matter of her own regal name. 'My own name, of course,' said the Queen when the formal question was put to her, 'What else?' She could, perhaps, have chosen to be known as 'Mary III' (Mary was her second name) to distinguish her from her mother, but Elizabeth she had always been and Elizabeth she would remain.

Just 24 hours later Queen Elizabeth II was descending the steps of the blue and silver Atlanta airliner to the tarmac of London Airport. The welcoming party included Winston Churchill, once again Prime Minister, and Clement Attlee his predecessor, newly hon-

oured with the Order of Merit by her father. On the morning of Friday 8 February, she held her Accession Council in St James's Palace – the first official act of her reign. Only then did she go to Sandringham, where lay her dead father and where her mother and sister awaited her.

The Queen's declaration of Sovereignty to her Accession Council was followed by her proclamation as Queen by heralds in their gaudy medieval costumes from the ramparts of St James's Palace, Temple Bar, and other historic sites in London. But much had changed in the world over the 16 years since her father's proclamation. Something of the change was echoed in her official title: 'Queen Elizabeth the Second, by the grace of God Queen of this Realm and of all Her other Realms and Territories, Head of the Commonwealth.' The last time the word 'Commonwealth' had featured in the officialese of England had been during the Protectorate of Oliver Cromwell. Now the venerable word, dusted off and given the gloss of internationalism, had been appropriated to the use of royalty in place of the unacceptable and outmoded 'Empire.'

But, as unchanging as the glitter of traditional pageantry, the dedication of the House of Windsor shone on in the new reign. In her 21st birthday message she had said: 'I declare before you all that my whole life, whether it be long or short, shall be devoted to your service and the service of our great Imperial family to which we all belong. . . . God help me make good my vow.' Now, in her 26th year she was put to the test of these lofty sentiments. A test which she has never yet failed.

Above: King George VI, Queen Elizabeth and Princess Margaret leaving the Argonaut airliner 'Atlanta' after saying farewell to Princess Elizabeth and the Duke of Edinburgh on departure for their Commonwealth Tour, 31 January 1952. The King, whose health had been failing, seemed on the road to recovery – there had recently been a service of thanksgiving for his restoration to health. After this leave-taking from his daughter at Heathrow Airport, he and the family returned to Sandringham where the King felt well enough to go shooting. Yet less than a week after this photograph was taken he was dead and on 8 February Queen Elizabeth II, her Commonwealth Tour cut short in Kenya, was holding her Accession Council in St James's Palace.

Opposite: After the christening of Princess Anne, 21 October 1950. Queen Mary, the baby's great grandmother sits to the left of Princess Elizabeth and her daughter. Behind stand King George and Prince Philip while the Queen Elizabeth looks after Prince Charles.

The duty began almost at once as she opened the 'boxes' containing the state papers her father had been working on. If application to paper work is the mark of a devoted monarch, the Queen has certainly fulfilled her vow. Incredibly, only hours after the birth of her third child, Prince Andrew, in February 1960, his mother – propped up on her pillows – was already back at her reading. Over the years, her prime ministers have consistently paid tribute to her excellent grasp of the details of government business. All learnt to do their homework before their weekly audience at the Palace. Sir Harold Wilson found that what he had supposed would be a pleasant, if formal break from his ministerial duties could prove a testing interview and Harold Macmillan found her 'astonishingly well informed.' Well before her accession, that austere socialist and opponent of monarchy Sir Stafford Cripps had said: 'This country is fortunate to have as future Head of State someone with such manifestly good judgement.'

However, she was to prove a great deal more than just a successful woman of business. Critics and admirers have both detected characteristics reminiscent of her great ancestor Queen Victoria, at least in her public image. Commended for her dedication and seriousness

Above: The five-year-old Prince Charles, now heir to the throne, and the Queen at Balmoral, 1952.

Right: The Coronation procession of Queen Elizabeth II, 2 June 1953. The accession of the young Queen the previous year had caught the imagination of the country. Her name coupled with a growing sense of liberation as the years of postwar austerity finally began to ease, had prompted a welter of euphoric speculation about the birth of a new Elizabethan Age which should match the glories of the first Elizabeth. The mood was ephemeral and was faltering by the time of the coronation. It received a boost with the news that the British expedition led by John Hunt had made the world's first ascent of Mount Everest. The historic climb was accomplished on 28 May but the news held back a few days, to be released on the eve of Coronation Day.

of purpose, she has also been censured for being stuffy and conventional. Yet few question her queenly bearing – 'the carriage of her head and that . . . indescribable something.' A 1969 Opinion Poll was to show that out of ten well-known personalities the Duke of Edinburgh was thought likely to make the best dictator . . . and his wife the worst. Whatever that 'indescribable something' is, it is not perceived by her subjects as a dictatorial quality.

Coronation Day 2 June 1953 demonstrated that the nation as a whole recognized its good fortune. The sky was overcast and drizzle was in the air, yet thousands had camped out under the hostile skies all night and many had travelled from distant parts of the country to wait for a glimpse of the Queen in her fabulous coach. Millions more tuned in to watch on television. Hers was the second coronation procession to be televised. Back in 1937 her father and mother's procession had provided the world's first ever major outside television broadcast, then for only some 50,000 viewers, within a 65-mile radius of London. For Elizabeth the BBC had an audience across the world.

The great event about to unfold had been prepared for by almost a year's work by the Coronation Commission, under the overall direction of the Duke of Norfolk, hereditary Earl Marshall of England. Prince Philip was chairman of the commission and brought his characteristic energy and thoroughness to the task the Queen, privy to the planning at every stage, insisted on careful rehearsals.

The participation of the Commonwealth heads of state was of course essential. From the outset of her reign the Queen was deeply aware of her role as head of the largest association of peoples with a common allegiance the world has ever seen. Her coronation might be held in the capital of her most ancient kingdom, but in her own mind her oath was taken to all the peoples who acknowledged her.

Old Sir Winston Churchill saw in the beautiful young monarch 'the young and gleaming champion.' In the streets the people cheered with almost embarrassing emotion, while in the Abbey all was kind hearts and coronets. Even Aneurin Bevan, passionate socialist and architect of Britain's National Health Service was there. He and the dead King had developed a mutual sympathy and admiration, both having been stammerers in their youth, and he approved the Queen as far as he could any monarch. His blue lounge suit may have jarred among the formal dress of the dignitaries, but it

Above: A pensive moment during the Coronation Service. Flanked by Queen Elizabeth the Queen Mother and by his aunt Princess Margaret, Prince Charles follows the ceremony with thoughtful attention. Princess Margaret may have had other thoughts on her mind as it was only shortly before the coronation that she had informed her sister of her love for Captain Peter Townsend and her wish to marry him. The fact that he was a divorcee faced the royal family with a crisis and when the news became public shortly after the coronation the ensuing public controversy and debate displaced the speculations on the dawn of a new 'Elizabethan Age.'

Above: Returning from the Coronation. Prince Philip precedes the Queen as she descends from the great state coach, which has been drawn up inside the porte cochère in the inner courtyard of Buckingham Palace. The photographer has caught the Prince in an almost awkward pose. As is proper the Queen dominates the picture and her consort seems almost to feel himself out of place – if so, it was much against the wishes of his wife. The year before she had been forced by establishment pressure headed by Prime Minister Churchill to exclude her husband's family name of Mountbatten from the royal family name which was to remain simply 'Windsor.' She resented this slight and in September 1952 ordained by royal warrant that he should rank second only to her. The phrase 'My Husband and I', which was to delight satirists for years to come, was a gentle assertion of her respect and love for her consort.
Opposite: Her Majesty Queen Elizabeth II enthroned in Buckingham Palace.

allowed him to be present while demonstrating his principled protest against the royal 'rigmarole.'

A year before her day of triumph the Queen had been forced to compromise even her principles by another kind of rigmarole. Technically speaking, the marriage of Princess Elizabeth to Philip Mountbatten could be considered to have changed her family name from Windsor to Mountbatten. The breezy Lord Louis was heard to remark early in the new reign that since February 1952 a Mountbatten had been sitting on the throne. The Queen, devoted to her husband, must have been delighted rather than otherwise. Old Queen Mary was outraged. Her husband had established the dynastic name of Windsor and so it would always be. Many in the British 'Establishment' agreed with her, they had always been antipathetic, even envious, towards a family which they considered pushy upstarts. For years the conservative Beaverbrook newspapers had waged a vendetta against the Mountbattens while Prime Minister Churchill disliked the part which as Viceroy of India, Lord Louis Mountbatten had played in the dissolution of Britain's empire. Furious, Churchill convened a cabinet meeting which

unanimously authorized him to advise the Queen that the name of the royal house was Windsor. Accordingly, on 9 April 1952, bitterly against her will, Elizabeth – in the age-old formula – proclaimed as her 'Will and Pleasure that She and Her children shall by styled and known as the House and Family of Windsor, and that her descendants, other than female descendants who marry, and their descendants shall bear the name of Windsor.'

Prince Philip, not unnaturally, was disgusted. A century back Prince Albert had once complained that he was not even master in the domestic home – it had been unfortunate for him to have married Victoria when she was already Queen. Prince Philip, by contrast, had been cheerfully accorded the preeminence in the family by his wife ever since their marriage. Now, she had been forced to 'expunge' his name from the family designation and he found himself, in his own colourful words, nothing better than 'an amoeba – a bloody amoeba.'

The Queen resented the enforced slight on her husband. In September 1952 a royal warrant ordained that 'HRH Philip, Duke of Edinburgh should henceforth and on all occasions have, hold and enjoy the Place, Pre-eminence and

Precedence to her Majesty.' Before this Order he had ranked behind the royal dukes and even behind his own children. When Philip returned from a long Commonwealth tour in 1957, the Queen demonstrated her feelings about yet another press campaign against the Duke – which even hinted he had delayed his return because of a rift between them – by creating him a Prince of the United Kingdom.

The final episode in the saga of the royal surname was to come in 1960. Meanwhile, few close to the court, had much doubt that Queen Mary was 'the real mover' behind the Mountbatten controversy. But this was forgotten in the mourning of her death in March 1953. Even in death her last thoughts were for the monarchy which she had unswervingly served all her life long. It was her wish that should she die before coronation day in June court mourning should not affect either the date or the celebrations. In the words of Countess Longford she had 'given a

protective venerability to the house of Windsor.' She had lived through six reigns and had helped her family weather the most dangerous storms. Her funeral was attended by her beloved but wayward son David but for the majority of the nation the old battles were best forgotten. It seemed a new age was about to dawn.

Even before the Coronation publicists and politicians were heralding the start of a new 'Elizabethan age' news of the conquest of Everest by the British expedition led by John Hunt was delayed a few days so that the announcement would coincide with the celebrations. The staid *Sociological Review* described the Coronation itself as 'a great act of national communion.' In a word, the sense of euphoria mounted almost to hysteria. By the wish of the Queen, and against the unanimous advice of her ministers under Winston Churchill, created Knight of the Garter for the Coronation, not only the procession but even the ceremony within the Abbey was televised. It seemed that Elizabeth II was determined to involve her subjects as fully as possible in the business of monarchy.

But the mood of euphoria was to be shortlived. Within days of the coronation a newspaper article gave notice that another problem, common currency in the gossip columns of the world's press for months, was about to break cover in Britain. The writer described as 'of course utterly untrue' the rumour that Princess Margaret, 'third in line of succession to the throne' was in love with a divorced man and wished to marry him.

Group Captain Peter Townsend, an RAF pilot in the Battle of Britain, had been appointed a royal equerry at the insistence of King George VI who wished one of the hero pilots on the palace staff as a small tribute to them all. Townsend, who was soon promoted to Deputy Master of the Royal Household, was a tall, slender, handsome and modest man who so impressed the King that he once said he would have been proud of a son like him. It seems to have been during the family's tour of South Africa in 1947 that Princess Margaret developed a teenage crush for him that was to blossom into a true and passionate love.

Alert and demonstrative and eager for life, the young Margaret was also aware of her eternally subordinate position to her sister in the order of things. Utterly self-confident, it is said that she reckoned she would make a better Queen than Princess Elizabeth. She was early enlisted into the work of the 'firm,' launching her first ship, the liner the *Edinburgh Castle* at Belfast in September 1947, and accumulating a clutch of official positions from Honorary Colonel-in-Chief of the Highland Light Infantry to President of Doctor Barnardo's Homes. But she

Below: Princess Margaret, aged 17, at one of her first official engagements, the launching of the *Edinburgh Castle* at Belfast in September 1947. Behind her right shoulder can be seen Group Captain Townsend, the first man in her life who was to cause her much heartache and, through their mutual love, was to threaten the royal family with crisis. A trusted and admired aide of her father King George VI, Townsend had first come into her life a few months before this picture was taken when he had accompanied the royal family on their tour of South Africa.

also had a vivid private life of her own. The gossip writers were delighted by her exploits in London's night life, attended by a bevy of aristocratic beaux, her 'wild' holiday in Capri and her rumoured indiscretions. The Germans called her the 'beautiful princess', Paris dubbed her the 'fairy princess,' her father indulged, almost spoilt her. She certainly loved the glitter of the high life. But there was a less well-known serious side to her nature, reading the classics, following classical music and above all the ballet, and taking a deep interest in religion.

The death of her father in February in 1952 hit her very hard. In the last months the King had relied more and more heavily on Peter Townsend and his respect for the young courtier may have reinforced Margaret's love for him. In the days immediately following the King's death Townsend was a pillar of strength to the royal household. He helped supervise the financial dispositions of the King's will, handled the domestic arrangements for the Queen Mother and Princess Margaret and the redecoration of Clarence House where they moved. Concurrently he was also tidying up the debris of his divorce from his wife Rosemary, winning custody of their two sons. The Townsend family had been living in a grace and favour residence before the divorce and there were those who wondered whether the Group Captain's increasing involvement with the Princess led his wife to seek companionship elsewhere. Whatever the rights or wrongs, his divorce meant he was free to marry and Margaret's hopes rose.

In April 1953 she told her sister that she wanted to marry. By the terms of the Royal Marriage Act of the eighteenth century she could not without the Queen's consent until she was 25. A public opinion poll conducted for the *Daily Mirror* revealed that 95 percent of those interviewed thought the Princess should have the right to choose her own husband straightaway. Establishment opinion recalled that the Abdication crisis was less than 20 years in the past; Princess Margaret was torn between her love and her religion.

In the event it was decided that the couple should be separated for a time. Margaret was sent on a tour of Southern Rhodesia with the Queen Mother – Townsend was sent to a posting in Brussels. The two maintained contact by telephone but the Princess was bitterly unhappy to find that he had left for Brussels before her return. The following year Margaret was off again, this time on a solo official tour of the Carribbean, her first contact with a part of the world to feature so prominently in her later life. As her 25th birthday approached so did the moment of truth. After that date she would be free to marry whom she wished but if she chose

Townsend she would have to renounce her royal privileges and prerogatives. As it was the pressures proved too great. In October 1955 Townsend returned for a visit with the Princess at a friend's country house. On the 31st of that month Princess Margaret issued the following statement:

I would like it to be known that I have decided not to marry Group Captain Townsend. I have been aware that, subject to my renouncing my rights of succession, it might have been possible for me to contract a civil marriage. But, mindful of the Church's teaching that Christian marriage is indissoluble, and conscious of my duty to the Commonwealth, I have resolved to put these considerations before many others.'

While Margaret was grappling with the dilemma of a royal and private persona, the Queen was swept up in the traditional business of the 'firm.' Between November 1953 and May 1954, she and Prince Philip made a grand tour of the Commonwealth which seemed to carry forward the high hopes of the coronation. The first stop was in Canada, the last, Gibraltar. There was a month each in New Zealand, where the Queen delivered that year's Christmas Broadcast to the Commonwealth, and Australia, where she opened Parliament; two or more days in Jamaica, Tonga, Fiji, Ceylon (Sri Lanka), Uganda and Malta, where her relaxed attitude to security was later to anticipate future 'walkabouts.'

The Queen made more than a hundred speeches, attended scores of banquets and receptions, received some 200 gifts and, wherever she went, was expected to smile. The schedules were punishing and Prince Philip more than

Above: Front page headlines of the popular London dailies on the morning of 15 October 1955. Speculation about the Princess and Group Captain Peter Townsend had now reached fever pitch. The night before, it was reported, the couple had gone to weekend at the house of Mrs John Wills, a cousin of the Princess, who, ironically perhaps, lived at a mansion at Windsor. When it was learnt that the couple had gone for a long walk alone, the immediate assumption was that they had decided to get married – in fact it was during this interview that the Princess sadly told the Group Captain of her decision to give him up. The problem at the heart of the romance was, of course, that Townsend was a divorcee. The Princess was placed in a tragic dilemma. By the terms of the eighteenth-century Royal Marriage Act she required the permission of the sovereign to marry before her 25th birthday. When she informed her sister of her love for Townsend, in April 1953, it was less than 20 years since a divorcée, Wallis Simpson, had precipitated the Abdication. It is not surprising that the Princess was denied the official sanction she sought. But on her 25th birthday she was free to choose for herself.

Opposite: The Queen with Prince Charles and Princess Anne on the course at Smith's Lawn, Windsor during a polo match.

Right: The Queen and the Duke of Edinburgh on an official visit to the flagship of the Royal Australian Navy, *HMAS Australia*, at Cairns, North Queensland during their Commonwealth Tour, March 1954. Leaving England on 24 November 1953, they were away for six months. They flew first to Canada where there was a brief refuelling stop. A day in Bermuda, where they joined the *SS Gothic* was followed by two days in Jamaica, one in Panama, two in Fiji and one in Tonga, where they were welcomed by Queen Salote. From here they went on to New Zealand where they stayed five weeks. It was here that the Queen delivered her 1953 Christmas Day message: 'I want to show that the Crown is not merely an abstract symbol of our unity but a personal and living bond between you and me.' During their month-long visit to Australia, the Queen's numerous official engagements included the state Opening of Parliament in February 1954. The long tour continued with visits to the Cocos Islands, 11 days in Ceylon, a day in Aden, and then to Tobruk in Libya. Here they were received by King Idris and were joined by Prince Charles and Princess Anne in the royal yacht *Britannia*. The homeward leg of the journey was via Malta and Gibraltar. At the Guildhall luncheon given to celebrate her homecoming the Queen said: 'The structure and framework of monarchy could easily stand as an archaic and meaningless survival. We have received visible and audible proof that it is living in the hearts of the people.'

once exploded at the harassment by the crowds of reporters. But there were many delightful moments too. Walking under a ceremonial umbrella beneath the tropical Ugandan sun, the Queen turned to the Prince to remark, 'I feel like an African queen.' 'You are an African queen,' he reminded his delighted wife. Years later, addressing a Nigerian audience, she was to speak of 'The Commonwealth, to which I personally attach great importance.' Her visits to these overseas territories of her allegiance have provided not only some of her happiest experiences but, in her own view, some of her most significant contributions as a head of state.

1954 brought Queen Elizabeth II triumph in another department though this time in her private capacity. Her horse Aureole capped a series of victories by winning the King George VI and Queen Elizabeth Stakes at Ascot, and the Queen ended the year as the leading winner owner. At stud, the famous horse was to sire many great progeny, among them the Derby winner St Paddy. Over the next 30 years the Queen's horses were to win every classic except the Derby. She is respected throughout the racing world for her knowledge of pedigree, as a show-ring judge and for her ability to read a race. When she has the time she attends the classics of the racing year and, of course, the horse trials at Badminton and Windsor.

The fading euphoria of coronation year evaporated entirely in the glare of the Suez debacle of 1956. The romantic idea of a 'new Elizabethan Age' could not survive the humiliation of Britain's failure to secure the Canal against its nationalization by Egypt's President Nasser. Her government's action in the affair divided the nation; the Queen's views on the venture are unknown. When Prime Minister Eden resigned the following year the constitution required that she summon a successor. Following consultation she called on Harold Macmillan. Many had expected the brilliant R.A. Butler to succeed. When Macmillan himself left office in 1963, Butler was again passed over, this time in favour of Sir Alec Douglas Home. This appointment astonished the country and angered many Conservatives outside the magic circle of wheeler-dealers who in those days decided who had 'emerged' as the new party leader. Some charged that the Queen had followed her personal inclinations in selecting the aristocratic Home – in fact she had followed the advice of the outgoing Prime Minister.

Her exercise of the prerogative back in 1957 met with little criticism, but it was a bleak year for monarchy nevertheless. That summer John Grigg (Lord Altrincham) fired a journalistic broadside against the Queen for her whole style, as of a 'priggish schoolgirl surrounded by a con-

Below: The Queen with her family at Balmoral on 9 September 1960. Prince Philip, still often called the Duke of Edinburgh by the press even though he had been created a 'Prince of the United Kingdom' by his wife three years before, holds the baby Prince Andrew in his lap. Born on 19 February, he had been given the names Andrew Albert in honour of his father's and mother's fathers. Shortly before his birth the Queen had announced a change in the royal family name, an intention which had 'long been close to her heart'. Thereafter any of her descendants who might at any time be in need of a surname could bear the name 'Mountbatten-Windsor.'

ventional upperclass entourage.' He criticized her voice and cartoonists and commentators had a high old time. Traditionalists attacked the critics; the critics attacked the Queen as 'dowdy' and for appearing bored at official ceremonies and functions that would have bored *them* stiff. When she and Prince Philip visited Canada and the United States that October the New York *Saturday Evening Post* carried an article published the year before by the English journalist Malcolm Muggeridge, under the title 'Does England really need a Queen?' In those days, it seems, the Americans were better royalists than the British. A television network interview with Muggeridge during the Queen's visit was blacked out in Washington in case the Queen was there. The occasion for the visit was the 350th anniversary of the founding of Virginia – in the opinion of the British ambassador in Washington the visit had 'buried' the memory of George III.

Whether, in fact, that memory meant much to the average American outside the realms of schoolroom fantasy can be questioned. The Queen's mother and father had been warmly welcomed in the United States and she herself had been there more than once. In 1959 she was once more in North America for a state tour of Canada. The schedules were as taxing as ever (they included the official opening of the St Lawrence Seaway) and the crowds as enthusiastic. However, the anthem sung at the Governor-General's inauguration was not 'God Save the Queen' but 'O Canada' – it was an overture to that surge in Canadian nationalism which was to reach a climax five years later.

For the Queen, now in her 34th year, the tour, was especially arduous as she was pregnant with her third child. The news was kept private until her return. In addition to the preparations made by any expectant mother, the Queen was also determined to settle the question of her children's name. In a statement issued early in February 1960 she explained: 'the Queen has always wanted, without changing the name of the Royal House established by her grand-

father, to associate the name of her husband with her own and his descendants. The Queen has had this in mind for a long time and it is close to her heart.' These were the concluding words of a complicated though short document which, so the Home Secretary of the day assured her meant that 'all the children of Your Majesty who may at any time need a surname have the name of Mountbatten-Windsor.' Prince Andrew Albert, named in honour of the fathers of his two parents, was born on 19 February 1960. A week later the family had another celebration to announce, the engagement of Princess Margaret to Anthony Armstrong-Jones, created the Earl of Snowdon in due course.

Their friendship seems to have begun two years before at a society wedding where Tony, already making a name for himself in his profession, had been the photographer. Through him she entered an exciting new world of designers, artists and actors, Peter Sellers being one of the more celebrated names in his circle of contacts and friends. He joined her party at a performance of the muscial *West Side Story* and soon she was a guest at his parties in Chelsea. If Townsend had been a natural hero for a teenage girl in the immediate post-war years, Tony Armstrong-Jones was the ideal companion for a vivacious and aware young woman in the London of the 'Swinging Sixties.'

The wedding on 6 May 1960 in Westminster Abbey, the first major royal event since the coronation, was a brilliant affair. The Mall was lined with silken banners and the entwined initial of 'M' and 'A', the guest list ranged from dukes and princesses to theatrical designers and model girls, the Abbey was packed with flowers and equipped with closed circuit television screens to give a view of the ceremony even to those in the remoter locations in the great Gothic church. The honeymooners sailed the Caribbean in the royal yacht *Britannia* and a large suite of rooms in Kensington Palace was lavishly reappointed for their London home. Their first child, David, Viscount Linley was born in November 1961, their daughter, Lady Sarah Armstrong-Jones, in May 1964.

Tony, who had accepted his title reluctantly, was determined to excel in his career and, like others before him, was wary of the royal rigmarole. His appointment as 'artistic director' at the *Sunday Times* naturally provoked snide comments from rival newspapers and his design for the aviary at London Zoo, now well regarded, came in for its necessary share of adverse criticism. Meanwhile, Margaret was beginning to cut out a new life for herself in her Caribbean retreat on the island of Mustique, to the delight of the gossip writers and the royalty hunters among the photographic fraternity. Les Jolies

Eaux, Margaret's house on Mustique, was designed for her by Tony's maternal uncle, the distinguished theatre designer Oliver Messel, but Tony himself did not take kindly to the plutocratic beach-comber life style. Before the end of the sixties strains were appearing in the marriage.

But the decade opened with promise both for the Princess and the Queen. Happy in the birth of her new son and in the prospect of the new world opening for her sister, the Queen embarked with confidence on the decade that was to confirm her mature assurance in her life role. She was soon presented with a challenge both to her courage and her diplomatic insight into world affairs.

Above: Lord Snowdon, Anthony Armstrong-Jones, and Princess Margaret, after their wedding in Westminster Abbey on 6 May 1960. It had been a brilliant affair and they followed it with a Caribbean honeymoon in the royal yacht *Britannia*.

Above: The Queen with her prime ministers at the 1961 Commonwealth Conference; on her left Mr Nehru of India, on her right Mrs Bandaranaika of Ceylon.

Below: Riding a magnificent royal elephant on her 1961 tour of India.

In November 1961, she was due to fly out on a state visit to Ghana, then ruled by its mercurial dictator Dr Khwame Nkrumah. Britain suspected that his regime was being wooed by Russia while Nkrumah himself was facing heavy opposition at home. There were rumours of plots against the Ghanaian leader's life and many at Westminster questioned whether the Queen would be safe in such a charged political atmosphere. She brushed doubts aside with the level-headed comment: 'How silly I should look if I was scared to visit Ghana and then Khrushchev (the Russian leader) went a few weeks later and had a good reception.' She went, and the visit was a tumultuous success.

Her state visit to Canada three years later was a different matter. Agitation for a French *Quebec libre* was at its height and some French Canadians viewed the forthcoming visit as an act of deliberate provocation, encouraged by the English Canadians. There were rumours of plans for an assassination attempt on the Queen herself, and she was greeted to 'Go Home' posters. As always, she fulfilled her schedule, but with security guards, surveillance helicopters and precautions of every kind much in evidence the visit was not a happy one.

At this time more serious troubles were brewing elsewhere as negotiations dragged on with the Rhodesian government of Ian Smith. Many White Rhodesians, apparently ignorant of Britain's constitutional history and almost certainly out of touch with the Queen's views on the matter, thought that she was only prevented from supporting their plans for continuing White Supremacy by a treasonable conspiracy of Harold Wilson's government. In fact, when Wilson flew to Salisbury (now Harare) during the negotiations before Ian Smith declared UDI, 'he carried a personal letter in the Queen's own handwriting.' This letter made it clear to Smith that he was not a true servant of herself or her

crown. Years later she was to preside at the 1979 Lusaka Commonwealth Conference which paved the way to the Lancaster House talks and the independence of Zimbabwe.

The mid point of the sixties was marked by a mournful ceremony recalling the past age of Britain's greatness. It was the Queen's decision that the death of Sir Winston Churchill should be honoured with a state funeral. On that January day in 1965, the widow and family of the famous statesman travelled the solemn processional route in the Queen's own carriage and, by her order, occupied the place of honour – the last – as she preceded them up the steps of St Paul's Cathedral. There are moments when even the pedantry of precedence and protocol can achieve the grand or significant effect and the Queen, like her predecessors, has an unerring touch in such matters.

The State Opening of Parliament in October 1967 provided another opportunity for the delicate manipulation of ceremony. On these occasions the sovereign's throne is on a dais beneath a canopy. Henry VIII had ordained that his children should sit on chairs outside the canopy, the Queen consort being enthroned beside him. As Queen regent, Vicoria had relegated Albert to a place outside the canopy and Philip had, perforce, followed precedent. But in 1967 Prince Charles and Princess Anne were to attend for the first time. Was their father to sit with them, or even with the royal dukes, off the dais altogether. The Queen had the consort's throne brought out of store to be placed next to hers on

the dais so that her husband should at least occupy the position which she had always considered rightfully his.

The now 19-year-old Prince Charles had begun his formal education at five with his governess in the Palace schoolroom. But his parents wanted to break with tradition and give their son as normal a schooling as possible. At eight,

Above: The State Opening of Parliament in 1959. The Queen reads the speech from the throne to her peers in the splendour of their, mostly hired, ceremonial robes in the House of Lords. Prince Philip occupies his place on the dais by right of the royal warrant of his precedence made by his wife in the year of her accession.

Left: Prince Charles arriving for his first term at Gordonstoun where his father had been educated. Imbued by the muscular tough 'whole man' theories of its founder the educationist Kurt Hahn, it seems to have been a hard slog for Charles.

Charles went to a pre-preparatory school and in the autumn of 1957 went to his father's old prep school of Cheam. Homesick, always shy and now in the glare of the press, he found it an unhappy time . . . the day the school listened to his mother's radio announcement naming him Prince of Wales was a purgatory of embarrassment. With the title the ten-year-old automatically became a Knight of the Garter.

The decision to go to Gordonstoun was left to him, but the desire to prove himself where his confident, extrovert father had excelled must have played its part. For Charles, the place proved tough going. A private, if tough personality was not immediately at home there. Academically, it was clear he would never distinguish himself. But determination brought its reward – seven 'O' Levels including maths and physics, a personal triumph over two old enemies. Then preparation for his 'A' levels was interrupted by two terms at Timbertop, Kenya, the Geelong Church of England Grammar School, Victoria. A naturally reserved, 'Pommie' Prince viewed the prospect with some trepidation. He was accompanied to Australia by Squadron Leader David Checketts, his private secretary up to 1979 and liaison-man between Prince and press during the Australian interlude.

In fact, within days of arrival Charles was entirely at ease and genuinely popular with his Australian classmates. Laid out along the slopes of the Australian Alps and surrounded by forests of gum trees the school, with its curriculum generously punctuated by physical hard work, open air adventure activities and shared comradeship was 'the most wonderful experience.' During the holiday he toured widely in Australia and on his return to Gordonstoun, tough and inwardly assured, he got down to make up lost time on his 'A' levels. He passed two and left the school as 'Guardian' or head boy.

After the Palace schoolroom Princess Anne, too, went on to boarding school – Benenden in Kent. There, her enthusiasm for riding continued and having got her six 'O' levels and two 'A' levels she was more interested in developing this expertise – 'the one thing I can do well and can be seen to do well' – than in going up to university. She was, of course launched on her own programme of royal functions and here the fences proved more difficult. She first attracted the criticism of the foreign press on tours overseas. The Australians thought they heard her swear in public; the Kenyans thought her 'arrogant'; and the Americans dredged the vocabulary of disapproval to come up with 'sullen' and 'disdainful', to name but two. Like her aunt, Princess Margaret whose occasional haughtiness earned her a reputation as 'acid drop', Anne became the royal even the British press loved to hate. Forceful and impatient she certainly was and, if it is possible to be rude to the press, rude. But her riding was to bring her a respite from the carping and behind the acerbic image lay honesty coupled with energy waiting for a worthwhile outlet.

As the younger generation of royals grew to maturity, so the institution of monarchy moved sedately with the times. The Queen's 1965 visit to Germany helped lay the ghosts of wartime memories, the royal plate being flown out to the British embassy in Bonn to lend urbane opulence to the ceremonial. The following year saw the inauguration of the Queen's Award to Industry, to provide a spur to the export drive. And the decade ended with a calculated if unprecedented move to humanize and popularize the monarchy through television.

Below: Princess Anne photographed during a polo meeting at Windsor in April 1960. She was already passionately involved in horses. As a young woman, her 'O' and 'A' levels behind her, she was to reject the idea of university, preferring to devote her energies to developing her considerable expertise as a horsewoman. In her own words riding was: 'the one thing I can do well and can be seen to do well.' She reached the top level . . . by her own efforts.

Left: Embargoed for publication until 20 June 1969, this picture was captioned 'The Informal Prince.' It was intended to show 'the informal life of Prince Charles . . . to be invested as the Prince of Wales on 1 July. Princess Anne looks on as Prince Charles gives the seven-year-old Prince Edward a ride in a go-kart in the grounds of Windsor Castle. At the time, shooting was going forward on the film *Royal Family* which was intended to transform the image of the whole family with an unprecedented informality of approach. Charles and Edward made a special impact as the heir to throne treated his young brother to a tune on the cello – one of the strings broke. Some feared that this new, open approach to the mystery of monarchy would undermine the institution itself. But there are few public relations teams more expert than the staff employed by the Palace. They are continually aware of the need to balance traditional dignity, which can verge on the 'fuddy duddy,' and new departures which may appear merely trendy.

The Queen, who had insisted on the televising of her coronation, moved a little nearer to the medium when, in 1957, her annual Christmas Broadcast to the Commonwealth was televised for the first time. Nervous and reticent, she proved at first an awkward performer. In the view of her private Secretary, Michael Adeane, television ruined the broadcasts. 'The Queen is gay and relaxed beforehand but in front of the cameras she freezes and there is nothing to be done about it.' As the years passed, so her camera presence improved. She steadily opposed any suggestion of fireside family shots, guarding the privacy of her home.

She yielded so far as to permit the making of a television film, *The Royal Palaces of Britain*. A cultured survey of history and 'the greatest private collection of art in the world' it was presented in reverential tones by the art historian Sir Kenneth Clark as he accompanied the Queen and Prince Philip. For the first time the public was admitted into hitherto private precincts of monarchy but the family, so to speak, was not in residence. But in June 1968 shooting began on a much more ambitious, some thought hazardous, project. Persuaded by the enthusiastic urgings of Philip, and Uncle Dickie, and judging the time was right, the Queen had consented to a documentary of that home she had so long guarded.

By May 1969 the film crew, its advisers including the film producer Lord Brabourne, husband of Philip's cousin Patricia Mountbatten, had shot 43 hours of film in 172 locations which was to be cut to a film of 110 minutes. Expecting red tape and protocol they were delighted to find that the Queen 'very naturally and very spontaneously played her part.' *Royal Family* proved the hoped for success. Prince Charles playing the cello for his brother Prince Edward, when one of the strings broke; the Queen browsing through the family album with Andrew and Edward; Prince Philip presiding over a family barbecue; and the Queen's famous corgi dogs; and many other 'homely' touches, shifted public perception of the monarchy almost overnight. This was clearly no 'ordinary' family, but equally its members were not remote from the ordinary world. Walter Bagehot, the great 19th-century theorist of the monarchy, had urged 'We must not let in daylight upon the magic.' Now the television arc lights had revealed that they did not 'sit down to breakfast wearing coronets as they munched their cornflakes,' which was all to the good, but there were those who wondered whether the glare might bleach out the aurora of monarchy itself. In some circles the film was dubbed *'Corgi and Beth'*, the right wing *Daily Mail* ran an article series 'Do We Need the Queen?' The answer was a resounding 'Yes.' Over the subsequent years, strengthened by a growing bevy of young royals, the 'firm's' position was consolidated and diversified.

Charles Comes of Age

Pages 140-141: Princess Anne and Captain Mark Phillips, with the royal family, on the balcony of Buckingham Palace after their wedding on 14 November 1973. Prince Philip, Prince Andrew, the Queen and Prince Charles stand on the right of the bride; the nine-year-old Prince Edward is on the right of the picture.

Below: Another of the pictures of 'The Informal Prince,' published in the run-up to Prince Charles' Investiture as the Prince of Wales. It shows him relaxing in his rooms at Trinity College, Cambridge. His studies there had to be interrupted for a term at the University of Wales at Aberystwyth, as part of his preparation for his Welsh title.

The investiture of Charles as Prince of Wales at Caernarvon Castle on 1 July 1969 was, against all expectations, a landmark in the history of the modern British monarchy. For the Prince himself it was the highlight of his 21st year even more brilliant than his birthday celebrations at Buckingham Palace that followed in November. For the Palace establishment it offered heartening proof that the archaic ritual of monarchy, even when wedded to so recent a tradition (the first investiture as such had been that of 1911), could work an undeniable magic in the sceptical and political atmosphere of late 1960s Britain.

The prelude had not been promising. The Prince had been obliged to break off his studies at Trinity College, Cambridge, studies which offered prospects of a respectable degree in archaeology and anthropology, for a final term in the University of Wales at Aberystwyth. Naturally enough many, and not only Welsh nationalists, regarded the whole thing as a gimmick. For their part, Welsh nationalists of all kinds opposed the idea of the investiture volubly and violently. On his arrival in Aberystwyth a hundred Special Branch plain clothes detectives descended on the town posing as students – and were frequently greeted with ribald cries of 'Good evening, officer.'

As the time for the ceremony drew nearer tension mounted. Plaid Cymru, the official nationalist party, decided to boycott the occasion; a satirical folk song featuring 'Carlo Windsor' topped the Welsh hit parade; impassioned orators inveighed against the parade of English 'oppression.' For months past there had been a sporadic and ineffectual but frightening bombing campaign by the Free Wales Army. On the morning of the day itself, while minesweepers patrolled the Menai Straits, two amateur terrorists blew themselves to bits with their own bomb. Even as the Prince's car approached the Castle another bomb went off on a street away from the official route.

But within the courtyard of the great castle, where fifty tons of turf had been specially laid,

Left: Prince Charles after the ceremony of his Investiture as Prince of Wales at Caernarvon Castle on 1 July 1969; with him are the Queen, Prince Philip and Princess Anne. The 'contemporary' coronet worn by the Prince was specially designed for the occasion and the whole ceremony had been embellished with various other examples of modernism, to give the traditionalism of the event significance to the contemporary world. The whole ceremony had been designed for presentation as a television spectacular. The dais on the greensward within the castle walls was protected against the possibility of rain by a transparent plexiglass canopy so as not to mask the ceremony from any of the numerous television cameras mounted on vantage points all round the battlements. The canopy bore a gilt emblem of the Prince of Wales's feathers and the walls of the castle were draped with banners bearing the Dragon of Wales, collared with a white 'label,' the heraldic mark for an eldest son. The whole event was master-minded by the Duke of Norfolk, Earl Marshal of England and the royal family's own 'contemporary designer,' Princess Margaret's husband the Earl of Snowdon, the former Anthony Armstrong Jones, appointed Constable of Caernarvon in anticipation of the event. Prince Charles, who wore regimental dress uniform was spared the excesses of the 'preposterous rig' foisted on his predecessor great-uncle David.

the pageantry began on schedule and the first State Occasion designed for television began to weave its spell on millions of viewers. The preparations had been supervised by the Earl Marshal the Duke of Norfolk, assisted by Lord Snowdon, Constable of Caernarvon and the royal family's own artist-designer. Television cameras had been installed at 81 vantage points; the Prince knelt before his mother beneath a great transparent perspex canopy; the helicopters patrolled the skies around the castle while below the glittering tabards of the heralds and historic robes of the high officiants provided the traditional backdrop as the Prince received at his mother's hands the newly designed insignia of his office.

As they were presented, piece by piece, Home Secretary James Callaghan intoned the Letters Patent creating Charles Prince of Wales and Earl of Chester ' . . . by girding him with a sword by putting a coronet upon his head and a gold ring on his finger and also by delivering a gold rod into his hand . . .'

Even his critics admitted that Charles made a personal success of a daunting occasion – 'They really loaded the dice against him in Wales,' admitted one politician in a comment on the Establishment. Part of the magic worked by the fact of his five-minute speech in Welsh. Admiringly, the Poet Laureate C. Day Lewis observed 'Anyone who learns that bloody awful language well enough to make a speech deserves our respect.' Less contentiously, perhaps, another observer commented 'No one but a gifted mimic could have learnt to pronounce it so well.'

Charles faced both radio and television interviews in 1969 and emerged in public esteem as a likeable, thoughtful, if not brilliant personality.

Asked by one interviewer when it dawned that he was heir to the throne, he gave a hint at the drawbacks. 'I think it's something that dawns on you with the most ghastly inexorable sense. I didn't suddenly wake up in my pram one day and say Yippee . . . But slowly you get the idea that you have a certain duty and responsibility.' In the years since the Investiture he has shown himself capable of discharging both.

But first he had to complete his studies and after the investiture returned to Cambridge. In October he spoke at the Mahatma Gandhi commemoration in the Albert Hall and the following month celebrated his 21st birthday with, among other things a concert featuring Yehudi Menuhin as soloist. His official and personal lives were fairly launched.

Ever since, Prince Charles's schedule has been packed with official duties – some routine, some hazardous, some fascinating. Here only some of the highlights of a difficult life for a young man can be mentioned.

Doubtless among his personal highlights of the early days were his performances in the college revues at Trinity. Amateur theatricals had always been a pastime in the family and Charles was able to represent the royal troupe with distinction on a public stage. In a sketch of his own he appeared with an umbrella, whispering to the audience 'I lead a sheltered life.' He left Cambridge with a decent second class honours degree; took his seat in the House of Lords, sponsored by the Dukes of Kent and Beaufort – a graduation with theatricals. The same year he and his sister accompanied their parents on a tour of North America and in Manitoba the heir to the throne confided 'I want to change the old image of remote royalty.'

In 1971 he began training at RAF Cranwell and followed this with a period at the Royal Naval College, Dartmouth. Later, on a helicopter training course with the Fleet Air Arm he was to say: 'I adore flying and can't think of a better combination than naval flying – being at

sea and being able to fly . . . exciting . . . stimulating . . . bloody terrifying at times.' During his naval service he spent a six-month tour of duty in the Caribbean with the frigate *Minerva* and a year later another tour took him to the Pacific in the frigate *Jupiter*, culminating in a truly royal reception at the US port of San Diego. All this military activity was not mere royal posturing – Prince Charles passed through the Royal Marine Commando course, one of the most physically demanding there is. He kept in close touch with the Royal Regiment of Wales of which he was Colonel in Chief, visiting it on its German postings and keeping fully informed of its activities.

During the decade, the Prince went in real danger of his life at various times, from the threatening intentions of the IRA. Large security operations were mounted to protect him. Then, late in 1975, he was in danger of being dragged into hazards of a political nature when a leader in *The Times* floated the idea that he become Governor General of Australia. Earlier that year constitutional crisis had flared in the Commonwealth when the Governor General Sir John Kerr dismissed the Labour Prime Minister Mr Gough Whitlam and called elections which resulted in a Liberal victory. Sir John's

Opposite: A formal portrait of the Queen, Prince Philip, Princess Anne and the 21-year-old Prince Charles, now Prince of Wales.
Left: Prince Charles, in the dog-collar befitting one destined in course of time to become Supreme Governor of the Church of England, takes part in an undergraduate revue. He made something of a name for himself with self-mocking sketches: in one he hurried across the stage with opened umbrella muttering 'I lead a sheltered life.' On a visit to Manitoba, Canada, he told his audience 'I want to change the old image of remote royalty.' Changes were already under way and many more were to follow.

Below: A pilot in the Fleet Air Arm, a combination, in his own words, of 'being able to fly while at sea . . . bloody terrifying at times.'

action had been sparked by financial and political crises from which, in his judgement, the only escape was to be found in the dramatic action he took. But though an Australian, Sir John was the representative of the Queen in constitutional terms – though in no way directed in his actions by Whitehall, still less the Palace. Australian republicans raised the hue and cry; *The Times* reckoned a new Governor General was required to 'wipe the slate clean' and, in the wisdom of its leader writer, reckoned Prince Charles would be an excellent appointee. Fortunately, no doubt, the idea quickly sunk without trace. Charles had real affection for Australia ever since his Timbertop days; he would make an excellent Governor General, no doubt. But the circumstances were hardly propitious.

The Prince had enjoyed a less controversial political occasion that year when he accompanied his father to Nepal for the coronation of King Birenda. For the visitors it was an exotic moment: for Nepal, home of Britain's famous Gurkha regiments, a high occasion of pageantry and constitutional importance. Charles was

shortly himself the centre of similar archaic and exotic ritual when he was installed as Grand Master of the Most Honourable Order of the Bath, by his mother the Queen. A more valued distinction, one guesses, was the appointment to his own ship as commander in the minesweeper HMS *Bronington*.

The decade was rich in many more personal events. In 1972 he and his sister Anne had organized the family party to celebrate their parents' silver wedding. At times he was to defend Anne in her contretemps with the press. At other times he was to find himself the focus of its attention – especially in the speculations about his love life. Among the names most prominently mentioned in this respect were those of Lady Jane Wellesley, Davina Sheffield and, finally, Princess of Luxembourg. In the middle of the decade the Prince decided to move into Chevening Park, Kent, a 'paradise' of a country house presented decades before by its millionaire owner as a residence for a Prince of Wales. Unoccupied for years, it required extensive renovation which amounted to £1 million, when all the bills were in.

Below: A family photograph at Windsor Castle, Christmas Day 1969. Prince Charles, Prince Andrew, Princess Anne and, at the right of the picture, Prince Edward pose with their royal cousins, the children of Princess Margaret, the Duke of Kent and Princess Alexandra of Kent, the Honourable Mrs Angus Ogilvy. Left to right: Lady Sarah Armstrong-Jones, James Ogilvy, the Earl of St Andrews, Lady Helen Windsor, David Viscount Linley and Marina Ogilvy.

During these years the younger members of the family were also coming into their own. Andrew and Edward, luckily for them, had so far been spared the press attentions that had pursued Charles and Anne in their childhood. But when it was realised that Gordonstoun now had girl boarders and that the personable young Andrew was to follow the family footsteps to the school, comments were sought – Charles understood that his 14-year-old brother was 'enjoying himself immensely'. Andrew was to follow his brother, from school into a shared passion for flying, qualifying as a glider pilot in 1976 – a flyer 'quick to learn and quite fearless,' according to his instructor – and some years later earning a glamorous reputation for his part on active service during the Falklands campaign. Like Charles, he had spent part of his school career overseas, in his case at Lakefield, a smart Canadian school east of Toronto, in Ontario.

Meanwhile, Charles was maturing intellectually. He read avidly, Solzhenitsyn, biographies and histories. He became an ardent fan of *Monty Python's Flying Circus,* television's natural successor to his one-time favourite radio programme, the *Goon Show.* He appeared in a TV film *Pilot Royal,* but also served as presenter in a TV programme on Canterbury Cathedral, and appeared in an interview with Alastair Cooke in which he argues passionately on behalf of his ancestor King George III – a man not mad but driven to torment by a rare disease, prophyrea. 'I am determined,' said the prince, 'to clear his name.'

As the seventies drew to a close, it appeared that in Prince Charles the House of Windsor had found a fine professional all-rounder. Naturally, the high point of the decade was provided by the Queen herself at her Silver Jubilee, but there had been sad moments. In May 1972 Charles had joined the family at the funeral of the Duke of Windsor, at Windsor Castle and, only weeks later that of the 31-year-old Prince William of Gloucester.

Although the Prince was, as son and heir of the Queen's uncle Duke Henry of Gloucester, in the royal second division, he was extremely popular with the British public and his death in a flying accident was felt as a real tragedy by thousands. The present generation of young royals descends from the children of King George V, the Queen's aunt and uncles: Mary Princess Royal (d. 1965) and her husband the sixth Earl of Harewood; Henry Duke of Gloucester (d. 1974) and George Duke of Kent (d. 1942).

Princess Mary's eldest son, George, seventh Earl of Harewood, has long been a distin-

guished figure in the world of British opera, having published books on the subject and played a central role in the administration of Covent Garden. It is an unusual achievement for a member of the royal family and Harewood made a somewhat controversial contribution to public debate with a speech in the House of Lords in 1965 in favour of the abolition of hanging. Two years later he was involved in real controversy and an embarrassing marital scandal which led to divorce from his first wife, Marion Stein. They had three sons, the eldest being David, Viscount Lascelles (b. 1950). Their divorce in 1967 was the first in the royal family and matters were hardly improved when the Earl had a child by his second wife to be before they were married. His mother died shortly afterwards. Her own marriage to 'Lucky' Lascelles had hardly been happy and it was believed the scandal surrounding her son finally broke her heart. The

Above: Crowds celebrating the returns of forces from the Falklands Campaign in 1982. Prince Andrew saw active service as a pilot during the operation.

Below: The 19-year-old Princess Anne. On her 18th birthday, in the tired cliches of women's journalism then in vogue, a woman's magazine had commented 'poor Princess Anne — she's 18 today and nobody thinks she's a pretty girl.' A year later a more perceptive writer described her as 'the wittiest, gayest and most natural of royal princesses.'

tragic death of her husband in the air crash in 1942 prostrated Princess Marina with grief. It also left her with financial problems as she faced the prospect of bringing up her young family: Prince Edward (now Duke), born in September 1935; Princess Alexandra, born on Christmas Day, 1936; and Prince Michael on 4 July, some seven weeks before his father's death.

Princess Anne has long been regarded as one of the most serious and hard-working members of the royal team. She was the subject of an authorised biography when only 19, an absurdity which she no doubt realised went with the job if it can be called a job, as she remarked in another context at the time.

When she was 19, a perceptive journalist described her as growing into 'the wittiest, gayest, and most natural of royal princesses.'

On her 18th birthday, a woman's magazine had commiserated, 'poor Princess Anne. She's 18 today, and nobody thinks she's a pretty girl.' Such was then the nature of women's journalism. Conventional opinion dubbed her a 'tomboy.' Sometimes 'horsey' in looks as she was undoubtedly horsey by interest, Anne had no interest whatsoever in conventional opinions of what a princess should be. Also she was fully aware that verve and an attractive figure are more vital ingredients of sex appeal than 'prettiness,' whatever that may precisely be.

In the autumn of her 20th year she proved herself as a driver – at least in the heavy goods division – driving a London bus, and a Chieftain tank at speed over rough country, in the space of a few weeks. As honorary Colonel-in-Chief of the 14th/20th King's Hussars she handled a sub-machine gun, firing from the hip like a professional – in the opinion of a dutiful instructor. In more conventional vehicles she could make one apprehensive. 'She's the wild one,' said a friend. 'I'd hate to go driving with her.' She created a minor sensation in the upper strata of society by attending a performance of the musical *Hair* (which had shocked by its uninhibited nude scenes) and dancing on stage trouser-suited with the cast after the show. A duke, rather surprisingly, observed, 'Anne, of course, is very like the late Queen Mary. She'll go crazy and dance around. And suddenly she'll remember who she is.' When she did remember who she was it could go hard with those who momentarily forgot. An Australian photographer who called out 'Look this way, love,' was royally snubbed with the words: 'I'm not your love, I am Your Royal Highness.' Her encounters with the press reached perhaps their lowest point during the family visit to President and Mrs Nixon in the summer of 1970, but there have been many more uneasy moments since then.

But in 1971 she was the darling of the press. It began at the Badminton Horse trials. The royal party staying as guests of the Duke of Beaufort at Badminton House that spring numbered the Queen, Prince Philip, the Queen Mother, Prince Charles, Prince Andrew, and Prince Edward – all there to see how the Princess would fare in her first great competition. She did not win – a Captain Mark Phillips emerged as outright winner – but she came fifth out of 48. Riding was then her life 'because it has nothing to do with my position. If I am good at it, I'm good at it – and not because I'm Princess Anne.' She was obviously good at it. Badminton was followed in August by her 21st birthday – a comparatively low-key affair celebrated at her grandmother's

home of Castle Mey. The Princess was already keying herself up for the year's next great event, the Burghley Horse Trials in September.

Three sleepless nights were followed by triumph. This time she was the winner. Her mother proudly presented her with the Raleigh Trophy as Individual European Three-Day Event Champion. The BBC viewers' poll made her Sports Personality of the Year, the Sportswriters' Association named her Sportswoman of the Year; she shared the nomination of the Daily Express with racing driver Jackie Stewart. Now she set her sights on the 1972 Olympics at Montreal. The Queen was to open them and the Princess planned to ride her horse Doublet, a present from her mother. Hardened competitors thought Anne over-ambitious but she trained remorselessly in the hope of selection. In February she accompanied her mother and father on a tour of the Far East, but went straight back to training on her return. Tragically, that spring, Doublet injured a leg and had to be destroyed – and it was the end of Anne's Olympic hopes.

But not of her competitive career. The following year, after official heart searchings, she and Prince Philip attended the European Equestrian Championships at Kiev – Philip as President of the International Equestrian Federation, Anne as an individual competitor. It was a small landmark in international affairs since no member of the British royal family had visited Russia since the overthrow of the Tsar,

Princess Anne at the European Equestrian Championships, Kiev, in 1973 (*above*) and with Captain Mark Phillips (*left*). After a golden year as a horsewoman in 1971, culminating as Individual European Three-Day Event Champion and nomination as Sports Personality of the Year, she had been hoping to be selected to ride for Britain in the 1972 Montreal Commonwealth Games. She had to abandon this ambition following a critical accident to her horse, Doublet. The following year, however, she was selected to go to Kiev. She was accompanied by Prince Philip, attending in his capacity as President of the International Equestrian Federation. It was the first time members of the Royal Family had visited Russia since the downfall of the Tsar in the February Revolution of 1917. It was in May 1973 that the Palace announced her engagement to Captain Mark Phillips.

Above: The wedding photograph of HRH The Princess Anne and Captain Mark Phillips. The son of a company director of one of Britain's largest companies, Captain Phillips was just two years older than his bride. An outstanding horseman, he had won the Badminton Trials in 1971, the year when Princess Anne had come fifth in the placings out of 48. Their shared interest inevitably brought them much into one another's company and the romance blossomed. There is little doubt that the Queen was delighted with the match but, a sign of the times, Mark was not ennobled. The country faced the prospect of a marriage between a princess of the blood with a commoner with delight. The wedding was the most splendid royal event for a generation.

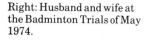

Right: Husband and wife at the Badminton Trials of May 1974.

cousin to King George V, in the February Revolution of 1917. It was a more important matter for Anne but unfortunately she was thrown and badly bruised. She reckoned the press saw the accident and the disappointment of her hopes merely as good copy. 'I hope they've got their money's worth now!' she barked. Inevitably she had to make her apologies in due course.

She had brushed with the press earlier that year for, having in March denied that she and Captain Mark Phillips planned marriage, in May she authorized the announcement of their engagement. The wedding, the most splendid royal event of its kind since the war, took place on 14 November 1973. Westminster Abbey was in the hands of the television producers for weeks as preparations were made for the great media event; the world audience was reckoned at half a billion and BBC World Service Radio broadcast commentaries in forty languages. The honeymoon couple, afterwards flew to Barbados to cruise the Caribbean in the royal yacht *Britannia*, Princess Margaret's haven of Mustique being among their ports of call. The wedding had been classed as 'private' by Buckingham Palace, but there were 4000 police on duty,

Below left: Princess Anne and her first born, Master Peter Mark Andrew Phillips. Born on 15 November 1977, he was not only a beautiful present to his grandmother, the Queen, in her Silver Jubilee Year, he was also that somewhat unusual phenomenon in the annals of British monarchy, a commoner born of a royal princess. Among those who witnessed his christening in the Music Room of Buckingham Palace on 22 December was Princess Alice, Countess of Athlone (then 94 years old), herself the grandchild of Queen Victoria (she can be seen second from the left in the wedding photograph opposite). Thus five generations of royalty were present at the christening.
Below right: Master Phillips some years later, apparently undismayed by the historic circumstances surrounding his arrival into the world.

so large were the crowds, while among the 1500 guests at the fabulous reception given by the Queen were 25 members of foreign royal families.

Early the following year the glowing happiness of the newly-weds was blighted when a deranged gunman attempted to kidnap the Princess as she, Mark and friends were driving down the Mall, on their way back to Buckingham Palace, on the evening of 20 March 1974. Her bodyguard, Inspector James Beaton was shot three times as he made a heroic defence, Mark protected her with his body throughout the incident; the chauffeur, a police constable and a journalist driving behind the royal car were all shot and a passing motorist, who tackled the gunman narrowly avoided injury before the man was overpowered. All received awards in the honours list.

Just two years older than his wife, Mark Phillips, then a career soldier, was the son of Peter Phillips, a director of Walls, one of Britain's largest food manufacturers. Mark was also an outstanding horseman and a member of the set from which the Princess drew her friends.

Eventing continued to be the centre of their life until in 1976 the Queen presented them with the magnificent 730-acre estate of Gatcombe Park in the Cotswolds, when the management of the farming land and the alterations to the Georgian mansion claimed something of their attention. Mark had been appointed by the Queen as one of her personal aides-de-camp, but he was granted no noble title. Anne became the Princess Anne, Mrs Mark Phillips and their first child also the first royal child to be born a commoner for some 500 years. Commoner or no Master Peter Phillips made an auspicious entry to the world.

Born on 15 November 1977, he was christened Peter Mark Andrew in the Music Room at Buckingham Palace on 22 December by the Archbishop of Canterbury. Among those present was not only his proud grandmother, Queen Elizabeth II, but also the 94-year-old Princess Alice, Countess of Athlone, grandchild of Queen Victoria and great-great-great aunt of the baby. Five generations of the family were thus present at this culminating royal celebration in the Queen's Silver Jubilee Year.

Above: Queen and Consort during the Service of Thanksgiving held in St Paul's Cathedral to celebrate the Jubilee on 7 June 1977.

Paul's Cathedral. The glittering procession of carriages and landaus through London's streets, the distant boom of artillery salutes and the dazzling though solemn pomp beneath the Cathedral's stupendous dome guaranteed another royal TV spectacular – but even viewers felt the mood of dedication and love flowing towards the monarch. Afterwards she went on royal walkabout with Prince Philip all over the capital and plaques let into the pavement and graffiti later recalled the happy and proud delight of the crowds who thronged about her that day.

The Palace was flooded with cards and messages of good will; there was a Buckingham Palace banquet for Commonwealth heads of state; a chain of bonfires and beacons sprang up in the night sky throughout the kingdom, signalled by the first, fired in Windsor Great Park by the Queen herself. In the weeks that followed she made royal progress through every region of the United Kingdom and Northern Ireland, protected there by heavy security precautions against IRA threats on her life. By the end of the year she had travelled 7000 miles through the kingdom, visited her troops in Germany and toured Canada and the West Indies, making the return flight by Concorde.

For her progress through Britain both the royal train and the royal yacht *Britannia* had been called into service. The train, ten coaches completely rebuilt and fitted out over the previous three years, comprises a saloon car each for the Queen and Prince Philip, a dining car for the royal party, a restaurant car and sleeping cars for the staff and other service coaches. Prince Philip's saloon is self-contained, with kitchen and dining facilities for up to ten people in addition to his private apartments, and can be used independent of the rest of the train. The Queen s saloon, approached from the platform through double doors and a vestibule, provides a lounge, with work desk and telephone among its fittings, the Queen's bedroom and bathroom and a second en suite bedroom-bathroom for her dresser.

Britannia, one of the world s most luxurious private yachts with a gross tonnage of some 5800 tonnes and more than 400 feet overall, seems a sea-going palace. The state apartments are approached down a majestic mahogany staircase. The dining room, which can serve also as a cinema, can seat up to 56 people round its great ebony-edged table, while a reception for more than 200 can be accommodated when the folding mahogany doors between anteroom and drawing room are thrown open.

With its royal blue and white livery, royal arms at the bow, royal cipher at the stern,

The Silver Jubilee, the 25th year of the Queen's reign, dawned on 6 February 1977. She marked it with a quiet family weekend at Windsor. Given the nature of English weather it had been decided that the celebrations should be held during the summer. Thus the people of the island of Western Samoa became the first of the Queen's subjects to offer her public congratulations, as her plane made a stopover there en route to Tonga, Fiji, New Zealand, Australia, and Papua New Guinea.

Meanwhile, Britain was gearing itself up. The souvenir factories were rolling, the chain stores were taking out insurance on the royal life against the possibility that death or other disaster should put a premature end to the bonanza; town councils and local organisations throughout the land were laying plans for civic receptions and street parties; brewers were busy bottling super-strong jubilee ales, and the Post Office and the Royal Mint launched memorial stamps and coins.

On 4 May both Houses of Parliament presented loyal addresses to their Queen to the accompaniment of pageantry and trumpets in Westminster Hall and on 7 June the Queen, Prince Philip and the Royal Family attended a Service of Thanksgiving in St

Britannia makes a handsome ambassadorial presence for Britain in foreign waters. But, perhaps inevitably, it is a favourite target for critics of the sheer cost of monarchy. With a complement of more than 250 officers and men all RN volunteers and running costs well in excess of £1 million a year it seems something of a luxury for official duties of little more than six months in twelve. The solemn pretence that it can be adapted in time of war for use as a hospital ship, kept up by its participation in NATO manoeuvres, was exposed during the three-month Falklands campaign of 1982 in which it played no part at all.

In 1979, the Queen continued her travels with a visit to Denmark, where attractions included a journey through the 'Tunnel of Love' in the Tivoli Gardens with Prince Henrik, Queen Margarethe II and Prince Philip in the boat behind; the following year Switzerland; and the year after that Norway. It is said that Norway is the one foreign country outside the Commonwealth where the Queen feels truly at home: 'Coming to Norway is a family occasion,' she said to King Olaf, a grandson of King Edward VII.

On 27 August, Bank Holiday Monday, Earl Mountbatten of Burma, the beloved Uncle Dickie of Prince Philip and hero of Prince Charles, was assassinated by IRA bombers. That holiday weekend the house party at Classiebawn Castle, the Mountbatten retreat on the coast of County Sligo included his daughters and their husbands and families. The young Nicholas Brabourne and the deck-hand Paul Maxwell died with the Earl in the blast which shattered *Shadow V* on that sunny morning fishing excursion. Prince Philip was in France at a four-in-hand driving championship Prince Charles on a fishing holiday in Iceland. Both broke down when the news reached them. Not a member of the royal family but was shattered by despair, and the nation at large found its anger at the outrage tinged also with mournful grief at the Palace. The state funeral, following the programme that Mountbatten himself had devised, was for most who saw it, even on television, a deeply moving occasion. It was certainly, as the dead Earl, Sea Lord and Viceroy of India would have been delighted to know, a stunning spectacular. He wanted no tears shed at his funeral, though in this he was to be disappointed. 'I am only sorry I will not be there to see the fun.'

Coming two years after the triumphs of the Silver Jubilee, the solemn processional marked a tragic downbeat at the end of the royal seventies. The new decade opened with the happy celebrations of the Queen Mother's birthday. The nation joined in the cheerful homage to the smiling matriarch and the family firm was back to business as usual.

Below: Prince Charles receiving the presentation at Cowdray Park polo ground from Lord Mountbatten, 22 July 1979. Five weeks later, Earl Mountbatten of Burma, 'Uncle Dickie' to Prince Philip and the adored hero of Prince Charles, was dead, assassinated by the IRA. The crime outraged the nation while the royal family was grief-stricken. The Earl's funeral was a stirring and above all magnificent spectacle and followed closely the programme he himself had devised. He had once lamented the impossibility of enjoying being a spectator to the pageantry: 'I am only sorry I shall not be there to share the fun.'

Charles and Diana

Pages 154-155: The Prince and Princess of Wales making an appearance on the balcony of Buckingham Palace after their wedding on 25 July 1981. After this picture was taken they were to delight the crowds below when the Prince gave his bride a kiss. Highly popular and also a truly joyous national occasion, the wedding was also a television spectacular on the grand scale, occupying hours of air time and immense resources and having a world-wide audience running to hundreds of millions. There were some who thought the marriage of the 33-year-old prince was not before time but none quibbled with his choice of bride when it was finally made.

The third daughter of Viscount and Viscountess Althorp, Diana Spencer was in a sense 'the girl next door.' She was born on 1 July 1961 at Park House on the Sandringham estate. Her family could trace descent back to King James I and also, through the 'Merry Monarch's' mistresses, to King Charles II. About half a mile from Sandringham House, Park House had once been the home of her mother's parents, Lord Fermoy and Lady Fermoy, Lady-in-waiting and the close friend of the Queen Mother. The baby girl was christened in Sandringham Church in the same font as had been used for the future King George VI. Her brother Charles, now Viscount Althorp, was born in 1964, a contemporary of Prince Edward.

The 20-year-old Prince of Wales, asked his opinions on marriage, responded to his interviewer: '. . . You've got to remember, in my position, you are going to marry somebody who perhaps one day is going to be Queen. You've got to choose very carefully. The one advantage about marrying somebody from a royal family is that they know what happens.' At the time these views were probably part of the staid public front needed in such interviews. In one of the hilarious sketches in the Trinity College revues he walked off stage arm in arm with a pretty girl, smirking at the audience 'I like to give myself heirs.'

When Charles wrote the now famous children's story *The Old Man of Lochnagar* for his five-year-old brother Edward, a copy was sent to Park House for the young Lady Diana. The younger members of the two families were friends, the Althorp's swimming pool being a chief attraction for Prince Andrew. But her eighth year was a sad time for Diana since it was then that her parents' marriage broke up Lady Althorp marrying Mr Peter Shand-Kydd after the divorce. Then, when she was 15, her grandfather inherited the title as Eighth Earl of Spencer and the family moved to the ancestral home of Althorp in Northamptonshire. It is a stately home on the grand scale with one of the country's finest collections of art. In 1976 Earl Spencer married a second time, to Raine, formerly Countess of Dartmouth.

Diana was so to speak 'formally' introduced to Prince Charles 'in a ploughed field' in November 1977 by her 22-year-old sister Lady Sarah, at that time a friend of the Prince. She and two girl friends took a flat in London's South Kensington and in the intervals of a happy social life Diana occupied herself with a cordon bleu cookery course and looking after children, quickly developing a natural sympathy for them. A bridesmaid at the wedding of her sister Lady Jane to the Queen's Assistant Private Secretary, Robert Fellowes, Diana, at 18, was a tall, beautiful and happy girl and a striking figure

Right: After finishing her schooling Lady Diana Spencer had taken a flat in London and in the autumn of 1979 took up a job as a teacher in a kindergarten school in Pimlico. She seemed to have an immediate rapport with children and to be able to win their love and confidence.

among the younger set in London society. Her love of children – and their immediate love of and response to her – decided her job and in autumn 1979 she started teaching at a kindergarten school in Pimlico.

That year she had been a guest at Balmoral with the royal house party, being a particular favourite with Prince Andrew, just one year her senior. Early in the following year she was at Sandringham House; in July, Prince Charles invited her to one of his polo matches and during Cowes week in August 1980 she was a guest on the royal yacht *Britannia*. The press began to see her as the favourite in the Prince Charles marriage stakes.

In his twenties, the Prince had fenced questions about romance with the observation that 'about 30' was a good time to marry. They were good years. At one Covent Garden Christmas Party he appeared, suitably attired, to give a spirited rendering of 'I am the Pirate King.' Music is very important in his life. Among the celebrations for his 21st-birthday he had requested a concert with Yehudi Menuhin as soloist. For relaxation he also dabbles in painting – his father has an amateur artistic talent above average – and is a keen swimmer. Play hard, work hard, might be the family motto and Charles undertakes a heavy load of official duties. As President of the Royal Jubilee Trust he is actively involved with youth projects, with particular concern for the needs of the handicapped and the deprived young people of Britain's inner cities. From funds raised in the Silver Jubilee year appeal, the Trust has some £3 million a year to spend. The Prince believes that motivating people is a prime function of leadership and under his direction the Trust's money is distributed among small groups and organizations in which people are helped and encouraged to cooperate and motivate each other to tackle their common problems and look

to the needs of others still worse off than themselves.

With the Prince's purchase of Highgrove House, a Georgian manor near Tetbury in Gloucestershire and not far from the home of his sister at Gatcombe Park in 1979, speculation that he was at last contemplating marriage mounted to near certainty. That November, Charles visited BL's plant at Longbridge near Birmingham for the launch of the company's new world beating car the mini Metro. Soon Lady Diana Spencer was to be observed negotiating London's traffic in a bright red little Metro, shortly to be a beacon for the press corps. Surely, Diana had to be the one. Charles was now in his 32nd year. But still no announcement was made.

Above left: Mrs Shand Kydd, the mother of the Princess of Wales and herself daughter of Lady Fermoy, long time member of the household of Queen Elizabeth the Queen Mother.

Above right: Earl Spencer, formerly Lord Althorp, father of the Princess of Wales. Here seen on a visit to St Mary's hospital in London where the Princess went for the birth of her son Prince William. It was when Diana was in her eighth year that the marriage and Lady Althorp broke up. Such an event can never be happy for a child but in this case, it seems, the breakup between the parents was particularly acrimonious. After the divorce Lady Althorp married Mr Peter Shand Kydd, director of a large company of quality wallpaper manufacturers while in 1976 Earl Spencer, as he now was, married Raine, formerly Countess of Dartmouth.

Left: Prince Charles with Mother Theresa of Calcutta during his tour of India in 1980. This Indian trip embraced the Taj Mahal and many other glories but one feels that for the Prince these took second place to his meeting with this saintly woman. For Prince Charles, at least, this encounter with the Institute and those who came for them must have been deeply moving. He once said: 'I suffer from the constant battering my conscience gets as to what I can try and do to help.'

off her splendid ring – a large oval sapphire surrounded by fourteen diamonds and set in eighteen-carat gold. Paste replicas were soon to be seen on the fingers of thousands of girls throughout the land; Diana's deceptively casual hair style was copied by millions; her choice in hats and dress became fashion leaders.

For months past the 19-year-old beauty, 12 years younger than her husband to be, had run the gauntlet of the press with the loyal support of her friends and impressive self control. Now she could relax a little within the protection of Palace protocol and official public relations. The Queen Mother took her under her wing and at Clarence House she also had the support of her grandmother, Lady Fermoy. She had been an intimate of the royal circle for some months, of course – November 1980 had seen her among the guests at Princess Margaret's 50th birthday ball at the Ritz – now she featured regularly in the Royal Circular. Rooms in Buckingham Palace were set aside for the wedding preparations chief among these, fitting with her dressmakers David and Elizabeth Emanuel.

The date of the wedding was set for 29 July and it was to take place in St Paul's Cathedral. This was a break with tradition, royal weddings being usually held in Westminster Abbey. The fact raised mild interest but it was of course the dress that provided the real talking point as preparations mounted.

The Emanuels provided the sensational black taffeta dress in which the Princess appeared at her first official public engagement with the Prince. It was a glittering occasion at Goldsmith's Hall, London which raised over £7000 for the Royal Opera House Development Appeal. The mixed programme of music and

Above: The official engagement photograph of Prince Charles and Lady Diana Spencer – always 'Lady Di' to the popular press – taken on the steps at Buckingham Palace. As 1980 advanced speculation that the Prince was planning to marry Lady Diana was continually mounting. She was pursued by reporters everywhere. Then in January 1981 she joined the royal family at Sandringham and finally, on 24 February 1981 the engagement was announced.

Right: Her beauty and public charm of manner made Diana a fairy-tale Princess. For her first official engagement with the Prince, at Goldsmiths Hall London, her couturiers the Emanuels made a stunning creation in black taffeta, seen here.

Late in 1980 Charles went off on a long scheduled tour of India. The crowded itinerary included a visit to the Taj Mahal but for the Prince, one feels, the highlight must have been his meeting with Mother Teresa, the saintly Albanian-born nun who has devoted her life to the daily personal care of poor people in the teeming slums of Calcutta.

The Prince returned to England in time to join the family Christmas at Sandringham; in January 1981 Diana joined the party for a few days the place was besieged by the press. And then Charles was off with the Duke and Duchess of Kent for the skiing at Klosters. Finally, on 24 February, Buckingham Palace put the press out of their misery and ended the expectant speculation throughout the country with the announcement that Prince Charles and Lady Diana Spencer were engaged to be married.

At the innumerable photo calls that followed Diana, smiling and confident, happily showed

literature included readings of her own poetry by Princess Grace of Monaco. On 27 March the Queen presided at the meeting of the Privy Council, convened at Buckingham Palace to give formal assent to the match as required by the Royal Marriages act of 1772. Two days later Prince Charles had to leave his fiance for a long arranged five-week tour of New Zealand, Australia, Venezuela and America, where he was to meet President Reagan.

On his return the couple had a short holiday at Balmoral before Charles, accompanied by Diana, was off again, this time to Broadlands to open the Mountbatten Exhibition, a permanent memorial to his great uncle. A happier family occasion was their visit to Princess Anne in hospital after the birth of her daughter Zara Phillips on 15 May. The following month the spotlight shifted dramatically away from the couple.

On the morning of Saturday 13 June 1981 Lady Diana, with other members of the royal family, from their vantage overlooking Horse-guards Parade awaited the commencement of the Trooping the Colour Birthday Parade. The Queen, riding as always the black mare Burmese, was approaching the parade ground at the head of her Guards when there were a couple of sharp reports and a scuffle in the crowd by the barriers. Two of the Queen's cavalry escort spurred forward, Burmese skittered momentarily on the tarmac before the Queen brought him back under control. Passing the Admiralty building she raised her hand to the window where stood the Queen Mother and Diana. It was all over so quickly that even alert television viewers who, despite their astonishment guessed what had happened, had to wait confirmation by the commentator ... the Queen had been shot at. The parade continued on schedule, Prince Philip and Prince Charles took up their appointed positions and the ceremony progressed upon its stately way. The 17-year-old perpetrator of the outrage had, it transpired, made his gesture with a replica gun loaded with blanks. But this could not be known at the time. The Queen's cool courage and the alarming ease with which it seemed her life could be endangered awakened both admiration and dismay throughout the country. The offender was sentenced to five years in prison under the Treason Act 1842, without leave to appeal.

Two days later, Lady Diana was among the congregation at the Garter Service of Thanksgiving in St George's Chapel Windsor and at the official opening of Royal Ascot week delighted the racegoers as she rode with Prince Charles along the race course in his state landau. As the day aproached ever closer the official programme of engagements was interspersed with re-

hearsals of various kinds. Lady Diana's 20th birthday celebrations were comparatively low key, but during Wimbledon she found time for three visits, including John McEnroe's victory in the men's finals and Chris Evert Lloyd's in the women's.

Souvenirs of all kinds were doing a brisk trade well before the wedding and the unveiling of Brian Organ's official portrait of Lady Diana attracted queues to London's National Portrait Gallery. With uncomplicated but direct symbolism it portrayed a relaxed, beautiful and unpretentious young woman seated on an upright chair in a four-square, formal setting provided by the frame of the picture itself and a background of a gilded panelled door and door case.

The build up to the wedding continued with a television documentary, *A Prince for Our Time*, on Prince Charles and a joint television interview of prospective bride and groom transmitted a day before the event; that evening Prince

Above: It is jokingly said that the 16-year-old Lady Diana was formally introduced to the Prince of Wales by her elder sister in a ploughed field. The Prince and Princess share a common love of outdoor activities.

Above: The official portrait of the Princess of Wales by Bryan Organ, 1981; it hangs in the National Portrait Gallery. The symbolism of a simple and charming girl framed, potentially confined, by the world of protocol is uncomplicated and direct. Soon after it went on public display the picture was vandalized; it was carefully restored.

Right: Lady Diana Spencer with Prince Charles at a polo meeting shortly before their wedding.

troops were marching to their precisely ordained positions along the processional route through the streets of London; hundreds of police security men, marksmen and dog handlers were also moving into position. At the Cathedral itself clergy, choir and organist were preparing themselves while the bellringers, who were to ring 5000 changes – a four hour stint – were limbering up. Soon the great church began to fill up with thousands of distinguished guests. At Clarence House the bride was putting the finishing touches to her appearance with the aid of a make-up artist specially flown in from Paris and dressers arranging the veil and train of that fabulous dress. The whole of London was *en fete* and families throughout the land were settling down before the television in anticipation of a spectacular of pageantry, romance and religious dedication unlikely to be equalled in their life time.

The crowds along the route were entertained by the massed bands of the guards and then, shortly after ten in the morning the first waves

Charles lit the first of a nationwide chain of bonfires and beacons. He then joined the crowds in Hyde Park to watch a fireworks display which featured a flaming palace facade, the world's largest Catherine wheel, massed bands and choirs and artillery salvoes, in the largest such display in Britain in modern times.

Wedding gifts had been pouring in from all over the world and a special area of Buckingham Palace was reserved for them to be stored and listed. The royal wedding licence on finest parchment had been prepared by a master calligrapher. Weeks of preparation had readied St Paul's Cathedral for the service and the television cameras – it was to be estimated that the viewing audience was 750 million world wide. The five-tier wedding cake, completed weeks before by the catering corps of the Royal Navy was maturing nicely towards perfection and a thousand and one other major and minor details efficiently seen to.

The 29 July dawned bright and glorious. Carriages were being readied in the royal mews;

of cheering began to break around Buckingham Palace as the cavalcade of state coaches and landaus bearing the members of the royal family – the Kents, the Gloucesters, the Ogilvys, the Queen, Prince Philip and Princess Margaret, Princess Anne and Mark Phillips, the Queen Mother and Prince Edward – began clattering out of the yard. The last to emerge bore the bridegroom and Prince Andrew. When they reached the Cathedral, Charles, with his two 'supporters' Prince Andrew and Prince Edward, advanced to their places preceded by two Admirals of the Fleet, acting as gentlemen ushers. The royal family, the bride's family, the congregation were in place and the buzz of conversation rose to a new pitch of expectancy as the cheers of the crowds outside the great church heralded the arrival of the bride, accompanied by her father, riding in the magnificent Glass Coach used by King George V at his coronation in 1910.

Before she began her approach to the altar down the ceremonial carpet stretching some

650 feet down the length of the Cathedral, the dress makers made the final adjustments to the fabulous dress of ivory silk taffeta with its 25-foot-long train. Then, preceded by the Cross, the Archbishop of Canterbury, the six officiating clergymen representing all the principal denominations the bride and her father began the majestic progress. She carried a deeply falling bouquet of white flowers, roses, trailing ivy and the traditional myrtle and veronica cut from bushes propagated from sprigs from Queen Victoria's wedding bouquet. A fanfare of trumpets echoed through the great building and the five bridesmaids and two page boys (costumed in Victorian naval cadet uniforms) brought up the rear of the bridal procession.

After the opening hymn the veiled bride joined her groom and the two advanced to receive the blessing of the Archbishop. At this point Earl Spencer who despite the constitutional frailty brought on by a brain haemorage many years before had stalwartly born the fatigues of the morning, gave his daughter away

Above: Prince and Princess, bride and groom, come out of the cathedral onto the steps of St Paul's to be greeted by the roars of the crowds on 29 July 1981. The decision to hold the ceremony in St Paul's was something of a break with tradition, royal weddings being generally held in Westminster Abbey. But the real talking point in the months leading up to the event was the bride's dress. A well guarded secret, the beautiful garment of ivory silk taffeta fully lived up to expectations.

Left: The bride on the arm of her father as they enter the Cathedral.

and was assisted to his seat by his son, Lord Althorp. The ceremony continued according to the age-old rituals of the church, to be concluded by the fervent singing of the National Anthem. Then, accompanied by the principal bridesmaid Lady Sarah Armstrong-Jones, the married pair were conducted into the sanctuary for the signing of the register. Their return was heralded by another fanfare from the trumpeters in the Whispering Gallery under the dome and the congregation gasped at the beauty of the bride revealed now that her veil was thrown back.

The bells pealed them home to the Palace; the crowds called them back time and again to the balcony; to everyone's delight the newly weds established a royal precedent with a royal kiss and finally they were free to retire and change for the ride in an open landau to Waterloo Station for the first stage of their honeymoon at Broadlands. On Saturday 1 August an Andover of the Queen's Flight flew them to Gibraltar, to the ecstatic delight of the Gibraltarians and the irritation of the Spanish government and from there the honeymoon continued in *Britannia*, visiting Egypt, where they were received by President Anwar Sadat and his wife. From there they flew back to Scotland to complete the honeymoon and holiday at Balmoral.

In October Charles took his new Princess on a tour of the Principality. Fittingly, Diana made her first appearance in Caernarvon dressed in red and green in tribute to the national colours of Wales. But it was her beauty, charm and warmth of personality that assured her instantaneous popularity. The Prince showed his wife round the Castle where he had been Invested in 1969 on the day of her eighth birthday; seated on a dais in the courtyard they were serenaded by a choir of school children having been welcomed to the precincts by Lord Snowdon. From there they went on to share in the 800th

Opposite: The bride and groom descend the steps of St Paul's; the train was some 25 feet long.
Above: Returning to the Palace through streets crowded with spectators along the whole route.

Below: The family wedding photograph.

Above and right: The Princess of Wales visits the Principality. Prince Charles took his wife on her first tour of Wales in October 1981 (above) three months after their wedding. She made her first appearance in Caernarvon dressed in red and green, a tribute to the national colours of Wales. Their itinerary included a visit to the great castle where the Prince had been invested back in 1969; the 800th anniversary celebrations of St David's Cathedral; the freedom of the city of Cardiff for the Princess and many other official engagements. But the Princess always seemed most at her ease meeting the people. In November 1982 she made a second visit to the Principality (right), after the birth of Prince William.

anniversary celebrations at St David's, the national cathedral of Wales. From there to Swansea and then on to Cardiff where Princess Diana received the Freedom of the City. Later that year she attended the State Opening of Parliament, the first Princess of Wales to do so in 70 years and then on 5 November, to the nation's delight, came the announcement that 'The Princess of Wales is expecting a baby next June.' The same day the Wales's were guests of the Lord Mayor and City of London at a Guild-hall luncheon. The year ended with the Princess, elegant and ravishing as always, performing her first solo public function on a balcony in London's Regent Street when she threw the switch to illuminate the Christmas decorations.

Meanwhile the wedding presents had gone on display to draw the admiration of thousands and earn thousands of pounds for charity and the bride's, bridesmaids' dresses and pages' uniforms were on touring exhibition and raising thousands more for the disabled. Apart from their official engagements, the young marrieds had the business of settling into their new home together at Highgrove so that the comparative seclusion of Christmas at Sandringham that year must have come as a welcome relief.

Even when the novelty of a Princess of Wales began to abate a little and her appearance gradually came to be accepted as another aspect of

the royal team at work, Princess Diana continued to exert her own personal magic on everyone she met and on the public at large. Criticism never surfaced above rumour and gossip. She was said to have a sharp tongue when it suited her and Charles was said to feel the edge of it at times. But as the public began to gear itself up to the birth of the new royal baby such disloyal sniping was treated with contempt.

In any case, there were other things to absorb the national attention with the outbreak of the remarkable Falklands War against Argentina, precipitated on 1 April. Naked jingoism soon overtook the healthier sentiments of national self esteem. The country watched excitedly as the Royal Navy, and Prince Andrew, got slowly but surely into position to fight a campaign halfway across the globe.

A new, if somewhat erratic star was beginning to twinkle in the royal firmament as the dashing, unpredictable and handsome Prince Andrew began to carve a career for himself through the photo pages of the world's press and to make his mark as a heart throb of almost Hollywood dimensions. His name was linked with various degrees of reliability with a string of young women of whom the actress Koo Stark seemed to make the strongest impact.

As a boy he had loved practical jokes and, in the Queen's words, 'was not always a little ray of sunshine.' The impish streak is clearly well established and he has managed to excel even his father in his 'handling' of the press. Back in the sixties, during a tour of the Caribbean, Prince Philip commiserated with a hospital matron whose wards were plagued by mosquitoes. 'I know what you mean,' replied the Prince. 'You have mosquitoes. I have the press.' Observed journalist Andrew Duncan in his book *The Reality of the Monarchy,* 'The sensitive souls of the reporters were deeply shocked . . . Incredible, an apology was demanded . . . and given.' Visiting the US in 1984 Andrew was to take more positive action, spraying an aerosol paint can in the direction of the camera corps. Naturally, the royal playboy apologised and paid compensation.

In the early hours of 21 June Diana entered the maternity wing of St Mary's hospital, Paddington. Barely a month earlier she had attended her last public engagement before her confinement – to open the Albany Community Centre in South East London while on 12 June

Left: The royal couple leaving St Mary's hospital with the baby Prince William on 22 June 1982. She was meeting her public engagements to within a month of her confinement and on 12 June attended a polo match in which the Prince was playing. She entered the maternity wing at St Mary's, Paddington, during the early hours of 21 June. At 9.03pm she gave birth to a baby boy, weighing in at just seven pounds. Mother and baby were reported to be doing well, which was evidently the case since the Princess left the hospital the following day and was back in Kensington Palace within 24 hours of leaving it. The bells of Westminster Abbey rang a special peal lasting one and a half hours; the Royal Horse Artillery fired a salute in Hyde Park and the Honourable Artillery Company one at the Tower. The choice of name was a cause of speculation and bets were placed. The eventual choice was not the favourite but, it is said, the Queen Mother put her money on it and made a handsome winning.

Right: Spring 1983, Prince and Princess with baby William, on shipboard. On a tour of Australia shortly before his marriage the Prince had promised to return with his wife. In fact, he went one better and returned with wife and baby son.

Below: Prince and Princess, tourists, photographed in front of Ayers Rock. A vast rocky outcrop rising sheer out of the Australian desert it is one of the wonders of the natural world and a mecca for tourists. For the aboriginal inhabitants it is a place of deep religious significance.

she had been among the spectators as Prince Charles took part in a polo match in Windsor Great Park.

On Monday 21 June the nation woke up to hear the news that Princess Diana had begun her confinement. Finally at 9.03pm she gave birth to a baby boy, blue eyed and weighing seven pounds. Mother and baby were said to be doing well and, indeed, the Princess was back in her London home in Kensington Palace within 24 hours. The bells of Westminster Abbey pealed from noon to 1.30pm; the King's Troop, Royal Horse Artillery fired a 41 gun salute in Hyde Park; the Honourable Artillery Company the same from the Tower of London. The little boy to be known as Prince William had been launched on life with full 'royal rigmarole.'

On his visit to Australia just before his marriage, Prince Charles had promised to return soon with his wife. On 20 March 1983 he went one better when he and the Princess arrived in Alice Springs, complete with the baby William, for the beginning of a month long tour. The royal arrival had been preceded by five days with freak monsoon rains. The resulting raging floods had brought tragedy into many families;

roads were washed away; and the royal couple had to be accommodated in a new hotel at the last moment because the one scheduled for their use was entirely cut off.

After his presentation, so to speak, to the people of Alice, the baby prince was flown off with his nanny to Woomargama, which was to be the Wales's base home during their trip, while his parents embarked on a heavy schedule. Among the first and most important sites they were to visit the remarkable Ayer's Rock, sacred to the aboriginal peoples of the continent for millenia before the coming of the white man. Over the ensuing weeks they travelled thousands of miles throughout the Commonwealth of Australia and everywhere the Princess was rapturously received. On 16 April they flew for two weeks in New Zealand.

Once again the welcome was ecstatic . . . but once again they were deluged with rain. Prince Charles was not sure 'whether we brought the rain from Australia or whether it's the same rain that soaked the Queen in California.' The trip was also troubled by Maori demonstrators protesting civil rights, which the Princess, in traditional royal style deflected with bland good

Above: The Princess of Wales on walkabout in Wellington, New Zealand. Some parts of the tour were disrupted by Maori demonstrators protesting in the cause of civil rights. The Princess proved adept at handling such occasions with the bland goodwill characteristic of the monarchy. Since, almost by definition, the royal family is excluded from everything concerning politics in the public arena, this is about the only reaction to such demonstrations left to them. Fortunately for the Princess, always at her best with children, the Maoris in this group of admirers do not seem to be politically motivated.

Left: Prince William takes a photo call in Auckland, New Zealand.

Right: Prince Charles is a skilled as well as an enthusiastic polo player. Here Princess Diana is clearly delighted with her husband's performance in a match held at Cirencester Park in June 1985.

nature. At Wanganui they paid a visit to Charles's brother Prince Edward, a college teacher there, who greeted them adorned in a handsome traditional cloak of kiwi feathers. At Gisborne they were given a traditional Maori tribal ceremony of welcome and admired an exhibition of Maori culture. A magnificent banquet in Auckland brought to a glorious end the first of no doubt many tours they would make together.

The Prince was again in Australasia in the summer of 1984. In August he ceremonially opened the new £20 million parliament building in Port Moresby, Papua New Guinea. He had been welcomed on arrival in the island state

to the drone of ceremonial conch shell trumpets and wood flutes and was cheered to the echo after his brief speech in Pidgin. From the celebrations in Port Moresby, 'Nambawan pikinini bilong Misis Kwin' progressed to the Island of Manus, there to be paddled shorewards in outrigger canoes and carried up on to the beach for his formal inauguration, in full regalia, as tribal chief. While he was taking part enthusiastically in one more colourful variation on the 'royal rigmarole', his mother back in London was approving the designs for the new effigies of her portrait head to appear on the British coinage in 1985.

The Prince's tour coincided with the Los Angeles Olympics and there his sister, on a flying visit found herself embroiled in yet another storm of rumour and press gossip. Her husband Captain Mark Phillips was already there, on attachment as commentator on the equestrian events to an Australian broadcasting network. When the Princess booked in at a different hotel speculation was rife that the couple were on the verge of a marriage break-up. When the Princess met the British decathlete Daley Thomson to congratulate him on his gold medal, the champion's joking comments as to whom he would like to be the mother of his children provoked a media 'storm of anger' in Britain and sympathy for the Princess. Her press officer issued the following statement: 'Princess Anne considers it totally absurd that anyone should think anything Daley Thomson said was offensive.'

The following month the royal family were among the spectators at another rather different athletic occasion – the Highland Games at Braemar. Traditionally one of the most important fixtures in the royal diary, these games are a world away from the hectoring commercialism that has overtaken the Olympic movement and among the happiest events in the royal year of the Queen of Scotland. The Monday following, 3 September, Princess Anne, with her well-known interest in children's charities, made the official opening of the International Conference on Concerned Technology in Education. Ten days later she was launching a three-year programme designed to encourage the women of Britain's Asian communities to take advantage of the ante-natal services of the National Health Service and so benefit the well being of their children to be.

But while the business of the 'firm' continued as usual – airport control towers were opened and ships named – the nation's interest was focussed once more on the Princess of Wales, now daily expecting her second baby. In the morning of Saturday 15 September she was admitted to the Lindo Wing of St Mary's Hospital, Paddington and at 4.20 that afternoon she was delivered safely of a boy. Prince Charles had been with his wife throughout the birth and emerged to receive the plaudits of the jubilant crowds outside the hospital. Barely 24 hours later, just after 2.30 on Sunday afternoon, Princess Diana, the baby Prince Henry Charles Albert David in her arms, was whisked off home by limousine to Kensington Palace. The birth was celebrated with artillery salutes in London and a three-hour ring from the bells of St Mary's Church, Tetbury, the neighbouring village to the Wales's home at Highgrove House in Gloucestershire. When it was learnt that the

boy was to be known as Prince Harry the nation looked back to the last monarch 'Harry' – Henry VIII – and tried to decide what, if any, significance to attach to the fact.

Still glowing with pleasure at the arrival of her latest grandson the Queen left England later that month for the royal tour of Canada, postponed earlier in the year because of a snap general election there. She was welcomed by Mr Brian Mulroney, the triumphant victor of the elections. The royal yacht *Britannia* provided a base for the royal party while the Queen travelled by train a good deal and thus saw and was seen by a number of small towns and com-

Above: Princess Diana lends a helping hand to Prince Harry, while Prince William follows closely behind her, as the Wales's arrive at Aberdeen Airport in August 1986 for the start of the annual holiday at Balmoral.

Right: Mother and son in pensive mood: Princess Diana and Prince William take a photo call during a family holiday in Majorca in August 1987. The Wales's were guests of King Juan Carlos and Queen Sofia of Spain.

munities. High on the list of priorities were the provinces of Ontario and New Brunswick. An elaborate banquet was thrown in her honour at Moncton, New Brunswick, to commemorate the 200th anniversary of the founding of the province by United Empire Loyalists, Americans loyal to the British crown who had left their homes at the time of the War of Independence rather than betray their allegiance. The Queen was also honoured by the Mohawk Indians with ceremonial dances and in turn dedicated the late 18th-century Chapel of the Mohawks as a national historic site. Unfortunately, the festive air of the whole tour was marred from time to time by small but irritating breaches of protocol and the visit was overshadowed by criticisms of the Queen in the Canadian press as 'over made-up,' 'middle aged' and dowdily out of fashion.

From Canada, the Queen flew south for a week's private visit in the United States, first as the guest of a millionaire stud farm owner near Lexington, Kentucky, and then to a polo ranch in Wyoming. Her one official public engagement during these relaxed days among fellow horse enthusiasts was the presentation of the Queen Elizabeth II Challenge Cup at the Keeneland races. She returned home to

tragedy for, in the early hours of 13 October, the last day of the Conservative Party Conference at Brighton, an IRA bomb shattered the Grand Hotel there, killing four delegates and severely wounding a cabinet minister and his wife. Prime Minister Thatcher's suite was wrecked by the explosion and a further intensification of security cover for public events ensured.

Evidence of the tightened precautions was to be seen when President Mitterand of France arrived at Gatwick Airport for a state visit towards the end of the month. The President and Mme Mitterand were met by the Duke and Duchess of Kent and welcomed, on their arrival in London, by the Queen. The magnificent carriage procession wound through the streets of London along streets lined by police and watched over by special branch men. This state visit saw another innovation when, for the first time, the television cameras were admitted to Buckingham Palace for the broadcast of a state banquet. In this opulent setting the diamond-studded figure of the Queen seemed the epitome of majesty.

Meanwhile, Prince Charles was struggling to carve out a meaningful role for himself within the royal family. It was apparent that his mother was not planning to step aside so that he could become King. And yet, his options were severely restricted. He was, essentially, a King in waiting. Or, as one writer put it, he was 'trapped in a gilded cage.'

The depth of his self doubt became clear in 1988 when Anthony Holden, who had written an authorized biography of the prince eight years earlier, announced that he was going to revise the book in commemoration of the Prince's 40th birthday. The Prince protested that there was no need for a new edition because he 'hadn't achieved anything' since the first edition was published.

The general tone of the press's coverage of him did not help matters. When Prince Charles took a trip to Africa's Kalahari Desert, he announced that he was doing so because he believed that the leaders of western civilization could learn something of value from primitive tribes. The tabloids reacted to this bit of news by suggesting that he might be a bit 'loony.'

Nevertheless, he continued to speak out on social issues ranging from unemployment and drug abuse to environmental pollution. As he did, some high-profile celebrities rallied in support of him. The rock musician Phil Collins, who had helped to organise concerts for the benefit of the Prince's Trust, told reporters that Charles's focus on social problems was completely understandable. 'He's going to inherit the country's problems,' Collins said, 'so he's trying to solve them now.'

Everyone, including Charles himself knew that he couldn't 'solve' the country's problems. He didn't have the power to do so. Moreover, many people believed that he was far too detached from the people to have any sort of impact on social problems. After he told an interviewer that he saw himself as a 'champion of the ordinary bloke,' one commentator responded that Charles refers to 'the people' as if they were 'an alien and distant race whom he would like to get to know better.'

But ultimately, his comments and concerns were overlooked for another reason. In comparison with Princess Diana, he was regarded as a bore. Given the choice between focusing on Prince Charles's social agenda or the Princess's glamour, reporters inevitably chose the latter. As Donald Spoto put it in his book *The Decline and Fall of the House of Windsor,* 'the slightest indications of [the Princess's] feelings were noted, amplified and discussed. Laughter, frowns, hesitation, boredom – each glance and manner was plumbed for profundities and interpreted for family ramifications.' A change in hairstyle was front-page news, while 'every word was revered [and] every touch considered sacred.'

In spite of the news media's snubs, Prince Charles persisted in his efforts to do something meaningful. It wasn't so much that he wanted more respect, according to those who knew him well at the time. He was, simply, very serious by nature. Lady Rusheen Wynne-Jones, a friend of the Prince, summed up the matter in March 1988, when she told *Newsweek* that the Prince 'doesn't want to spend the rest of his life opening hospitals. He'd go mad.'

At times, the public seemed to appreciate Charles's seriousness even if cultural commentators did not. When Charles's book, *A Vision of Britain,* was published in 1989, there was evidence that the majority of the British people agreed with its premises. The book focused on post-modern architecture. Charles had harshly criticised several high-profile architectural projects, and when architects tried to dismiss his criticisms, he suggested (somewhat ironically) that they were being elitist. 'The good folks,' he said, shared his love of traditional design. Nevertheless, reviewers on both sides of the Atlantic were less than kind. Herbert Muschamp, writing in *The New Republic,* sarcastically referred to the Prince as 'that killer wit' and suggested that his criticisms were essentially 'sophomoric insults.'

It is difficult to determine the degree to which such comments bothered Prince Charles, but one thing is certain: by 1989, disrespectful commentators had become the least

of his problems. In part because of his seriousness, the emotional distance between him and Princess Diana was growing.

With increasing frequency, the press was focussing on the contrast between the Princess's fun-loving ways and Charles's intellectualism. As Anthony Holden had pointed out in a 1987 article for *Life* magazine, Charles was fond of art, classical music and serious conversation. The Princess, by contrast, was in the habit of listening to the music of Genesis and Dire Straits and reading 'the shallow romances of her step-grandmother Barbara Cartland.'

As the Prince and Princess drifted further and further apart, Diana's sense of loneliness was aggravated by what has come to be called 'empty-nest syndrome.' William and Harry

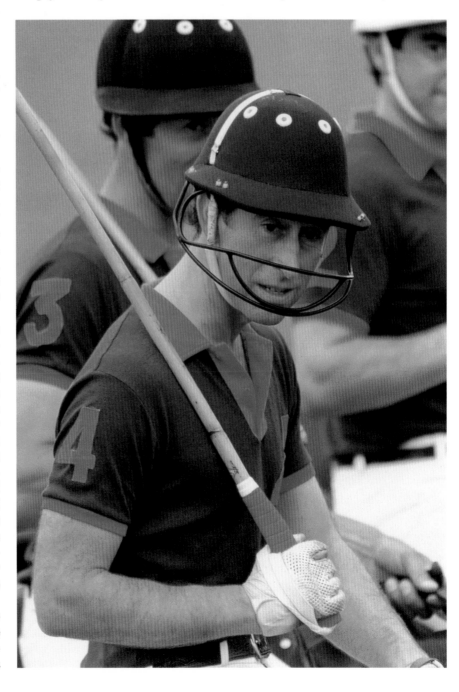

Below: Prince Charles pauses during a polo match. Polo has been the royal family's favourite sport for generations, but Charles' passion for the game is especially strong. Princess Diana dutifully attended the Prince's polo matches during the first few years of their marriage, but she later revealed that she had little interest in the sport.

Above: Princess Diana shares a moment with a young handicapped woman at a hospital in Angola. The Princess was widely admired for her efforts to help victims of injury, disease and poverty. In the last years of her life, she made a special commitment to helping victims of land mines.

'darling' during public appearances, and the Princess returned the affection with 'adoring gazes,' according to several news accounts. One British paper even dubbed the trip 'The Tender Tour,' and several others ran articles suggesting that the reconciliation might be genuine.

Other observers remained unconvinced. 'They may have laughed and joked,' wrote one reporter, 'but the magic wasn't quite there.' Another observer commented that the couple's show of togetherness was 'just a bit too calculated and contrived.' There was evidence to support these more cynical assessments. As *People* magazine noted, 'when the cameras weren't rolling. . . Diana was conspicuously less responsive.' Nevertheless, the couple continued to demonstrate a renewed solidarity. The following spring, *Newsweek* reported that the royal marriage 'seems to have subsided into a workable arrangement.' But as late as 1989, some reporters still believed that real love had been rekindled.

They were wrong, of course. Both the Prince and Princess, as the world would learn later, had long since given up on the marriage and turned to others for the affection they craved.

For Prince Charles, that person was Camilla Parker-Bowles, a longtime companion. According to Donald Spoto, the Prince had 'regularly gone off on trysts' with Parker-Bowles since 1983. The public would not learn the full truth about the relationship until 1993, when a telephone conversation between the Prince and Parker-Bowles was leaked to the press. During the conversation, which was actually recorded in December 1989, Prince Charles expressed his desire to be with her constantly, and she reciprocated by telling him that she couldn't 'bear' to be without him.

That same month, an amateur radio operator named Cyril Reenan recorded similar conversations between Princess Diana and James Gilbey, an heir to the Gilbey's Gin fortune. These recordings later became known as the 'Squidgy' tapes, in reference to Gilbey's term of affection for the Princess. The true nature of the Princess's relationship with Gilbey has never been revealed, but the transcripts of the telephone conversations make it clear that they felt a great deal of affection for one another. In any event, this was not Princess Diana's first extra-marital relationship. Earlier that year, she had been involved with James Hewitt, her riding instructor.

Prince Charles and Princess Diana were not the only members of the royal family who were experiencing marital problems in the late eighties. In 1989, it was announced that Princess Anne and her husband Mark Phillips

had left home in 1987 to attend school, and the Princess – who came to be known as an extremely devoted mother – could find nothing to fill the emotional void.

Their private despair notwithstanding, the Prince and Princess struggled to maintain the appearance that their marriage was strong. They were encouraged in this effort by the Queen, who was growing concerned about the effect the gossip might have on the institution of the monarchy.

In the fall of 1987, the Queen summoned her son and daughter-in-law to her private sitting room at Buckingham Palace and told them that they needed to work harder to put an end to the rumours. Shortly thereafter, there was a noticeable difference in the way that the royal couple dealt with each other – at least in public. The new attitude was especially evident during a trip to Germany in November. Prince Charles made a point of calling the Princess

were separating. They had been married for 16 years, but it now appeared that the marriage had been a sham for much of that time.

The marriage between Prince Andrew and Sarah Ferguson appeared at the time to be somewhat stronger than the other royal marriages, and the birth of their daughters Beatrice and Eugenie – in 1988 and 1990 respectively – reinforced that view. But it is now clear that their marriage was also on the rocks during this period, although it would remain legally intact for several more years.

Needless to say, all of this was profoundly distressing to Queen Elizabeth II, who had spent four decades faithfully upholding the institution of the monarchy. What she could not have known, of course, was that the worst was still to come.

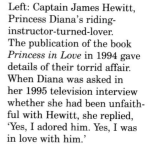

Left: Captain James Hewitt, Princess Diana's riding-instructor-turned-lover. The publication of the book *Princess in Love* in 1994 gave details of their torrid affair. When Diana was asked in her 1995 television interview whether she had been unfaithful with Hewitt, she replied, 'Yes, I adored him. Yes, I was in love with him.'

Below left: Camilla Parker-Bowles participating in a hunt near Highgrove House in Gloucestershire. A lifelong companion of Prince Charles, Camilla married Andrew Parker-Bowles after Charles went to sea with the Royal Navy in the spring of 1973. Nevertheless, she continued her relationship with Charles. Princess Diana reportedly learned of this fact on her honeymoon and became deeply depressed as a result.

The 1990s

Pages 174-175: Members of the royal family celebrate the Queen Mother's 97th birthday in August 1997. From left, in the front row, are Princess Margaret, Prince Charles, the Queen Mother, Queen Elizabeth, and Prince Harry.

Above: Princess Diana visits an AIDS clinic in London in June 1996. With her is AIDS patient Aileen Getty (dressed in red), daughter of billionaire J P Getty.

In 1991, Queen Elizabeth II officially put an end to rumours that she might abdicate the throne for the sake of her son. 'Voluntary renunciation of the Throne strikes at the root of the Monarchy,' she said in an official statement, because it would 'destroy some of the magic' of the institution.

Much of the magic, however, had already been destroyed. Over the years, many people in Britain and elsewhere had come to view the monarchy as an anachronism. Its very existence, in a democratic era, seemed absurd, if not downright offensive. The wedding of Prince Charles and Princess Diana had restored some of the magic. But in the years since, it had become clear that the life of the young royals was no fairy tale.

Given the persistent rumours that Charles and Diana's marriage had soured, it was only natural for observers of the monarchy to won-

der whether the Queen was being completely honest in her comments about abdication. Was she really against it, in principle? Or did she decide against it because of the problems between her son and daugher-in-law? We may never know the full truth, but common sense suggests that concern over the faltering marriage was a factor in her decision to remain on the throne.

In any event, it was clear that the marital problems between Prince Charles and Princess Diana would continue to have a negative effect on the monarchy. Thus the royals renewed their efforts to persuade the press and the public that the marriage was sound.

'Don't worry about me, my marriage is fine,' Diana told a reporter early in 1991. The notion that the marriage had been revived was reinforced by an article in the April 1991 issue of *Good Housekeeping.* The writer was Andrew Morton, whose book *Diana: Her True Story* would subsequently paint a very different picture. For now, however, Diana was playing along.

'Diana watchers have speculated about Prince Charles's selfishness and Diana's preoccupation with her children,' Morton wrote. 'Yet their closest friends – and Diana herself – say the marriage is happier than ever.'

Several months earlier, rumours of a separation had taken on new life when Prince Charles retreated to the royal estate at Balmoral – without his wife or children – to nurse a broken arm. (He had been injured while playing polo.) When the Prince and Princess were reunited to pose for a photograph that would appear on the Waleses' 1990 Christmas card, Charles remained sullen, according to observers. But that simply gave Diana an opportunity to work some public-relations magic. At one point, according to Morton, Diana leaned toward Charles and stuck out her tongue. 'The Princess,' Morton wrote, 'had demonstrated a quality that Charles loves about her – the ability to make him laugh.' Based on what we know now, it is safe to say that in private neither the Prince nor the Princess was laughing very often. But they recognised the importance of maintaining the illusion of domestic bliss.

Not long after the appearance of the article in *Good Housekeeping,* the Waleses went to Brazil on an official tour. When they returned, Princess Diana retreated to Kensington Palace to spend time with Harry. Charles, on the other hand, immediately went to Aston Down polo field, near Highgrove, to play a pre-season match. He was, by all accounts, elated to be back on the field, and he was looking forward to regular-season play, which would begin in

May. His sense of exhilaration was understandable. After all, the polo field was one of the few places where the Prince's public and private selves were completely in harmony. Here he could his pursue his passion, while polishing his image as a dashing Prince.

The Princess, meanwhile, was indulging in a passion of a different sort: the acquisition of a stunning wardrobe. By 1991, according to some sources, Diana had spent more than £833,750, or approximately $1.8 million, on more than 3,000 outfits, 600 pairs of shoes and 400 hats. Her fashion sense – cultivated with the help of editors at *Vogue* magazine – immeasurably enhanced her glamour. At the same time, however, it increased the distance between her and the other members of the royal family.

The contrast wasn't due simply to the royal family's stodginess in matters of fashion. Queen Elizabeth II is known for her frugality, and she passed this trait on to her son. Thus it is not surprising that Prince Charles was reportedly appalled by his wife's extravagance. There was little he could do to rein her in, however, since any attempt to do so would have highlighted their differences. Those differences had already been well-documented, of course, and the Prince's silence on the matter did little to diminish them.

Given the obvious differences between the Prince and Princess, it was only a matter of time before rumours about problems in the royal family would re-emerge. By the summer of 1991, members of the press were again speculating that the marriage might be over. The *Daily Mail*, for example, suggested in a headline that there was 'cause for concern,' and other papers followed suit.

Meanwhile, the press seized on another flurry of rumours about problems between the Duke and Duchess of York. The suggestion that Prince Edward was a homosexual, which had surfaced a year earlier, caused further problems for the House of Windsor. The Queen tried to minimize the impact of these stories by stating that all families have their share of 'impetuous, wayward youngsters and family disagreements,' but the argument did not carry a great deal of weight. After all, the much-celebrated 'magic of the monarchy' was because of the royal family's uniqueness. The royals were *supposed* to be different from everyone else. It was futile to ask people to embrace this myth while also asking them to regard the royals as a family just like any other.

As it turned out, 1992 brought far more than a fair share of problems to the House of Windsor. On 19 March, the *Daily Mail*

announced the official separation of 'Andrew and Fergie.' The Duchess, it was reported, would receive £500,000 in cash, plus £1.4 million to be held in trust for her daughters.

The following August, a photographer caught the Duchess and her lover, American financier John Bryan, snuggling on a beach, while her two daughters played nearby. The publication of the photos, she later said, was the 'most humiliating experience' of her life. Undoubtedly, it was humiliating for Andrew and the other royals as well, since it further reinforced their image as a dysfunctional family.

The 'Fergie' stories, however, paled by comparison to the bombshell that was to come. Andrew Morton, who only a year earlier had written that rumours about the Prince and

Below: Prince Andrew and Sarah Ferguson embark on an outing with their daughters. Not long after they were married, Andrew decided to go back to sea. The move put a strain on the marriage, and Fergie eventually sought comfort in the arms of Texas millionaire Steve Wyatt. Andrew and Fergie were separated in 1992.

Right: Queen Elizabeth II. When critics lashed out at the royal family toward the end of 1992, the Queen responded by delivering a conciliatory speech. 'There can be no doubt that criticism is good for people and institutions,' she said. Nevertheless, she asked for 'a touch of gentleness, good humour and understanding.'

Below: Windsor Castle in flames on 20 November 1992. The blaze marked the culmination of what Queen Elizabeth II called an *annus horribilis*. Shortly after the fire, officials announced that public funds would be used to pay for the restoration. The announcement was not well received by the British public.

Princess of Wales were 'greatly exaggerated,' was now bringing out a book called *Diana: Her True Story.* According to Morton, Diana had loved Prince Charles but that his ongoing affair with Camilla Parker-Bowles had driven her to despair. (Among other things, the book included disturbing accounts of the Princess's battle with bulimia nervosa, an eating disorder.) But these were not simply the ruminations of another gossip mongerer. The Princess herself – as well as members of her family – had cooperated with Morton.

The crisis within the royal family was now completely out of control. There was certainly nothing more that the Queen could do. She was virtually helpless as she watched the veneer of royal decorum gradually being peeled away. The crisis was further compounded on 20 November, when the private chapel at Windsor Castle caught fire. Before the blaze could be extinguished, much of the castle had been destroyed.

News of the fire might have elicited sympathy for the Queen had there not been an

Left: Princess Anne with her second husband Commander Timothy Laurence (far right), Prince Andrew (left) and Prince Edward at St Paul's Cathedral after the service of Thanksgiving in July 1995. Princess Anne had been divorced from Mark Phillips in 1989.

announcement, immediately afterward, that public funds would be used to restore the castle. This announcement seemed to prove that the royals – and their supporters in the British government – were out of touch with the people. Britain was in the midst of a deep recession at the time, with nearly three million people out of work. The idea that the royal family, with its exorbitant wealth, would expect an impoverished public to pay for the restoration of the castle was too much to bear for many people. Even those who normally supported the monarchy were disenchanted by this latest turn of events.

A week after the fire, Prime Minister John Major responded to critics of the monarchy by announcing that the Queen had volunteered to pay tax on her annual private income. The sovereign's income had not always been tax exempt. Queen Victoria had agreed to pay taxes on all of her income, regardless of the source. But in 1910, George V had managed to gain exemption for the Civil List – the annual sum voted by Parliament to cover immediate expenses for the royal household. Gradually, the Royals' private income was exempted as well, and by 1936, during the reign of George VI, the precedent of tax exemption had been firmly established.

Although Queen Elizabeth II's offer to pay taxes marked a major change in policy, it was perceived as nothing more than a public-relations manoeuvre and thus did little to diminish the criticism of the Royal Family. The Queen

had no choice but to issue a public plea for compassion. At a lunch given by the Corporation of London, the Queen slyly referred to 1992 as an *annus horribilis.* This was a play on the words *annus mirabilis,* a term that had been applied to the year 1666 – the year the first Anglo-Dutch war ended in defeat of the Dutch. She then went on to suggest that she had learned valuable lessons from the experiences of the past year.

'There can be no doubt,' she said, 'that criticism is good for people and institutions that are part of public life. No institution – City, monarchy, whatever – should expect to be free from the scrutiny of those who give it their loyalty and support, not to mention those who don't. But we are all part of the same fabric of our national society, and that scrutiny, by one part of another, can be just as effective if it is made with a touch of gentleness, good humour and understanding. . . .He who has never failed to reach perfection has a right to be the harshest critic.'

While the Queen's speech did elicit some sympathy from the British public, it was soon forgotten. Approximately two weeks after the speech, on 9 December 1992, Buckingham Palace acknowledged what had long been expected: Prince Charles and Princess Diana were officially separating.

The Prime Minister quickly reassured the British public that the separation would have no effect on the succession to the throne. 'The children of the Prince and Princess,' he said,

Below right: The cover of the July 1997 issue of *Vanity Fair* featured Princess Diana wearing a dress by Gianni Versace. The feature article and interior photo spreads suggested that Diana had transformed herself and had finally found happiness. The following month, Diana and companion Dodi Al-Fayed were killed in a car crash in Paris.

'retain their position in the line of succession, and there is no reason why the Princess of Wales should not be crowned Queen in due course. The Prince of Wales's succession as head of the Church of England,' he added, 'is also unaffected.'

Over the next few years, Princess Diana's popularity continued to grow, in large part because of her beauty and her evolving sense of style. She had become the most glamorous woman in the world. But she was not just another self-absorbed celebrity. On the contrary, she became known as one of the world's great humanitarians. Her concern for AIDS patients and the victims of land mines became especially noteworthy. Meanwhile, she also

VANITY FAIR

DIANA

EXCLUSIVE: A STUNNING PORTFOLIO OF
PRINCESS DI'S
NEW LOOK BY MARIO TESTINO
PLUS: THE PRINCESS REBUILDS
HER LIFE BY CATHY HORYN

managed to spend time with her beloved sons.

William and Harry were in the news more often after the separation. In particular, there was much speculation that William would some day bypass his father and ascend directly to the throne. There appeared to be a great deal of public support for this idea, since William was growing into a handsome young man and had a reputation for being mature beyond his years.

But there was also a growing number of people who didn't much care who was in line for the throne; they wanted to see the monarchy abolished altogether. Indeed, between 1984 and 1994, the number of people who favoured eliminating the monarchy tripled. These anti-Royalists remained in the minority, but many commentators suggested that if the younger members of the royal family continued in their self-destructive ways, opposition to the institution would continue to grow.

The future of the monarchy was again thrown into question in 1996 when Prince Charles and Princess Diana were finally granted a divorce. The possibility that the two might reign together, in spite of their estrangement, had now been eliminated. Many people also questioned how a divorced man could serve as official head of the Church of England.

As part of the divorce agreement, Diana received $36 million. More importantly, she was granted joint custody of the children. The settlement also stipulated that she would lose her royal title, but in time it became clear that she did not need it. Eventually, the people came to regard her as 'the Queen of Hearts.'

A year after the divorce was granted, Diana announced her decision to auction off 79 of the dresses she had worn in her capacity as the future Queen of England. *Vanity Fair*, which ran a cover story soon afterward called 'Diana Reborn,' called the decision 'a powerful symbol of her changing life.' The writer added that there was now 'a kind of serenity' about her. 'She's found herself – the way she wants to live.'

The same could scarcely be said for Prince Charles. Theoretically, he was now free to openly pursue his relationship with Camilla Parker Bowles, but, according to insiders, he remained frustrated by the ambiguity of his role in life. As the Prince of Wales and the official heir to the throne, he continued to attract media attention. But the exposure he received was nothing in comparison to the publicity that attended Diana's every move.

When the press revealed that Diana had a new love in her life – Harrods department store heir Dodi Al-Fayed – photographers began to trail her with even greater determination. Diana herself seemed ambivalent about the

Left: Princess Diana with Mother Teresa in June 1997. Both women, who coincidentally died within days of each other, were admired for their depth of compassion and for their commitment to helping ordinary people around the world.

attention she was receiving. She apparently wanted the world to know that she was happy in her new relationship, but, understandably, the relentlessness of it all became tiring.

The pursuit of gossip about Di and Dodi reached a climax in Paris, in the early morning hours of 31 August 1997. After enjoying a late-night dinner together, the couple climbed into the back of a chauffeur-driven automobile. As usual, there was a swarm of paparazzi nearby. Minutes later, a high-speed chase was on, and, as the car was racing through a tunnel, it crashed into a barricade.

News of the Princess's death stunned the world. As *People* magazine put it, 'The shocking and sudden loss of a vibrant beauty plucked at her peak – too early to achieve her happily-ever after, to see her elder son, William, inherit the throne, to watch Harry blossom into manhood – pierced Britain and the world to its core.' Within a matter of hours, mountains of flowers and other mementos had been piled outside the royal palaces and other sites around London.

Queen Elizabeth II and her advisors were taken aback by this outpouring of grief. Protocol dictated that the members of the royal family remain silent. But the tabloids, which had been vilified by the people for indirectly causing Diana's death, now spoke out on the public's behalf. It was the duty of the Queen, commentators suggested, to comfort the people with some sort of public statement. After several days, the Queen relented and agreed to go before the television cameras. 'We

have all been trying in our different ways to cope,' she said. Her entire statement took only a few minutes to read.

The Queen's official statement was received with some skepticism. Commentators, especially in America, took note of her 'cut-glass' tones and her apparent lack of emotional warmth. Nevertheless, it did indicate that the royal family was not completely out of touch with the people.

Meanwhile, there was still some question as to how the funeral would take place. The Queen had initially felt that a private service would be appropriate. But it was clear that the public would not accept an understated tribute. The people wanted to be a part of the ceremony. And that they were.

On 6 September, mourners lined the streets of London, while family members and friends – including many celebrities – poured into Westminster Abbey where the ceremony was to be held. Around the world, some two billion people watched the proceedings on television. It was the largest audience in the history of broadcasting.

The ceremony reflected Diana's personal style. It was, on the one hand, very much rooted in the traditions of British culture and of the Church of England. On the other hand, Diana's love of popular culture was well-repre-

sented. One of the most moving moments of the day came when Elton John, a close friend of the Princess's, sang a special version of his hit song 'Candle in the Wind.' But the most riveting moment by far came when her brother, Earl Spencer, delivered the eulogy.

'I stand before you today the representative of a family in grief, in a country in mourning before a world in shock. We are all united not only in our desire to pay our respects to Diana but rather in our need to do so.' He went on to remark that Diana was loved because she was 'the very essence of compassion, of duty, of style, of beauty. All over the world,' he said, 'she was a symbol of selfless humanity.'

In an obvious swipe at the royals, Spencer went on to pledge that Diana's 'blood family' would see to it that William and Harry enjoyed the kind of upbringing that the Princess had wanted for them. 'We fully respect the heritage into which they have both been born,' he said, 'but we, like you, recognize the need for them to experience as many aspects of life as possible. . . .'

When the funeral was over, the world watched in stunned silence as Diana's casket was taken to Althorp House, the estate where she had spent her childhood. She was buried there in a private ceremony on a small, private island in the middle of a lake.

Opposite: Princess Diana's coffin is carried into Westminster Abbey on 6 September 1997. Millions of mourners lined the streets of London to watch the funeral procession, while family and friends – including many celebrities – gathered inside for the service.

Below: Earl Spencer, Princess Diana's brother, joins Prince Charles, Prince William and Prince Harry after Princess Diana's funeral at Westminster Abbey. An estimated two billion viewers around the world watched the funeral on television.

The Future

Pages 184-185: Prince William greets the public in Vancouver, British Columbia, in March 1998. It was the first official visit to North America by Princes Charles, William and Harry after the death of Princess Diana.

Right: Prince Charles tours the Kyichu Temple in Paro, Bhutan, on 9 February 1998. The Prince arrived in the tiny mountain country on the final leg of a three-nation Asian tour.

In the weeks and months following the funeral of Princess Diana, editors and television news producers assembled one 'Diana' tribute after another. Meanwhile, representatives of the press promised to honour a request made by the royal family. They pledged that no pictures of William and Harry would be taken, except during official photo opportunities. Still, journalists could not help but wonder how Prince Charles and the boys were coping with the tragedy.

Charles, it was noted, had not been unmoved. 'The public cannot have had anything but sympathy when they saw Charles crying, arriving home with the coffin,' said royal correspondent Peter Archer. 'Charles is a melancholy man, and this tragedy will affect him more than most people.'

Ironically, Charles's display of emotional vulnerability boosted the public's confidence in the Prince. A few weeks after the funeral, Archer and others suggested that Charles's abilities had long been underestimated. 'Diana's death will have many consequences,' Archer wrote. 'One will be that the royals will have to be responsive to the public. And it's a change [Charles will] embrace. The Windsors are constantly reinventing themselves.' In the months that followed, Charles reinforced this impression. During public appearances, observers said he seemed warmer and more down to earth. Whenever he referred to William and Harry, he did so with great affection, and on several occasions he even went so far as to talk about his own grief.

'He has taken the death very badly,' said one royal insider. 'He's not eating well, he's very distracted, he's finding it difficult to concentrate. I think he is racked by self-doubt and guilty feelings, rightly or wrongly, and it will take a long time for him to get back to normal.'

In spite of this outpouring of sympathy for Charles, many people continued to focus their attention on the boys. One royal expert argued that the fate of the monarchy now lay in their hands. 'The only thing the royals have going for them now,' he said flatly, 'is William and Harry.'

William seemed to have just the right qualities for a young prince. If anyone could save

Below: Prince Charles with his sons on holiday at Balmoral Estate in 1997. For the two boys, the estate will always be associated with a tinge of sadness. It was here that they learned of their mother's death.

Right: Princes William and Harry explore the banks of the River Dee. After Princess Diana's death, most newspaper editors promised not to invade the boys' privacy. In exchange, Prince Charles promised that there would be plenty of official photo opportunities.

Below: Prince Charles and Prince Harry pose for photographers during a January 1998 ski trip in Klosters, Switzerland. Charles was a dedicated father from the very beginning. After Diana's death, he redoubled his efforts to give his sons the support they needed.

the monarchy, observers suggested, it was him. The handsome young man, who had already become a teen idol, had been raised to respect British tradition and to accept his assigned role within that tradition. At the same time, however, he seemed to possess Diana's spirit. This had been evident in the aftermath of the Princess's death, when he put aside his own grief in order to comfort mourners who had never met his mother. Not long before she died, Diana herself had noted these special qualities in her eldest son. 'When you discover you can give joy to people,' she told a writer for The *New Yorker*, 'there is nothing quite like it. William has begun to understand that too. And I am hoping it will grow in him.'

William has also become good student and is

reported to have displayed some talent as an artist. But he has a fun-loving side as well, according to observers who note that his interests include go-cart racing, riding mountain bikes, playing video games and listening to rock music.

Less is known about Harry because the press has paid far more attention to his brother. As the so-called 'spare heir,' he will undoubtedly have a difficult time defining a role for himself. Nevertheless, there is every indication that Diana loved her sons equally, and Prince Charles appears to be devoted to Harry as well. Two months after his mother's death, in fact, Harry joined his father on a trip to South Africa while William stayed behind in England.

During the tour, Charles expressed his belief that the royal family had no choice but to change with the times. It was not the first time he had made such a remark. Ten years earlier, he had stated bluntly that the monarchy's survival was 'not guaranteed.'

'Something as curious as the monarchy,' he had said, 'won't survive unless we take account of people's attitudes. If people don't want it, they won't have it.' The scandals that erupted in the early nineties highlighted the reality of that statement. Ironically, however, the response to the death of Princess Diana was indication that the monarchy probably will survive. The widespread expression of grief over her passing revealed a deep-seated need for larger-than-life heroes and heroines. In recent decades, many people have looked to Hollywood and to professional sports for such inspirational figures. But in Britain, the royal family has long provided inspiration in a more meaningful context. Kings, queens, princes and princesses are not only glamorous; they represent a link to tradition. They symbolize the nation's glorious past.

The younger members of the royal family, of course, have behaved in ways that cannot exactly be described as glorious. But the public's desire to hold onto the institution remains significant And, perhaps because of that desire, people have demonstrated a willingness to forgive Charles for his shortcomings.

The question remains, of course, what will happen when Queen Elizabeth II dies. Polls have shown widespread support for the idea of William by-passing his father and acceding directly to the throne. But that prospect seems unlikely. Brian Hoey, an author who has written extensively about the royal family believes that Charles 'absolutely will be king' if he outlives his mother.

'There's no question of William bypassing him,' according to Hoey. 'William wouldn't want it, the Queen wouldn't want it, and I

don't think the country would want it. It's [Charles's] destiny' to sit on the throne.

Only time will tell whether Hoey and others who share this belief are correct. Observers agree that if Charles is to live out his destiny, he must continually demonstrate his willingness to change. He must become more open with the public. He must clarify a vision for himself and for the monarchy—and, most important, he must continue to demonstrate that he is a devoted father. After all, barring some tragedy, William will one day be king. It will remain incumbent upon Charles not only to prepare for his own reign but to nurture his successor as well.

Above: Prince William accepts flowers from a well-wisher outside Buckingham Palace, shortly after the death of his mother. The young prince was praised for putting his own grief aside so that he could comfort mourners who never personally knew his mother. His behaviour during this period reinforced the widespread belief that he will one day make a fine king.

Index